MELTDOWN
IN
TIBET

CHINA'S RECKLESS DESTRUCTION OF ECOSYSTEMS FROM THE HIGHLANDS OF TIBET TO THE DELTAS OF ASIA

MICHAEL BUCKLEY

palgrave
macmillan

MELTDOWN IN TIBET
Copyright © Michael Buckley, 2014.

First published in 2014 by
PALGRAVE MACMILLAN® TRADE
in the United States—a division of St. Martin's Press LLC,
175 Fifth Avenue, New York, NY 10010.

Where this book is distributed in the UK, Europe and the rest of the world,
this is by Palgrave Macmillan, a division of Macmillan Publishers Limited,
registered in England, company number 785998, of Houndmills,
Basingstoke, Hampshire RG21 6XS.

Palgrave® and Macmillan® are registered trademarks in the United States,
the United Kingdom, Europe and other countries.

ISBN: 978–1–137–27954–5

Library of Congress Cataloging-in-Publication Data

Buckley, Michael, 1950–
    Meltdown in Tibet : China's reckless destruction of ecosystems from the
highlands of Tibet to the deltas of Asia / Michael Buckley.
        pages cm
    ISBN 978–1–137–27954–5 (hardback)
        1. Environmental degradation—China—Tibet Autonomous Region.
2. Tibet Autonomous Region (China)—Environmental conditions.
3. Environmental policy—China. 4. Natural resources—Government
policy—China. 5. Water-supply—Government policy—China.
6. Water-supply—Asia. I. Title.

GE160.C6B84 2014
363.700951′5—dc23   2014014138

A catalogue record of the book is available from the British Library.

Design by Newgen Knowledge Works (P) Ltd., Chennai, India.

First edition: November 2014

10 9 8 7 6 5 4 3 2 1

Printed in the United States of America.

Contents

Abbreviations   v

Preface by His Holiness the Dalai Lama   vii

Why Tibet Matters   1

Chopping Tibet in Half   5

Eco-Snapshot: The First Casualties

PART ONE   LISTENING TO GLACIERS   11

1   Rafting the Drigung   13
       What on Earth Are China's Engineers Getting Up To?

2   Crisis at the Third Pole   23
       What Does a Rain of Black Soot Have to Do with This?

PART TWO   ECOCIDE IN THE LAND OF SNOWS   41

3   Valleys of the Dammed   43
       What Is the Fate of the Mighty Rivers of Tibet?

4   Stealing Water   75
       Where Is the Thirsty Dragon Going to Guzzle Next?

5   Vanishing Nomads, Vanishing Grasslands   91
       Why Are Tibet's Grasslands Being Usurped by Desert?

6   Paper Parks, Theme Parks   115
       Why Is China Snuffing Out Tibetan Nomad Culture?

7   Plundering the Treasure House   137
       How Much Can an Ecosystem Take before It Collapses?

CONTENTS

PART THREE   THE POLITICS OF WATER   165

8   Downstream Blues   167
        Southeast Asia: What Is at Stake for Food Security?
9   Himalayan Water Wars   189
        Why Can't They Just Leave the Rivers Alone?
10 Running Wild in Bhutan   215
        Does Bhutan Hold the Key to a Brighter Future?

APPENDICES
        Water Justice   225
        Links   228
        Notes   231
        Acknowledgments   239
        Index   240
        Author Bio   248

Abbreviations

$	indicates estimated cost in US dollars, converted from Chinese yuan
AQI	Air Quality Index
CCP	Chinese Communist Party, in sole power since 1949
EIA	Environmental Impact Assessment
GW	gigawatt, equivalent to 1,000 megawatts
IPCC	UN Intergovernmental Panel on Climate Change
MRC	Mekong River Commission, an organization supposed to protect the Mekong River's ecosystems
MW	megawatt
NGO	non-governmental organization
PLA	People's Liberation Army
PRC	People's Republic of China
TAR	Tibet Autonomous Region, or Xizang, created by Chinese authorities in 1965
UHV	ultra-high voltage power lines, used to transfer electricity from dams to industrial hubs several thousand miles away

THE DALAI LAMA

PREFACE

The condition of the river systems on the Tibetan plateau directly impacts the development and even the survival of more than a billion Asians who live downstream. Therefore, it is encouraging to see increasing attention being given to the critical importance of Tibet's environment to Asia and the world at large. I welcome Michael Buckley's *Meltdown in Tibet* as another step in that direction.

Economic development is undoubtedly important for social well-being. Material development enhances society's ability to provide its citizens with decent health and education. In this connection, China has made amazing progress.

However, I believe that pursuing economic development at the expense of the ecological balance will lead to drastic and unforeseen consequences. In the case of China, many environmental experts consider economic accomplishments are already exerting a heavy environmental price. They bemoan the threat of China's disappearing lakes, shrinking and increasingly polluted rivers and smog-filled skies that will have long-term consequences for public health. The ability to breathe clean air and drink clean water is a human right. But it is a right threatened by focusing only on economic development that pays inadequate attention to ecological well-being.

As far as Tibet is concerned, there are Chinese scientists who recognize the importance of the plateau's fragile environment, even referring to it as the "Third Pole." Therefore, the question of river and water management in Tibet transcends mere political concerns because of its far-reaching impact in this part of the world. This book, therefore, should be part of a wake-up call to the international community and China to seriously assess ecological and environmental conditions on the Tibetan plateau and take remedial measures before it is too late.

July 30, 2014

Why Tibet Matters

Glance at a physical map of the Tibetan Plateau and you will see why the rivers of Tibet are so important to Southeast Asia and the Indian subcontinent. The Tibetan Plateau is the source of the major rivers of this vast region, stretching all the way from the coast of China in the east to Pakistan in the west. Ninety percent of the run-off from Tibetan rivers flows downstream into China, Vietnam, Cambodia, Laos, Thailand, Burma, Bangladesh, India, Nepal, Bhutan, and Pakistan. At the tail end of those same rivers lie the world's largest deltas. One way or another, close to 2 billion people rely on Tibet's waters—for drinking, for agriculture, for fishing, for industry.

Water, not oil, is now becoming the world's most important resource. Though we live on a planet covered by water, very little of it is accessible. More than 97 percent is seawater, which is too salty: at this point in time, desalination plants are very costly, in terms of both money and energy. Roughly another 2 percent of water resources are locked in ice and snow. That leaves a paltry 1 percent to supply drinking water, grow crops, run factories, cool power plants, and handle all the other key roles that water plays. And it's possible that up to half of that paltry 1 percent is polluted or contaminated water, which is not usable. As nonrenewable groundwater resources are used up, the global supply of freshwater is dwindling at an alarming rate. This will lead to great tensions between nations over shared water resources.

Although there is freshwater derived from the ice in the Arctic and Antarctic, most of it cannot be funneled into usable freshwater for human consumption. Tibet is often referred to as the "Third Pole," because it is the third-largest source of water locked in ice and snow. Tibet is unique in the world as a mass provider of freshwater, via rivers, to a dozen nations downstream. It is the source of major headwaters for the rivers of Asia and the Himalayas, and additionally provides key tributaries or feeders for other major rivers, such as the Ganges. There is no parallel to this situation anywhere else on the planet.

Tibet's glaciers are melting rapidly, and its lakes are drying up. The plateau is under siege from climate-change factors, but instead of seeking ways to minimize the impact of all this, China is aggravating the situation. Chinese hydro consortiums are damming the heck out of the rivers of Tibet, blocking their flows. Extensive mining by Chinese companies is degrading the land, with high potential to pollute rivers downstream. The grasslands of Tibet are being encroached upon by desert.

Why should this matter to someone sitting halfway across the world? Well, for reasons that you will discover in this book, environmental meltdown in Tibet is going to have a huge impact. The initial impact will be on the nations downstream. Any water shortages will disrupt rice or wheat harvests and drive grain prices to record highs, causing great social unrest—and causing nations like China or India to import massive quantities of grain.

What appears to be just a Tibetan Plateau problem or a Chinese problem is going to become an Asia-wide problem. Ultimately, this will become a global problem because there are no boundaries when it comes to environmental impact. A volcano erupts in Iceland and spews volcanic ash into the atmosphere—which shuts down flights over the whole of Europe. A tsunami triggers a meltdown at a nuclear reactor in Fukushima, putting Japan on alert for radioactive fallout—and leaking radioactive water into the Pacific Ocean, impacting marine life. Massive clear-cutting of forests in Tibet and expanding desertification of grasslands have severely impacted regional ecosystems and may influence extreme weather patterns in Asia. Tibet sits on the largest permafrost layers outside of the two poles. As the permafrost starts to thaw, it releases significant amounts of carbon dioxide and methane into the atmosphere. Methane is a superpotent greenhouse gas, thought to be some 20 times stronger than carbon dioxide.

We only have one Tibet. There are no backups, no second chances. If the water resources of the Tibetan plateau should be blocked or diverted, or become polluted, then Asia will tumble into chaos. His Holiness the Dalai Lama, a great believer in interdependence and the interconnectedness of all living things, captures the heart of the matter in a few sentences: "Destruction of nature and natural resources results from ignorance, greed and lack of respect for the earth's living beings. . . . Our ancestors viewed the earth as rich and bountiful, which it is. Many people in the past also saw nature as inexhaustibly sustainable, which we now know is the case only if we care for it."[1]

Chopping Tibet in Half

Eco-Snapshot: The First Casualties

The definition of *Tibet* depends on who is doing the defining. The Chinese and the Tibetans refer to different-sized areas when it comes to Tibet. The Tibetans refer to the entire Tibetan Plateau region within the confines of the People's Republic of China (PRC). The defining element of Tibet is its extreme altitude—hovering above 13,000 feet—and its "extreme people," the ethnic Tibetan groups that have adapted to life in this harsh, high-altitude environment. Ethnic Tibet, or Greater Tibet, covers 830,000 square miles, or almost a quarter of China's land area.

Because this book focuses on environment and water resources, it takes the wider view seen by Tibetans: so the use of the word *Tibet* refers to Greater Tibet—the entire Tibetan Plateau within the PRC.

China redrew Tibet's borders in 1965, creating Xizang Province, or the Tibet Autonomous Region (TAR), with an area of 460,000 square miles, which is around half the original size of Tibet. TAR is an Orwellian twist—there is nothing autonomous about this region. Under the rule of the Dalai Lamas, Old Tibet (historic Tibet) was composed of three vast regions: U-Tsang (central Tibet), Amdo (northeast Tibet), and Kham (eastern Tibet). In 1965, Amdo was absorbed into the Chinese provinces of Qinghai and Gansu, while Kham was donated to the neighboring

Chinese provinces of Yunnan and Sichuan. Chinese geological surveys refer to the Tibetan Plateau as the "Qinghai-Tibet Plateau."

But China's chopped-down version of Tibet—the TAR, or Xizang Province—is still huge. It is roughly the size of France and Spain put together. Buttressing the southern flanks of Tibet, the great Himalayan range stretches over 1,550 miles from east to west.

The Tibetan population was also cleaved in half by these Chinese divisions. A census taken in 2010 says there are 6.2 million ethnic Tibetans, with an estimated 2.7 million Tibetans inside the TAR, and another 3.5 million living outside the TAR.

★ ★ ★

ONE OF THE FIRST ENVIRONMENTAL CASUALTIES IN TIBET WAS DEFORESTATION. THE Chinese occupiers have cut down half the forests of eastern and southern Tibet. Central Tibet is mostly above the treeline, but the eastern and southern slopes shelter vast old-growth forest. In 1985, I first entered Tibet as a truck passenger, heading overland from Chengdu to Lhasa. In eastern Tibet, I saw long lines of Dongfeng trucks filled with huge logs going the other way. I was witness to China's highly destructive practice of clear-cutting the forests of eastern Tibet. Those long lines of trucks had shifted logs from Tibet for decades, stripping entire regions of trees.

By some estimates, over 50 percent of Tibet's forests have disappeared since China invaded Tibet in 1950.[1] Over $50 billion worth of oak, pine, larch, and rhododendron has been logged and hauled out to mainland China, where the wood is used in construction, manufacturing, and making furniture. Ongoing since the 1950s, the repercussions from this massive deforestation are evident in mudslides, landslides, and flooding all the way from western China to Bangladesh. It's possible the scale of logging here has even altered monsoon patterns over the region.

Tibetans culled large trees from eastern and southern Tibet for use in temple construction, but only on a very small scale. Tibetan Buddhism promotes great respect for trees: the Buddha was born under a tree, attained enlightenment under a tree, and died under a tree. The same Buddhist ethos of respect for trees was present in pre-1949 China to some degree, with temples protecting nearby forests. But that ethos was swept aside with the ascension of Mao Zedong in 1949. Mao Zedong launched a new battle: he called for the conquest of nature.

The entire population of Old Tibet was never more than 6 million. China's population is over a billion today. That's a very different footprint when it comes to matters like logging. Tibetans never had the advanced machinery or technology to log on a large scale, even if they wanted to. But China does have that capability. The logging went on relentlessly at the edges of the plateau until 1998. That year, the Yangtse River saw devastating flooding that killed thousands, left millions homeless, and caused billions of dollars in damage. A panel of scientists persuaded the government that the cause of this disastrous flooding was massive soil erosion, which was in turn caused by extensive logging at the river's headwaters. In response, the government imposed a complete ban on logging virgin forest in the mountainous western provinces.

This had a peculiar side effect: out of nowhere China became a bigger importer of timber than Japan (another voracious consumer of wood). At stake here are the virgin rainforests of Borneo, the Philippines, New Guinea, and other parts of Asia.[2] Chinese companies have been linked to illegal harvesting of the forests of Siberia and Madagascar.[3] Chinese timber companies are trucking in rare teak logs from neighboring Burma and Laos. The logging trucks are rolling again—but down different roads, destroying different habitats.

★ ★ ★

THE SECOND MAJOR ENVIRONMENTAL CASUALTY IN CHINESE-OCCUPIED TIBET was wildlife. The wildlife was decimated in the 1960s and 1970s. This is not a case like losing 50 percent of the trees. This is a case of erasing the wildlife from the grasslands of Tibet.

In July 1939, when he journeyed from his birthplace in Taktser in eastern Tibet to Lhasa to be formally enthroned as the fourteenth Dalai Lama, Tenzin Gyatso was just four years old. The caravan traveled slowly, by horse. He says his chief memory of this three-month journey across Tibet was the wildlife encountered along the way: "Immense herds of *kiang* (wild asses) and *drong* (wild yaks) freely roamed the great plains. Occasionally we would catch sight of shimmering herds of *gowa*, the shy Tibetan gazelle, of *shawa-chakar*, the white-lipped deer, or of *tsoe*, our magnificent antelope. I remember, too, my fascination for the little *chibi*, or pika, which would congregate on grassy areas. They were so friendly. I loved to watch the birds: the dignified *gho* (the bearded eagle) soaring high above the monasteries and perched up in the mountains; the flocks of geese (*nangbar*); and occasionally at night, to hear the call of the *wookpa* (the long-eared owl)."[4]

In 1979 and 1980, the Tibetan government-in-exile dispatched three fact-finding missions to Tibet. The delegates were profoundly shocked by the plight of Tibetans under Chinese rule, shocked by the repressive conditions they witnessed. They were shocked by what they saw—and also shocked by what they did not see. They did not see any wildlife. There was an eerie silence on the grasslands—no honking of bar-headed geese, no flocks of brahminy ducks, no thundering hoofs of wild asses or wild yaks. In less than two decades, the wildlife of Tibet was annihilated.

The Dalai Lama writes: "We always considered our wild animals a symbol of freedom. Nothing held them back, they ran free. Without them something is missing from even the most beautiful landscape. The land becomes empty, and only with the presence of wild animals can it gain its full beauty. Nature and wild animals are complementary. People who live among wildlife without harming it are in harmony with the environment. Sadly, the profusion of wildlife that once thrived in the region is no longer to be found."[5]

Traveling around Tibet from the 1980s to the 2000s, I came across very little wildlife. In 1995 in far-west Tibet, roaming for a month in remote areas, I saw only a few wild asses and some raptors. I sighted a small flock of black-necked cranes wading in wetlands near Yamdrok Tso. In Lhasa, I spotted some bar-headed geese sunning themselves at the lake at the back of the Potala Palace. The biggest "wildlife" sightings were at a mini-zoo inside the grounds of the Norbulingka summer palace in Lhasa. This hosted a motley collection of bears, spotted deer, foxes, lynxes, Argali bighorn sheep, bar-headed geese, and bearded vultures—none of which looked especially thrilled about living on bare concrete. The wild yak once roamed the grasslands in huge herds; it is now a highly endangered species in Tibet, with fewer than a thousand thought to remain. This is a home where the wild yaks no longer roam, where the musk deer and the antelope no longer play.

Where did all that wildlife go? Well, most likely the Chinese military and settlers ate it. The wildlife was machine-gunned, butchered, and cooked up on the spot, or else exported to east-coast Chinese cities, catering to high demand for exotic species like wild yak, gazelle, and blue sheep as gastronomic delicacies. There is a similar demand for exotic creatures for use in Chinese traditional medicine: this has decimated numbers of the musk deer and the snow leopard, for instance. The snow leopard was also hunted for its valuable pelt, along with animals like the Himalayan marmot. Herds of Tibetan antelope remain today in very remote parts of Tibet, but their numbers have plummeted. In the 1980s and 1990s, Tibetan antelopes were slaughtered for their valuable underwool, the finest on earth, woven into shawls in Kashmir. Other animals were hunted for sport.

Chinese hunters even ate the exotic birds of Tibet. Birds are considered a delicacy on the Chinese menu. The national bird of Tibet is no longer the black-necked crane. It is the Construction Crane.

PART ONE

LISTENING TO GLACIERS

This center of heaven
This core of the earth
This heart of the world
Fenced round by snow
The headland of all rivers
Where the mountains are high
And the land is pure

     —Tibetan poem, written about 1,200 years ago★

★ Source: Translation from text of the *Tibetan Chronicle*, written on the back of Chinese Buddhist scrolls. The scrolls were part of a large hidden library discovered in 1908 at the Dunhuang caves in Gansu by Western scholars Auriel Stein and Paul Pelliot. The *Tibetan Chronicle* was probably compiled in the period AD 800 to 840, and represents the earliest surviving record of Tibetan literature. It is kept as part of the Pelliot Collection at the National Library of France, in Paris.

CHAPTER ONE

Rafting the Drigung

What on Earth Are China's Engineers Getting Up To?

There are things you take for granted in Tibet: magnificent snowcaps, powerful gushing rivers, hearty nomads, yaks grazing the grasslands under vast open skies. I never imagined I would have to write the following lines: *Tibetans have experienced waves of genocide since the 1950s. Now they are facing ecocide—the reckless destruction of their fragile high-altitude environment.*

The Himalayan snowcaps are in meltdown mode due to climate change—accelerated by a rain of black soot from massive burning of coal and other fossil fuels in both China and India. The mighty rivers of Tibet are being dammed by Chinese engineering consortiums to feed the mainland's relentless quest for power. There are plans to divert water from some major rivers sourced in Tibet to feed China's desperate thirst for clean water. The grasslands of Tibet are being usurped by desert—partly due to climate change, but mostly due to the shortsighted Chinese policy of forcibly removing Tibetan nomads from the grasslands and settling them in concrete hovels. Even yaks—the iconic creatures of Tibet—are vanishing from central Tibet: the yaks are sent to slaughterhouses when nomads are settled. There is high demand for yak meat among wealthy Chinese.

When I first reached Tibet in 1985, little of this was apparent—at least, not at the sites where foreign "big-noses" were allowed to go and sniff around. This has all come to pass in a few short decades, unfolding right before my eyes. After Tibet opened up to individual travelers, I entered overland with an assignment to write a guidebook. It was published in 1986 by Lonely Planet—the first-ever English guidebook to modern Tibet. In the 1980s, 1990s, and the 2000s, I traveled all over the Tibetan world—and central Tibet itself—in the course of gathering research material, later for the British publisher Bradt Travel Guides.

In 2005, I traveled to Tibet not only to update the Bradt guidebook, but also to work on a story about the new railway arriving in Lhasa and its potential impact on Tibetans. I did some firsthand railway research, taking pictures of the new line and its bridges and tunnels. But I fell into a much bigger story—a black hole of a story—about dam building in Tibet. In fact, I stumbled into a story about impending disaster for Tibet and beyond.

So let me be your guide on a very different journey in *Meltdown in Tibet*, as we take in the glaciers, moraines, grasslands, sacred mountains, and lakes of Tibet—and roll on past railway tracks, dams, and mining sites. *Meltdown in Tibet* is an alternative guide—a guide to disaster, a personal take on environmental issues in Tibet based on my observations on the ground and on a mountain of research.

This book is about looming water crisis in Asia—and about looming environmental chaos in Tibet, India, and Asia. I believe *looming* will almost certainly translate to *real* because absolutely nothing is being done to stop China's wholesale destruction of the rivers, forests, mountains, and grasslands of Tibet.

China's official response to environmental degradation in Tibet repeatedly blames everything on climate change (which, it should be pointed out, is largely sparked by humans). For Tibetans, this is not about climate change, it's about the climate of fear that prevails—ruthless Chinese repression that renders Tibetans powerless to do anything to stop the reckless destruction of their sacred land. At the time of this writing, there have been more than 130 self-immolations by Tibetans since 2009—with over 100 deaths resulting. Tibetans have set themselves on fire in the ultimate act of desperation to protest what is happening to their land and their culture.

★   ★   ★

AUGUST 2005: MY INTRODUCTION TO THE TREMENDOUS POWER OF THE RIVERS of Tibet comes via a rafting ride on the Drigung River, a few hours' drive from Lhasa. This is a baptism fueled by pure adrenaline, a baptism that raises lots of questions—and gets me going on research.

Feeling rather ridiculous—decked out in a flashy wetsuit, rubber booties, lifejacket, and helmet—I waddle over to the big blue raft. All the gear is in the interests of warmth and waterproofing—and safety. Georgia gives us a briefing on what to do if ejected from the craft (don't try and tie a rescue rope around your neck). Georgia, from Australia, is conducting safety rescue courses for the Tibetan rafting trainees. She's our safety kayaker on this day trip, scouting rapids ahead and trolling for any body that happens to be floating past.

Instructions over, we turn to face the river itself, which is swollen by monsoon rains—definitely moody—frothy and foaming in parts. No room for error here. From this point, rapids are class III and IV—and our lives are in the hands of Captain Ram. Ram is a bearded young Nepalese with long hair tied back in a ponytail, and a warped sense of humor. Happily, Ram has ten years of white-water rafting and kayaking experience on rivers in Nepal. He gives us a briefing on when to paddle forward, backward, stop, jump to the left side of the boat, jump to the right.

There are not many rivers in the world where you can raft above 13,000 feet. In Tibet, most terrain starts at this elevation, and it's all uphill from there. I check my watch: the altitude at the put-in point is 13,400 feet.

We push off into the swirling Drigung Chu, nerves on edge. The majestic landscape flashes by in a blur—not much time to take it in when your energy is concentrated on remaining glued to the raft. But you feel the raw power of the river as no onlooker can. And you begin to realize that rivers are not all that simple—a point emphasized by the menacing waves crashing around your head. Rafters have more specific lingo for them: standing waves, pillow waves, eddies, seams, and drops—and deadly "holes."

On the river today are two matching inflatable blue rafts, both with a Nepalese Captain Ram at the helm. They provide a sort of stereo rafting effect for those with altitude-induced illusions. Injected into this is a dose of high spirits created by competitiveness among rafters—broadsiding boats, and drenching occupants by batting paddles on the surface. In the rafts: a couple from Germany, two Swiss guys, a brother and sister from the United States, a Dutchman, a Tibetan woman. I have missed most names, but remember the nationalities. Apart from high water, there's a lot of adrenaline floating around. The symphony of first-time rafters: high-pitched yelps, yahooing, and the occasional scream as waves crash over the bows, drenching all in frigid water. A good deal of the vocalizing emanates from Lodol, the young Tibetan woman on board next to me. She's on the lam: everybody at work has been told she's taken a day off to deal with family problems—and lord knows what she has told her family, as they would surely fear for her safety.

I'm trying to figure out if Captain Ram is bent on deliberately steering us into troubled waters at times to increase the excitement. In any case, he's a wizard at reading the river—looking for the best line through the rapids, steering clear of submerged rocks—and avoiding "holes" (like the spin-cycle of a washing machine, only much magnified) that can flip a small craft. *Forward! Forward!* yells Ram, urgently at one point. That translates as *Fast forward!* I think. There's no special command for *Jump out of your skin!*—which could easily be applied when we reach a spot with barely enough space for the raft to squeeze through. It's a kind of gate formed by rocks, so our raft has to be very precise. But we pull it off. *Everybody good?* inquires Ram. He calls for a group high-five with upright paddles.

Woman overboard! We have lost the college student from Virginia, along with the Dutchman—both swept out of the raft by a freak wave. But they are soon back with us, all in one piece though somewhat shaken. To the rescue is Phuntsok, the Tibetan trainee rafter aboard. In a few more seasons, he should be able to take over the helm from experienced rafters like Ram. Tibetan trainees have to overcome cultural taboos about fast-flowing rivers—normally places to stay well away from because they are associated with drowning. There is no tradition of pleasure boating in Tibet. Tibetans don't spend any time on rivers, they don't fish, and they look down on the boatmen who ply traditional yak-skin coracles at river crossings.

In calmer waters, we finally relax on the paddle and take in the scenery. And wave at Tibetans lining the banks. Some wave back, others just stare, open-mouthed. Foreigners are alien enough, but ones dressed in colored wetsuits and helmets must surely appear quite bizarre. When we stop for lunch at the river's edge, curious Tibetans edge closer—not so shy.

On the Drigung, you get to experience just how powerful Tibet's rivers are. The rafting gives you a huge adrenalin hit. I'm on a euphoric high that stays with me for the rest of the day. But lunchtime conversation takes a surprising turn. The rafting guides are not talking about first descents, they're talking about *last* descents. The Drigung River is the site of the first commercial rafting trip in Tibet, only started a few years back. But the run may soon be inaccessible; dam building could block the river, according to one guide.

After lunch, we resume the rafting descent: more bouts of being heaved around and showered in freezing water. This alternates with more tranquil stretches where I even relax enough to indulge in bird spotting: I sight a hoopoe, an exotic-looking bird with a spiky orange crest and black-and-white wings.

All too soon, the wild ride comes to an end. The gear is stowed away. The rafts are deflated, rolled up, and packed onto a minibus. We help ourselves to mugs of hot tea, which is good because my fingers are numb from the icy Drigung waters. And yet while most of me feels numb, my brain is exceedingly clear and calm. I have survived the ride.

But something leaves a bad taste. At the tail end of the rafting run, we passed a small dam under construction. The guides mentioned there's a much bigger one downstream on the Drigung. Hydro megaprojects are popping up all over, one guide said, to supply the Chinese industrial ventures with power. Chinese engineers want to bore tunnels to divert rivers from Tibet to the north and east, to supply water-starved Chinese cities. That sticks in my head. The water diversion, the dams, the huge tunnels. What on earth are China's engineers getting up to?

This new information surprises me. As a guidebook writer I have traveled to the Tibetan world numerous times, and have read everything I could lay my hands on. But this is the first time I have heard of dam building in Tibet. And yet it makes sense: Tibet has very powerful rivers, with the potential to generate huge amounts of hydropower. The more I dwell on this, the more I am convinced I should get cracking and research it—and relay this news to others.

★ ★ ★

AND SO I START DELVING INTO THE ENGINEERING PUZZLE. DELVING IS PERHAPS NOT the word I am looking for: it sounds too casual. Gathering any kind of research on Tibet is extremely difficult because there's a virtual blackout on media in Tibet. It is an information black hole. Information doesn't get in, information doesn't get out. Foreign journalists are refused entry to Tibet; a select few manage to make it there on brief, carefully orchestrated tours where every step is monitored by Chinese minders.

And gathering information can be a risky business in China. Information disappears, along with the messenger. Anything to do with

Tibet is classified top secret by Chinese authorities. Therefore, getting information out of Tibet is regarded as "leaking state secrets." For Tibetans, the penalty for being accused of this could be years in jail, though it is never specified what these state secrets are. Reporting a protest by Tibetans via e-mail or on the phone amounts to leaking state secrets. And to cover all bases, there are other absurd accusations such as "splitting the motherland" or "spreading rumors."

The Party definitely does not like criticism. The immediate reaction to any criticism is to silence the critic. Facebook, YouTube, and Twitter are banned in China. It gets worse in Tibet. In a restive place like Aba in eastern Tibet, Internet access is either sporadic or it completely vanishes. This is not a technical problem: it is because of Aba's rebellious citizens. The police and propaganda department in Aba appear to have functioning Internet connections. In other parts of this region, monasteries have been raided and satellite dishes seized. Police routinely go through cell phones looking for forbidden images such as the Tibetan flag or a picture of the Dalai Lama. Finding such items is justification for arrest and imprisonment.

Pre-1950 Tibet was run by the strangest form of government ever devised: a theocracy ruled by a lineage of reincarnate Dalai Lamas. After the Chinese takeover, Tibetans were told their former masters were parasites, and that the way forward lay with socialism introduced by the Chinese Communist Party. Happy smiling Tibetans are depicted in posters and propaganda as living in a Maoist socialist paradise where all their needs have been taken care of by the benevolent CCP. But it seems that Tibet has gone from theocracy to "thugocracy"—a term coined by veteran journalist Paul Mooney to describe the Chinese leadership, which qualifies for the dubious distinction of being the longest-lasting repressive regime in modern history.

In 2013, and also in 2012 and 2011, China spent more on its budget for internal security than it did on its defense budget for external security. For 2013, the military defense budget was announced at 740.6 billion yuan

($119 billion) while domestic security spending was allocated at 769.1 billion yuan ($124 billion).[1]

Chinese authorities spend extraordinary amounts of money on surveillance equipment, and on weapons and riot gear for China's vast network of official and undercover police and paramilitary forces. Huge amounts are dedicated to maintaining an elaborate complex of jails and prison labor camps. This is intended to keep the nation's people in check as discontent mounts over issues such as corruption, illegal land-grabs, inequality, and pollution. Government-backed studies indicate that the number of officially reported "mass incidents" of unrest across China skyrocketed from 8,700 in 1993 to around 90,000 in 2010 (those figures could actually be much higher).[2]

Ethnic unrest is particularly treated with brute force. Indeed, some ethnic groups such as Uighurs and Tibetans have been accused of "terrorism" by Chinese authorities. Protests in Tibet are dealt with by People's Liberation Army (PLA) troops and paramilitary forces in overwhelming numbers, armed to the teeth. For Tibetans, their homeland has become a place of great sadness and little hope—a psychological black hole, a downward spiral of feeling helpless and desperate. For Tibetan nomads, it is a black hole with little prospect of employment.

★   ★   ★

FIRST COME THE TUNNELS. THE FIRST THING THAT CAUGHT MY ATTENTION WHEN I stepped off the plane in Gongkar in 2005 and caught a taxi to Lhasa was a huge tunnel that had not been there on my previous visit. The entrance was painted with Tibetan auspicious motifs—rainbows and black-necked cranes.

I whipped out my video camera and pointed it at the front windscreen, thinking that this tunnel would finish in a matter of seconds. It didn't. It went on and on, boring through an entire mountain—quite a feat of engineering. Galashan Tunnel turned out to be 8,028 feet long.

It was built to shave an hour off the trip from the airport to downtown Lhasa. But was this tunnel really necessary? It saved time, but at what cost to the environment? For Tibetans, with their belief in deities resident in mountains, such tunneling could well be seen as defilement of their land. For me, it's symbolic of something else: Tunnel Vision, a one-sided view of problem-solving.

Chinese engineers are the most advanced moles in the world now. They have the most advanced tunneling technology. Tunnels boring through mountains, diversion tunnels for dam building, tunnels for mineral extraction. The 710-mile railway from Golmud to Lhasa bores through some 18 miles of tunnels, including the world's highest tunnel, Fenghuoshan, at 16,093 feet. The train crests two 16,400-foot passes and crosses more than 400 bridges, running past more than 30 stations before reaching Lhasa.

The railway line got under way in 2001 and was completed in 2005 (becoming fully operational in 2006) at a cost of $4.1 billion. In fact, over a four-year period, the railway racked up bills that surpass the entire budget spent in Tibet on education and health care since it was invaded by China in 1950. Obviously, the railway was not built for philanthropic purposes. Later, Beijing admitted that mining was a major factor in the decision to build the railway and that the income and benefits from mining would easily cover the cost of building it. Mining is not possible without the railway, which allows for shipping minerals economically.

For Chinese engineers, the Golmud-to-Lhasa railway is a case of conquering the impossible—an achievement up there with launching a man into space. The technical challenges were immense for building rails on unstable permafrost terrain, which accounted for 340 miles, or about half the length of the Golmud-Lhasa line.

The train is a game-changer, fast-tracking the destruction of Tibet's environment. The railway is the first megaproject in Tibet, and it opens the door to a host of other engineering megaprojects. The train has made possible a huge influx of Chinese settlers, migrant workers, and tourists, and has enabled large-scale exploitation of Tibet's resources. Large-scale mining in Tibet would not be possible without the train to export minerals economically. Nor would the export of Tibet's spring water in the form of bottled water. Nor would the construction of megadams on Tibet's rivers be possible, as the train brings in materials, technology, and migrant workers for construction of the new dams. The railway is Beijing's opening salvo in the Open-Up-the-West campaign, which got under way in 2000. This is more of a Plunder-the-West campaign, as the railway was specifically built to exploit Tibet's mineral resources and to enable dam building on the plateau.

I am appalled to learn of Canada's involvement in the Tibet railway. Montreal-based companies Bombardier and Power Corporation supplied the high-altitude railcars (the locomotives modified for high altitude are supplied by General Electric USA). Nortel Networks, headquartered in Ontario, supplied the digital wireless communication network for the line. Nortel later went bankrupt due to scandal and mismanagement—and unethical practices. The UK-based Free Tibet Campaign, criticizing Bombardier's involvement in the railway, asked this startling question: *Does Bombardier's Code of Ethics include cultural genocide?*[3] This is a reference to plans for the railway to bring in large numbers of Chinese settlers, allow for rapid deployment of Chinese military, and export Tibet's mineral wealth on a huge scale. Bombardier tried to distance itself from involvement in Tibet by saying they only made the railcars.

The railway tracks won't stop in Lhasa. New tracks are snaking toward large mining sites both east and west of Lhasa. In 2014, the railway reached Tibet's second largest town, Shigatse, with a line 157 miles in length. The line runs along the Yarlung Tsangpo valley: about 45 percent of the line passes through tunnels, including one tunnel 6.4 miles in length—a major feat of engineering. Road infrastructure is expanding considerably in central Tibet. New airfields have been opened. All with an eye to exploiting Tibet's powerful rivers and its abundant mineral resources.

CHAPTER TWO

Crisis at the Third Pole

What Does a Rain of Black Soot Have to Do with This?

Tibet will take your breath away. Initially, it's not the views, it's the altitude. Arriving in Tibet is like entering a different world—you need to adapt to the rarefied air at 13,000 feet, and pace yourself over the first few weeks while the body adjusts to changes. Altitude is what defines Tibet: often hovering above 12,000 feet, and sometimes reaching 18,000 feet or more on high passes. Peaks topping 23,000 feet form the original boundaries of Tibet—with the Himalayan range to the south, the Karakoram range to the west, the Kunlun range to the north, and the Hengduan range in the east. And within this icy wonderland are tens of thousands of glaciers: around 46,000 glaciers in the Himalayas, for starters.

When cresting a high pass, Tibetans tie prayer flags to rock cairns and pray for safe passage by shouting *Lha Gyalo! Victory to the Gods!* Altitude has shaped everything on this high plateau—from its otherworldly landscape and majestic snowcaps to its unique flora and fauna and its special people and culture. The Tibetan Plateau is a fragile ecosystem. Once damaged, it takes a long time to recover.

The fauna of Tibet is superbly adapted to altitude. The bar-headed goose offers a spectacular example. It resembles a normal goose with some black bars at the back of its head—that's where the name comes from. This bird, however, is extraordinary: it is an astronaut on the wing. Bar-headed geese can fly at altitudes of up to 29,500 feet, high enough to cruise over the top of Mount Everest. Flying in formation, bar-headed geese clear the Himalayas twice a year to complete an epic migration. When winter is over, the geese leave their breeding grounds in the lowlands of Nepal and India, going from near sea level straight up to 20,000 feet, heading over high passes and Himalayan peaks to breeding grounds in Amdo (Qinghai Lake), Outer Mongolia, and Kyrgyzstan. Tagged bar-headed geese, tracked by satellite, reveal that this journey from sea level up to 20,000 feet is accomplished in an astonishing seven or eight hours on the wing.[1]

The bar-headed goose has been clocked flying at 50 mph, but with a tailwind it can rocket along at speeds up to 100 mph. An inner layer of down feathers prevents the bird from freezing to death, while an outer layer of tightly woven feathers apparently waterproofs the goose and prevents buildup of body ice that would cause it to plunge to its doom. The bar-headed goose is the ultimate high-flier of the avian world. Ornithologists have dubbed its migration the most extreme on earth.

Other species are attuned to high-altitude snowy conditions. The snow leopard has large paws that act like snowshoes, and it uses its enormous bushy tail to stabilize acrobatic leaps. At night it wraps its tail around its body and face like a scarf to withstand freezing temperatures. The wild yak's long shaggy coat enables it to withstand violent winds and snowstorms. Males can weigh in at up to a ton, making this one of the largest land mammals in Asia. Species like the wild yak are so attuned to altitude that they have trouble surviving at lower altitudes.

★ ★ ★

TIBETANS HAVE ADAPTED SUPERBLY TO THEIR HARSH ENVIRONMENT. THEY HAVE A physiology that is attuned to altitude—their blood has a greater red-cell count and their lung capacity is larger than normal. But more than this, they learned how to live in harmony with the land upon which their survival depended. They developed a great respect for nature—and a spiritual reverence for the landscape.

Light years ahead of the West, Tibetans developed the concept of sacred mountains, sacred valleys, sacred lakes—where the fauna and flora were to be left totally untouched. This essentially derives from Bon, an ancient Tibetan faith. Bon is an animist faith, with belief in powerful spirits dwelling in trees, lakes, and mountains that are not to be disturbed. If disturbed, they can unleash demonic forces. Seals specifically prohibiting fishing and hunting in certain valleys date back to the fifteenth century in Tibet. Local rulers and high lamas brought in a system of sealing off whole regions—including forests, grasslands, lakes, and rivers—as sanctuaries.

It would be erroneous to paint a picture of perfection here. Tibetans were not environmentalists. They had no concept of sanitation, plumbing, or garbage disposal. However, the fact that they were out of sync with modernity made Tibetans from the pre-1950 era rather eco-friendly. No wheeled vehicles, no machinery, no heavy mining equipment to chew up the scenery or change it. No high-powered weapons to decimate wildlife. No population density at all: there were fewer than 6 million Tibetans scattered over an area the size of western Europe. Tibetans did not have to patrol or police the environment. The environment was simply left alone. The rivers were freeflowing. And the wildlife was abundant.

★　★　★

MOUNT KAILASH, WESTERN TIBET, SEPTEMBER 1995: I SET OFF WITH A SMALL group of travelers to drive to the most sacred peak in all Tibet. That involves a week of bouncing around in a Land Cruiser, negotiating some very rough roads. So rough that I have taken to wearing a woolen hat to soften the blows caused by hitting the interior roof when the vehicle goes over a rut. Tibetan pilgrims travel much less comfortably, crowded into the back of a truck. Tibetans take time out to pay homage to key temples across the plateau, and to make walking circuits of sacred lakes and mountains. An arduous circuit of Mount Kailash on foot is the goal. For our small group, this is a major trek. For Tibetans, Kailash is the top pilgrimage circuit.

At Kailash, I am mesmerized by the vastness of the place—drinking in the pristine Himalayan vistas and the majestic wilderness. We take our time at Kailash—a day hike for acclimatization, three days for the circuit, and one day off to visit a glacier. Tibetans often do the entire circuit in one long day. And then they might come back and do another circuit for more merit the following day. Then there are hardier pilgrims who perform full-body prostrations all the way around the mountain. At a rest stop, a man with a rubber apron, rubber knee pads, and mittens cut out of old tires comes past us, standing up in prayer posture, throwing himself outstretched to the ground, then inch-worming forward to perform the next prostration. I donate a chocolate bar, which he gratefully pockets. If I were in his shoes, I would have wolfed that bar down on the spot.

Day two on the circuit dawns crystal clear. I step outside the monastery guesthouse and am stunned to see, looming right in front of me, the north face of Kailash, which up to now has been shrouded in mist. The dome-shaped peak glistens with icy walls—bewitching, hypnotizing, powerful. Which is why the Tibetans call the mountain Kang Rinpoche—Jewel of the Snows. The symmetrical dome looks like an uncut diamond.

For Tibetan Buddhists, Kailash is the center of the universe—the earthly manifestation of Mount Meru, the abode of the gods. The peak is modest by Himalayan standards at around 22,000 feet high. The sacred mountain draws pilgrims from all over Tibet, with wide variations in dress and hairstyles. And makeup: at a small chapel en route, I notice some pilgrims are not only shiny-eyed, but green-faced. These women wear green "makeup" that is made from concentrated buttermilk or roots: a cross between cosmetic and sunblock, it is applied to ward off the high-altitude sun and to counter skin dryness. With the pilgrims, one thing stays the same: the ready smiles that show dazzling white teeth. Early Western explorers in Tibet remarked that although toothbrushes were not in use, the Tibetans had superb teeth. It's in the DNA. And Tibetan pilgrims are very tough. As I huff and puff my way toward the 18,400-foot Drolma La pass, hardy grandmothers keep overtaking me, with big grins spread over their wrinkled faces. They must be at least 65. Fried by the altitude and fighting a headache, I go slowly. The grandmothers, I reason, must be very well acclimatized to 18,000 feet. At the top of Drolma La, a large boulder carved with an image of the deity Tara is festooned with prayer flags. Here pilgrims throw paper wind horse squares into the air, tie on prayer flags, and make offerings and prayers to the resident deities of the mountain, asking for safe passage for the rest of their journey. They leave coins, paper bills, locks of hair, and photos of themselves or other mementoes of their passage.

When people see the photos I took in this region, they ask me what kind of software I used to alter the colors—how did I get such a brilliant blue in that lake, or a deep ochre in the hills, or a stunning green in the valleys? But I didn't use any software. That's the way the place is—colors seem to glow with intensity at this altitude. Tibet has an otherworldly high-altitude environment. And a fragile ecosystem—known to Tibetans as "Ghangjong," the Land of Snows. Or should it be renamed the Land of Melting Snows? The glaciers are in meltdown mode due to climate change and human interference.

★　★　★

OUTSIDE OF THE ARCTIC AND ANTARCTIC, THE TIBETAN PLATEAU HAS THE largest store of ice on earth, leading to its designation as the "Third Pole." The north and south poles get all the attention when it comes to the impact of ice melting, with studies on polar bears and emperor penguins. In terms of human impact, however, meltdown of Tibetan Plateau glaciers will have far greater repercussions. Many Western climatologists are not familiar with the impact of changes on the plateau, most likely because there is far less scientific data available, whereas the Arctic and Antarctic have seen many scientific expeditions. Within Tibet, expeditions to remote parts of the plateau are mostly conducted by Chinese scientists, not Western researchers (though some joint Chinese-Western research has been permitted). Most of the plateau lies within the region of Chinese-controlled Tibet.

With its myriad glaciers acting as major water-keeper for the entire region, Tibet is the icebox of Asia. There are numerous sources of water in Tibet—lakes, rivers, wetlands, permafrost, glaciers, snowpack, groundwater, and springs. With some 37,000 glaciers in Chinese-controlled Tibet alone, Lonnie Thompson, glaciologist at Ohio State University, calls the Himalayan region "Asia's freshwater bank account." It's an icebox where massive buildup of new snow and ice (deposits) has traditionally offset its annual runoffs in rivers (withdrawals). But now the region is facing bankruptcy because rapid "withdrawals" are depleting the account.[2]

Glaciers are slow water-release mechanisms, keeping the rivers alive during dry spells and allowing for storage of water. When annual Indian monsoon rains hit Tibet, they are converted into snow, which settles on glaciers and thus makes monsoon rain usable over long periods as a meltwater source that enters the rivers. The snowpack acts as storage for monsoon rainwater that would otherwise dissipate. Of the 680 glaciers currently monitored by Chinese scientists, 95 percent are shedding more ice than they are adding, particularly at the southern and eastern edges of the plateau. "The glaciers are not simply retreating, they are losing mass from the surface down," says Thompson.[3] And if the glaciers disappear, the rivers will essentially dry up. "Fifty percent of the glaciers were retreating from 1950 to 1980 in the Tibetan region; that rose to 95 percent in the early 21st century," claims Tandong Yao, director of the Chinese Academy of Science's Institute of Tibetan Plateau Research.[4] Chinese scientists believe that 40 percent of Tibet's glaciers will be gone by the year 2050.[5]

The biggest question of all is, *When will Himalayan glaciers all melt down and vanish?* Nobody knows.

In 2007, the UN Intergovernmental Panel on Climate Change (IPCC) put out an extensive assessment report, running to 2,800 pages, that asserted that climate change is accelerating: ice is melting faster, glaciers are discharging ice to the sea faster, temperatures are rising faster—and that humans are the principal driver of all this change. Climate-change skeptics attacked the report based on a number of errors. One of these errors was that Asian glaciers would disappear by the year 2035. The source of the error was a transposition of numbers from 2350 to 2035. In other words, another 300-year reprieve for Himalayan glaciers—perhaps. But it's equally possible that the ice will disappear much sooner. Henry Pollack, a key member of the IPCC, puts it this way: "During the past three centuries, rapid population growth and the rise of industrial economies have pushed the relationship between ice and people to a tipping point. Soon, for the first time in human history, we may live on a planet without ice."[6]

★ ★ ★

GLACIERS ARE LIVING ENTITIES—AWE INSPIRING AND DANGEROUS IF YOU GET TOO close. They creak and groan, and crackle and rumble. And sometimes they roar. These days glaciers have lots to complain about. But are we listening? American climber Ed Viesturs developed a survival strategy he calls "listen to the mountain." Before setting off on a dangerous climb to the summit, he sits and meditates, and takes time to listen to the mountain and the glaciers—to figure out if the mountain sounds welcoming or dangerous, to determine if it is about to unleash avalanches or not. For Viesturs the climber, listening to the mountain is a matter of life and death.[7] And for millions of South Asians, reading the glaciers may be a matter of urgent survival. Here's why.

You need time-lapse photography to show retreating glaciers. The melting is slow. But dramatic visual evidence of meltdown comes in the form of glacial lakes, pooling at the foot of melting glaciers. These lakes can be seen on Google Earth, and they are extremely hazardous. They are found in Tibet, Bhutan, Nepal, and in mountain regions such as Kashmir. After a sudden landslide or debris flow interrupts a river that would naturally drain a melting glacier, these lakes build up in size behind a wall of mud and debris. When that wall breaks, it sends a glacial flashflood cascading down the valley below, destroying all in its path, like a Himalayan tsunami that sweeps away roads, bridges, entire villages.

These flashfloods, known as glacial lake outburst floods, have occurred more than 30 times in the last 70 years in Nepal. There are around 3,300 glaciers in Nepal, roughly two-thirds of which contain glacial lakes. Scientists come to study Imja Tsho in northeast Nepal because it is one of the fastest-expanding glacial lakes in the Himalayas: it is over half a mile long and up to 300 feet deep. If the lake walls burst, it would take out the entire town of Dingboche below. Similar problems exist in Bhutan and Tibet. Bhutan has identified scores of sites for potential glacial flashfloods within its borders, of which 25 are at extremely high risk of bursting. Lungge Tsho, a glacial lake in Bhutan, had a dangerous outflow in 1994.

★ ★ ★

LHASA, SEPTEMBER 2010: AT THE HOTEL, I HEAR A HIGH-PITCHED WHINING. Could it be? Minutes later, I have zapped the culprit: a mosquito. In most parts of Asia, this would not be news. In Lhasa, it is. Mosquitoes and other bugs have an altitude barrier, not usually flying above 11,000 feet. I have never seen a mosquito in Lhasa before. Lhasa sits at 12,000 feet. Intrigued by this, I later conducted some research and discovered that since 2009 many Lhasa residents have complained of being bitten by mosquitoes—for the first time in living memory. Mosquitoes are moving beyond the normal altitude threshold. They have been found at Namche Bazaar in Nepal, at 11,280 feet. Butterflies have been sighted at 15,000 feet. And houseflies have even been spotted at Everest base camp in Nepal, at

17,300 feet. Malaria and other mosquito-borne ailments are unknown in Tibet, but it looks like that could change. Explanations for the arrival of mosquitoes in Lhasa range from increased tourism and infrastructure (such as the Lhasa railway) to global warming. Whatever the case, the march of the insects upward in altitude is a sure sign that environmental conditions are changing.

★   ★   ★

IN LATE 2013, THE IPCC RELEASED A REPORT THAT SAID GLOBAL WARMING attributable to human factors was "extremely likely" (translating in scientific terms to 95 percent confidence). In its previous assessment in 2007, the UN-sponsored panel said it was "very likely" (equating to 90 percent confidence) that global warming was man-made.[8] This is the greatest moral crisis of our time—the problem that dwarfs all others. But the world's greatest carbon emitters—China, the United States, and India—have failed to address the pressing issues of climate change. Temperatures on the Tibetan Plateau have warmed by 0.5°F per decade over the past 30 years, about twice the rate of observed global temperature increases.[9] There is no doubt that greatly elevated carbon dioxide emissions from both China and India are leading causes of warming on the Tibetan Plateau. But for glacial meltdown, another significant factor may be the rain of black soot.

Back in the thirteenth century, explorer Marco Polo reported to incredulous Europeans that the Chinese burned a "black rock" for heat. Today, more incredulous news: burning these black rocks is destroying the planet—and speeding up the meltdown of Himalayan glaciers. Lumps of coal burned in Chinese households results in a tremendous output of black carbon, also referred to as black soot. In India, the burning of dung, wood, and crop residues in households (for cooking and heating) sends huge amounts of black carbon into the atmosphere. Black carbon from cities in both India and China travels on air currents and gets trapped on the Tibetan Plateau.

Black carbon is a tiny particle that is generated by the incomplete combustion of fossil fuels, biofuels, or agricultural waste due to a shortage of oxygen. The dark-colored pollutant absorbs heat from the sun both while floating in an air column or once settled on the ground—or the ice. When inhaled, black carbon is harmful to human health, as the particles are so small they can be absorbed into the lungs. Black carbon is different from greenhouse gases like carbon dioxide (emitted from coal-fired plants) and methane. Black carbon is actually not a gas: its damaging power comes from its absorption of heat. The Himalayan range sits between the nations of China and India—the world's worst offenders for carbon dioxide emissions from coal-fired power plants and producers of great quantities of black soot. Both pollutants affect the glaciers of the Himalayas and other ranges, but surprisingly, black soot may be the greater problem. Its impact is now being given greater prominence by scientists. James Hansen, a director at NASA and coauthor of a study on the Himalayan region released in 2009, says, "Black soot is probably responsible for as much as half of the glacial melt, and greenhouse gases are responsible for the rest." His coauthor, Junji Cao, a researcher from the Chinese Academy of Sciences in Beijing, notes, "During the last 20 years, the black soot concentration has increased two- to three-fold relative to its concentration in 1975."[10]

In a report released in January 2014, Chinese scientists in Beijing revealed that the amount of black soot generated in China and India has been greatly underestimated. Their studies show that certain regions of the two countries experience two to three times greater levels of this pollutant than previous models have suggested.[11]

Shimmering white glaciers reflect the sun's heat, while "dirty" glaciers—caused by black carbon depositions—will do the exact opposite: they will absorb the sun's rays, thereby accelerating glacial meltdown. Highly reflective white ice sheets near the Arctic and Antarctic normally bounce 70 percent of incoming sunlight back into space. If melting turns ice sheets into open ocean, this surface will no longer bounce light back. Instead, the open ocean will absorb 90 percent of the sunlight striking it, and convert it back into heat. Soot in the Himalayan region comes mainly from burning of agricultural fields, diesel engines, and residential cooking and heating stoves. Multiply the cooking stoves by several billion to get an idea of how much black soot may be floating around in the air.

There are solutions for the black carbon problem: ensuring proper filters are used for diesel engines, and reducing the burning of forest and other areas for land clearing. But the greatest step forward would be to give villagers and urban dwellers access to cleaner, more efficient forms of energy. Change the cooking and heating methods, preferably to systems that are smoke-free. Atmospheric scientist Veerabhadran Ramanathan has done simulations that suggest that removal of traditional cooking methods (wood, dung, and crop residues) eliminates 40 to 60 percent of black carbon emissions.[12] While greenhouse gases may stay in the atmosphere for decades, black carbon emissions are washed out within a few weeks and then replaced. So tackling the problem of black carbon would have an immediate effect.

Across Asia, governments have attempted to introduce cleaner-burning cookstoves—with varying degrees of success. A large program to disseminate improved cookstoves has been ongoing in China since the 1980s, making big strides in improving efficiency for cooking and heating. A more recent initiative is the introduction of solar cookers, which produce zero black carbon—but these are expensive and require access to strong sunlight on a regular basis. Chinese-made solar stoves and solar panels used in Tibet are highly effective due to the intensity of the sun and the frequent number of sunny days. But a lot more needs to be done to tackle the problem of black carbon emissions from traditional cooking and heating methods.

★   ★   ★

SOMETIME IN 2006, CHINA SURPASSED THE UNITED STATES AS THE WORLD'S TOP emitter of carbon dioxide and other heat-trapping gases. China thus attained the dubious distinction of taking the lead role in driving climate change. Since then, China's carbon dioxide emissions have spiked significantly, due to increases in coal burning. According to the Global Carbon Project, the world's top carbon emitters in 2012 were China (responsible for 27 percent of world total emissions), the United States (14 percent of total), and India (6 percent of total).[13] Burning of coal accounted for roughly 43 percent of global carbon emissions in 2012, followed by oil (33 percent of emissions) and gas (18 percent of emissions).[14] Statistics for global carbon emissions vary by source. For 2013, one study showed China was responsible for 23 percent of global emissions, the United States responsible for 15.5 percent of emissions, and India for 5.1 percent. But there is one constant statistic: China is way out in front of the pack—an environmental nightmare that is spiraling out of control. There was a time when environmental damage was localized to specific regions. That time is gone. Carbon emissions are a global problem. China is exporting pollution: filthy emissions are carried by powerful winds across the Pacific Ocean within days, and they contribute to air pollution on the west coast of the United States. The first landfall on this Pacific pollution route is Hawaii.

In May 2013, Mauna Loa Observatory in Hawaii showed levels of atmospheric carbon dioxide peaking at 400 parts per million (ppm)—a grim milestone for humankind. The last time carbon dioxide levels were this high was between 3 and 5 million years ago, in the Pliocene epoch. The climate of the planet was hotter then, and sea levels were much higher. It was a very different-looking planet.[15]

Atmospheric carbon dioxide has been accurately measured since 1958 in Hawaii, in testing developed by Charles Keeling. Then the level was recorded at 315 ppm. Keeling's son, Ralph, carries on his work—not just to monitor the levels of carbon dioxide, but to make people aware of what the research means. Levels of 350 ppm would be ideal, but what would it take to stop emissions, even at 400 ppm? Ralph Keeling attempts a reply: "The answer is that we would have to reduce immediately our burning of fossil fuels by something like 55 to 60 percent. So it's a pretty drastic change. That is clearly not going to happen. If it did happen, it would be an economic catastrophe. So, it's not in the realm of something we should hope for, but it tells you where we have to get to at some point. We have to actually move away from fossil fuel burning in such a way that we practically go fossil-fuel-free within the next half a century or century, if we're going to avoid going above considerably higher levels like 500 parts per million."[16]

But those reductions in carbon emissions are simply not happening in China and India. As author Lester Brown points out: "Ironically, the two countries that are planning to build most of the new coal-fired power plants, China and India, are precisely the ones whose food security is most massively threatened by the carbon emitted from burning coal. It is now in their interest to try and save their mountain glaciers by quickly shifting energy investment from coal-fired power plants into energy efficiency, wind farms, and solar thermal and geothermal power plants."[17]

Tibet's glaciers are in meltdown mode, which threatens the very existence of China and Asia. So what is being done? The Chinese Communist Party has no immediate plans to reduce coal burning, arguing that coal is cheap and that the nation is entitled to experience the same coal-fired industrial revolution phase that Western nations passed through. There are plans to tap into big coal reserves in both Inner Mongolia and Outer Mongolia, and to expand coal use until the year 2020, adding on average 38 GW (gigawatts) of coal energy a year—which is equivalent to adding three large new coal-fired plants every month.[18]

After 2022, a drop in coal production is envisaged, as coal burning is gradually replaced by gas-based energy, hydropower, and renewable energy. The long-range aim is to reduce coal-fired power generation from 68 percent in 2014 to 44 percent in 2030. But even that figure of 44 percent is heavy dependency compared to coal consumption in other nations. Those are projected figures, and what China says on paper may not tally with reality.[19]

China is spending huge sums on security on the Tibetan Plateau, and on the largest standing army in the world—and spending huge amounts on cyber eavesdropping. And huge sums on destructive megaprojects. Could not this money be put to better use for preserving the environment? Bring in more solar power, more wind power: Tibet is second only to the Sahara for solar potential, and in certain seasons sees fierce winds.

In Ladakh, northwest India, solutions are being worked on. There is a major initiative to make use of solar panels for power, using the intense sun at these altitudes. To counter the effects of melting glaciers, a retired civil engineer named Chewang Norphel has built "artificial glaciers." These consist of stone embankments that trap glacial meltwater in the fall and freeze it, to be released for use in the spring growing season, thus mimicking what a natural glacier does.[20] On the Chinese side, there is little sign of initiatives like this. China is more interested in generating artificial rain to increase the amount of water available. They have been launching rain-inducing silver iodide into the clouds. There is no evidence that this cloud-seeding actually works.

★   ★   ★

DR. JOHN STANLEY, DIRECTOR OF ECOLOGICAL BUDDHISM, OUTLINES THE STARK implications of ignoring glacial meltdown: "The essential challenge is to design national energy policies to save the glaciers upon which Tibet, China, the Indian subcontinent and Indochina all depend. Right now China and India are pursuing a 'suicidal' economic policy of growth based on carbon fuels. In truth they need to cut carbon emissions by 80% as soon as possible. Asian civilization will not survive inaction or half-measures like partial decarbonization by mid-century. To date, proposals made by politicians for the convenience of the fossil fuel industry have no authentic bearing on the survival of billions of people, or civilization as we know it."[21]

China has a much harder time pinning the blame on climate change when it comes to toxic smog in China's northern cities. In November 2013, the smog appeared immediately after the start of domestic coal-burning season, when people are allowed to turn on the heat as freezing conditions of winter move in. Winter 2013 weather reports from Beijing and Harbin talk about pale-yellow skies, brown haze, foul smells, and industrial effluent. In Harbin, visibility was reduced on some days to 30 feet due to toxic smog, attributed to coal burning mixed with industrial pollution. China's manufacturing sector is a heavy coal user.

Dubbed the "airpocalypse," the smog continued on through the winter. In December 2013, Shanghai disappeared. It was so shrouded in smog that flights were canceled and cars were ordered off the road. Around the same time, in Nanjing, dense smog led to the announcement of a Red Alert, indicating pollution levels that are off the charts. Citizens were warned to stay home and wear protective masks. The sun in Nanjing was described as being the color of a salted egg-yolk.

To the great annoyance of Chinese authorities, US embassies in Shanghai and Beijing have monitoring stations that analyze five major air pollutants as the basis for readings released publicly under the Air Quality Index (AQI), developed by the US Environmental Protection Agency. The most significant pollutant monitored is PM2.5, which is microscopic particulate matter less than 2.5 micrometers in diameter that can embed deep in the lungs, causing lung disease and respiratory problems. Black carbon from domestic coal burning is a component of particulate matter. The AQI uses a formula to convert PM2.5 readings into values. An AQI value of 50 or less represents good air quality, an AQI value under 100 is satisfactory (though a problem for sensitive individuals), while 300 constitutes a health hazard. Speaking about the environment in the United States, the Environmental Protection Agency says, "AQI values above 300 are extremely rare—they generally occur only during events such as forest fires."[22]

The AQI chart maxes out at 500, which indicates serious health hazards. Readings over 500 are "beyond index." On January 12, 2013, an astonishing AQI value of 755 was recorded in Beijing, based on US Embassy readings.[23] That corresponded to a PM2.5 density of 886 micrograms per cubic meter.

The World Health Organization regards acceptable air quality as less than 25 micrograms per cubic meter over a 24-hour exposure period, so the reading in Beijing was 35 times higher than the safe level. Chinese authorities complain about the American embassy's insistence on independently monitoring air quality: there is often a gulf between those readings and China's official ones, which tend to be less dire. Cell phone users in Beijing can scare themselves by viewing both sets of data on air quality apps.

Smog in Beijing mainly comes from domestic coal burning and car exhaust fumes. There have been some half-hearted attempts to deal with the toxic smog issue. One is a typical Beijing band-aid solution: confiscate barbecue grills and destroy them. At a cost of $5 million, Beijing International School put up two huge domes over its playground area and piped in filtered air to give the students a breather. New requirements have been introduced to train pilots to fly through dense smog for a successful landing. A social media commentator joked that Chinese officials are waiting for the smog to get so thick that they can slice it up with a knife and sell it as tofu.

Toxic smog is not the end of Beijing's air quality problems. In March 2013, a blogger at Sina Weibo posed this question: "Seriously, which is more harmful, the lingering smog caused by industrial pollution or the sandstorms from Mongolia?"[24] That month, the toxic smog became mixed with a rain of fine yellow dust from the Gobi Desert in Mongolia. Every year large amounts of yellow dust rain down on Beijing—a phenomenon that has been dubbed the "Mongolian cyclone." The sandstorms are due to large-scale erosion of soil in both Inner Mongolia and Outer Mongolia—which in turn is directly due to Chinese interference that has caused the grasslands of those regions to turn to desert. The yellow dust from Gobi sandstorms has blown as far afield as Hong Kong and South Korea.

★　★　★

Chinese travel agencies have been luring domestic tourists to Tibet with promises of a veritable Garden of Eden—with towering snow mountains, crystal-clear lakes, and charming villages set in pristine valleys. Particular emphasis is placed on phrasing such as "pure blue sky" or "intensely blue sky" or "deep azure-blue sky." Add a large number of days with direct, dazzling sun in Lhasa, as well as visibility for miles and miles, and you can see why Chinese tourists flock there by the millions. However, a strange weather report played out on December 19 and 20, 2013. Thick smog descended on Lhasa—so thick that it obscured the Potala Palace. The smog's origin is mysterious—it possibly drifted over from the industrial hub of the Sichuan Basin to the east. The AQI indicator in Lhasa hit the extraordinary level of 243, meaning very unhealthy. Tibet's reputation for having the cleanest air in the People's Republic of China took a nosedive.

Weather report for the Asian monsoon: unpredictable. As Himalayan glaciers melt, more dark areas are exposed, causing temperatures to rise faster. Some climatologists believe that this warming could intensify the Asian monsoon and lead to more extreme weather patterns in the region, as evidenced by intense cyclones battering the coastal regions of Bangladesh and Burma to major flooding in Pakistan. However, the question of how the Asian monsoon system will evolve has proven difficult to model.[25] Tibet could be the driver of Asian monsoon patterns because of jet streams passing over the Tibetan Plateau, but further studies are needed. Some climate models predict that India's seasonal rains will grow more intense, but other evidence seems to indicate weaker monsoon patterns. In any case, the monsoon patterns appear to be changing in India, with rains arriving late or finishing early. The monsoons are no longer predictable.

★   ★   ★

There's another kind of meltdown going on in Tibet: the permafrost is starting to thaw. Glaciers above, permafrost below: not as permanent as the name suggests, a vast underground layer of permafrost is located across the Tibetan Plateau. The permafrost varies from frozen subsurface soil to layers hundreds of feet underground. The Tibetan Plateau comprises the largest sub-Arctic permafrost region on the planet. Frozen for millions of years, the permafrost is now in danger of thawing. As with glaciers, this process is irreversible. Permafrost plays an important role as part of the Tibetan Plateau ecosystem. If subsurface permafrost melts, it can affect subsoil water supply in wetlands and lakes, and can impact the growth of plant life.

Though there are scores of research reports about Tibet's permafrost, there are many unknown factors about the rate of thawing. But human interference in the way of extensive mining and railway building could play a role in the degradation of permafrost. Chinese engineers encountered a major problem building the railway line to Lhasa: over half of the line goes over permafrost terrain. Permafrost thawing could cause the rail line to bend and slump, and bridges to crack. So engineers drilled 25-foot-long steel tubes into the soil to act as "cooling sticks," designed to refrigerate vulnerable parts of the soil along the railway tracks. These cooling sticks are filled with ammonia to draw latent heat out of the soil.

In the process of thawing, permafrost could release large amounts of trapped carbon and methane. In permafrost regions, methane hydrate is found trapped in layers between 500 and 6,500 feet deep. As a greenhouse gas, methane is thought to be over 20 times more potent than carbon dioxide in its ability to trap heat in the atmosphere. It is not known what effect the release of large amounts of methane into the atmosphere would have. It would likely set in motion a vicious cycle of more global warming—which in turn would trigger even more methane release.

PART TWO

ECOCIDE IN THE LAND OF SNOWS

The authorities' appetite for resources has proved voracious. They mine for ores wherever there are hills and dam wherever there are rivers for power—all in the name of development.

The nightmare that the Tibetan highlands' fragile ecosystem will be destroyed is becoming a reality.

—Tsering Woeser, *Voices from Tibet*★

★Tsering Woeser and Wang Lixiong, *Voices from Tibet*, trans. Violet Law (Hong Kong University Press, 2013).

CHAPTER THREE

Valleys of the Dammed

What Is the Fate of the Mighty Rivers of Tibet?

The kayakers' conundrum: 50 years ago, they didn't have the technology to run these rivers. And 20 years from now, the rivers could be dammed. So the race is on to explore the rivers of the Tibetan Plateau while that's still possible. Western kayakers are an excellent source of information on dam locations: they have to know exactly where the dams are, and whether new ones are under construction. Up-to-date information on dam activity is a matter of survival. While running a river, for instance, a kayaker could get sucked into a newly constructed water-diversion tunnel. Several rivers, the kayakers tell me, are no longer runnable due to huge dams popping up—the lower Mekong River in Yunnan, for instance.

Though the Mekong is sourced high on the Tibetan Plateau, the following two megadams mentioned lie in Yunnan lowland areas. They give an idea of the colossal scale of Chinese dam building, which will eventually move northward into Tibetan areas.

Xiaowan Dam on the Mekong in Yunnan, southwest China, was completed in 2009. With its huge reservoir slowly filling over a number of years, Xiaowan is among the tallest arch dams in the world. It has a capacity of 4,200 MW and a reservoir stretching back 105 miles. With a wall height of 960 feet, Xiaowan Dam is the height of an 80-story building—and roughly the same height as the 300-meter Eiffel Tower (without its present broadcast antenna). From 1889 to 1930, this engineering marvel held its place in the record books as the tallest man-made structure on earth. Downstream from Xiaowan Dam, another monumental structure, Nuozhadu Dam, started operation in 2014. Its capacity of 5,850 MW is roughly equivalent to that of five nuclear power plants. For reasons of inaccessibility, the Mekong River was untouched by dam builders until China started building a megadam in 1994. There are now five megadams operational on the lower Mekong in Yunnan, and more slated to be built upstream. Together, these dams will wreak havoc on the Mekong's ecosystem in the five nations downstream.

Xiaowan and Nuozhadu are part of a cascade of dams under construction by Huaneng Group, which has a concession to build, own, and operate dams on the Mekong within the People's Republic of China. In Thailand, hydroprojects are controversial and have been blocked by environmental campaigns, but Huaneng doesn't seem concerned about Chinese protesters. Huaneng has no shareholders who might call for environmental impact surveys.

The turbines of these megadams are giant money-spinners for corporations like Huaneng. Megadams mean big business for dam builders, subcontractors, investors, and others—which can trigger corruption and bribery on a large scale. In China, business is all about having the right connections, and cronyism and nepotism are rife. Take, for instance, the family of former premier Li Peng, a megadam advocate who was instrumental in getting the Three Gorges Dam built. From 1999 to 2008, Huaneng Group was essentially run by Li Peng's son, Li Xiaopeng. Consolidating the family's influence in the power industry, Li Peng's daughter Li Xiaolin moved up the ranks to take the reins of energy giant China Power International Development.[1]

Huaneng Group is notorious for secrecy—and for its determination to rush through controversial dam projects despite the impact on local people, the environment, and the nations downstream.[2] The corporation rarely makes any details about its plans public until a project is actually under way—and highly visible to the locals. Huaneng Group has been reprimanded by the central government for initiating projects that were not submitted for approval. The 1,900 MW Huangdeng Dam on the Mekong was half finished before it was brought to the attention of the central government—which had not given approval. Dam construction without approval is supposed to be illegal, but Huaneng Group somehow manages to get away with it.

★ ★ ★

AROUND THE WORLD, IN MANY NATIONS, HYDROPOWER PROVIDES AN AVERAGE OF 20 percent of energy resources; in some nations the percentage is much higher. Dams are here to stay. Hydropower—done right, with properly sited, operated, and mitigated dams—is an important part of the energy mix. But when hydropower is done wrong, it can have enormous impact on river health. The controversial issue is what kind of dams are beneficial and what kind are destructive. Small-scale dams and run-of-the-river dams (with no reservoir)—when properly managed and of benefit to the local population—are viable energy generators that reduce the carbon footprint. For instance, construction of small dams built to impound rainwater in India's desert state of Rajasthan has recharged groundwater supplies and increased food security for hundreds of thousands of farming families.

But big dams can mean big problems in the long run—especially when built by greedy consortiums that seek to exploit hydropower resources on a massive scale for use in industry, mining, or for export via power transmission lines. This is destructive damming. In such cases, the local population will suffer severe environmental consequences but will see no benefits. When megadams are built without consulting the indigenous population—or when they are completely opposed by the locals—it becomes a human rights problem. And that is the case for Tibet. Megadams with large reservoirs result in massive displacement of locals, who are subject to land grabs to clear them from dam sites. Dams become the perfect excuse for taking land from the poor and giving it to officials who make large profits from the deals. In Tibet, where local power demand is tiny, these megadams simply do not need to be built. The hydropower is intended to power Chinese mining and industrial operations, or slated to be exported elsewhere.

International Rivers, a California-based NGO, calls for new thinking on destructive damming: "Over the last 20 years, a growing international movement has emerged to challenge destructive dams, promote sustainable and equitable alternatives and secure reparations for dam-affected people. This movement has forced the indefinite postponement or cancellation of numerous projects around the world. Despite what critics say, most activists are not opposed to all big dams. What they are opposed to is current development planning processes that promote dams that benefit a few at the expense of the human rights, livelihoods and dignity of the poor."[3]

The World Commission on Dams defines a "large dam" as one being "at least 15 meters [40 feet] in wall-height from the base up, or having a reservoir containing at least 3 million cubic meters of water." Height-wise, that would be the equivalent of a four-story building. There is no firm definition for a "megadam," but roughly ten times larger than a large dam would seem to qualify, with wall-height over 150 meters (500 feet, the height of a 40-story building), and output at over 300 MW. But what do you call a dam over 250 meters (800 feet) in wall height and capacity over a gigawatt? I would call that a monster dam.

And yet all these dams are dwarfed by another colossus. Up and running at full capacity in mid-2012 is the Three Gorges Dam, trumpeted by China as being the greatest structure built since the Great Wall. And indeed it is the largest concrete object on earth. So you could call this dam the Great Wall of Concrete. The Three Gorges Dam is in a class of its own. It is the biggest dam in the Motherland, or the Mother of All Dams. Almost 20 years in the making, the Three Gorges Dam has a colossal power output of 22.5 GW, also stated as 22,500 MW. It is 600 feet tall and more than 1.2 miles wide. It was built at a cost of over $28 billion. The dam submerged an astonishing 13 cities, 140 towns, and 1,350 villages, displacing more than 1.3 million people. Another 300,000 people had to be evacuated because the constantly rising and falling reservoir level has triggered landslides in thousands of sites around the reservoir, which stretches back 375 miles.

And here the parameters run out: large dam, megadam, monster dam, Great Wall of Concrete. So what do you call a dam that is *double* the size of the Three Gorges Dam? Well, you could call that a Great Bend Dam. There is a gargantuan dam called Motuo on the drawing board for the Great Bend of the Yarlung Tsangpo River in eastern Tibet. The Great Bend is widely regarded to have the greatest hydropower potential in the world.

In 2008, I came across a terrifying map posted on the website of HydroChina Corporation, a state-run outfit from Beijing. This map is in Chinese only—no English translation given.[4] I find it terrifying because for the southwest region in Sichuan and Yunnan you can hardly see the rivers: they've been obscured by the circular symbols used for dams. In case the map should disappear from that website, I copied it and placed it on my own website, MeltdowninTibet.com, and added English annotations for the map keys and symbols used. The HydroChina map probably dates from around 2003, and shows a complete inventory for dam-building plans across China.

How accurate is the map? Very accurate, according to Agent Griffon, a researcher who prefers to remain anonymous. He used the HydroChina map as the basis for an English-language version. He cross-checked a host of Chinese websites and used Google Earth to confirm locations for dams both existing and recently completed, and those under construction. Agent Griffon continues his work, producing more dam and mining maps for Tibet, also found on my website.

Motuo Dam appears right on that HydroChina dam-inventory map. Named by the Chinese surveyors after the nearest village—Motuo in Chinese, or Metok (Metog) in Tibetan—the projected capacity of this dam is indicated on the map at 38 GW, which dwarfs the output of the colossal Three Gorges Dam. Another dam called Daduqia, also proposed at the Great Bend, is projected at 44 GW output, which is double the output of the Three Gorges Dam. If ever built, Daduqia's power output would be roughly equivalent to that of 30 nuclear power plants.

No river is more closely identified with Tibet's long history and culture than the Yarlung Tsangpo, which runs through the heartland of Tibet from west to east. It is often referred to in its short form, the Tsangpo, and is also known as the Brahmaputra (referring to the river within India) and the Jamuna (in Bangladesh).

The Tsangpo is the highest river in the world, with a length of 1,800 miles from source to sea. Rising close to Mount Kailash, the river surges through braided channels in central Tibet. To the eastern side of Tibet, the river performs a neat trick—it makes an abrupt hairpin turn (dubbed the Great Bend) and flows westward to India. Here, the Tsangpo thunders through a 16,000-foot cleft between two towering snowcaps—Namche Barwa (elevation 25,446 feet) and Gyala Pelri (23,461 feet). Over a distance of almost 310 miles the Tsangpo plummets some 8,800 feet through what is now known as the Yarlung Tsangpo Grand Canyon. Rapids on some stretches flow at 53 mph. This is the world's deepest gorge: it is more than twice the depth of Arizona's Grand Canyon—and 35 miles longer.

Richard Fisher, the American wilderness guide and river runner credited with identifying this great depth on a 1992 expedition, says the Yarlung Tsangpo is the only chasm he has encountered that compares with the Grand Canyon for sheer beauty. Fisher says the Yarlung Tsangpo is so vast and diverse that it must contain many mysteries yet to be discovered. In 1998, explorers Ian Baker and Ken Storm discovered a waterfall 108 feet high in the Great Bend region—the highest yet found on a major Himalayan river.

Although barely explored, the Great Bend is not seen as fantastic natural splendor by China's officials. Rather than regard the Yarlung Tsangpo as a living ecosystem, China's engineers see it as a huge water pipe—the greatest potential source for hydropower ever. In May 2010, the *Guardian* interviewed Zhang Boting, the deputy general secretary of the China Society for Hydropower Engineering, who confirmed that research has been carried out on Motuo Dam at the Great Bend, but the project is still at the drawing-board stage.[5] Zhang Boting was enthusiastic about the massive dam, saying that it could generate energy equivalent to all the oil and gas in the South China Sea. Plans for Motuo Dam are not clear, but it would seem that Chinese engineers want to drill a vast tunnel through the Himalayas to divert water before it reaches the Great Bend of the Tsangpo River—and direct it to the other side of the bend (there was even talk of using nuclear explosives to make the tunnel, but that idea appears to have been shelved). Instead of dropping thousands of feet around the Great Bend, huge volumes of water would gush through the tunnel, driving massive turbines at Motuo. Motuo lies in a very remote region, with virtually no demand for electricity. The plan is to connect Motuo Dam to an ultra-high-voltage grid, enabling power to be transferred to industrial bases in western China. Zhang Boting told the *Guardian*, "This dam could save 200 million tonnes of carbon each year. We should not waste the opportunity of the biggest carbon emission reduction project. For the sake of the entire world, all the water resources that can be developed should be developed."[6]

China's engineering spin doctors use arguments like this to make megadam building sound eco-friendly, and to make dams look like a viable method of countering the effects of climate change. However, Zhang Boting seems to have overlooked some key factors. Tibet's water resources are being developed for whom exactly? Tibetans don't need a dam the size of Motuo, which could power up an entire country like Iceland. Megadams are not as green as Zhang Boting makes out: for one thing, damming spews out greenhouse gases, particularly carbon dioxide and methane emissions from rotting trees and vegetation in a dam reservoir. Methane emissions are far more potent than carbon dioxide emissions: any carbon reductions saved by building a dam may be offset by methane output. Emissions depend on the climate where the dam is built, the amount and type of vegetation flooded, and the depth and age of the reservoir.

Megadams mean megaproblems. Huge dams have the potential for creating environmental chaos—turning free-flowing waterways into lifeless lakes, blocking fish migration and breeding, killing plants and trees, flooding and fragmenting ecosystems, and reducing biodiversity. Large amounts of water may simply disappear into thin air at reservoirs due to surface evaporation. Water quality may be severely degraded in stagnant reservoirs, which capture chemicals, fertilizer runoff, human waste, and all kinds of trash, thus potentially increasing water-borne diseases. Dam reservoirs capture nutrient-rich silt, which no longer reaches communities of farmers downstream. Eventually, dams can silt up, reducing their power generation.

Then there is the human cost: whole communities must be relocated for areas flooded by a dam reservoir. These people are often shifted to degraded land, where they live in poverty—driving many to migrate elsewhere and start again. Estimates vary, but it is thought that more than 22 million Chinese have been relocated for hydropower projects since the 1950s. Dams have a life span of perhaps 50 years: a huge dam itself poses a significant safety hazard as the structure ages, particularly if there is earthquake activity in the vicinity.

Dams may look like a way of reducing carbon emissions, but if China wants to be taken seriously about this, then it should be looking at reducing its heavy dependence on coal-fired power plants. Currently, China has absolutely no intention of reducing the number of these CO_2-spewing coal-fired plants. In fact, the opposite is true: there are plans to considerably expand construction of coal-fired plants in the coming years.

Motuo Dam must rank as the world's most dangerous hydro-engineering project. If a gargantuan dam goes ahead at the Great Bend of the Tsangpo, it will be curtains for the Tsangpo as a free-flowing river. Peter Bosshard of International Rivers says about Motuo Dam: "A large dam on the Tibetan Plateau would amount to a major, irreversible experiment with geo-engineering. Blocking the Yarlung Tsangpo could devastate the fragile eco-system of the Tibetan Plateau, and would withhold the river's sediments from the fertile floodplains of Assam in northeast India and Bangladesh."[7]

Alarm bells have been sounded by environmental activists about the building of a dam on the tremendous scale of Motuo. For one thing, the dam would be sited right in the region of Metok, considered sacred by Tibetans—and sited right in an earthquake-prone zone that is the axis on which the thrusting Indian plate pushes its way both north and east, ever deeper into China. The sacred valley of Metok has been inaccessible to outsiders for centuries due to torrential rains that wash away any attempt to build roads into the region. Chances are that Motuo Dam will only be realistically considered when there is sufficient infrastructure to support the construction. In 2010, there was an ominous turn of events: a tunnel over 1.8 miles long was constructed by Chinese engineers as the key structure for a road linking Metok with the outside world. The outside world here means Chinese dam builders and military. What was thought to be impossible—building a dam at the Great Bend—edges a notch closer to reality with the building of that tunnel.

★ ★ ★

BECAUSE OF EXTREME WEATHER CONDITIONS AT ALTITUDE, DAM BUILDING ON THE plateau involves complex engineering. In 2010, when construction started on Zhangmu Dam at 10,700 feet in elevation on the midreaches of the Yarlung Tsangpo, customized materials and technology were developed by the Chinese space agency. They used a special cement made at the laboratories of the Xichang satellite launch center.

Once Chinese engineers can solve the technical problems of building dams under extreme weather conditions at altitude, you can be sure they will move on to other parts of the plateau. Already half a dozen dams are in operation on the Tibetan Plateau, located above 8,200 feet in altitude. At around 8,850 feet in elevation are Banduo (capacity 360 MW, wall height 255 feet), Longyangxia (capacity 1,280 MW, wall height 580 feet), and Laxiwa (capacity 4,200 MW, wall height 820 feet) dams—all on the upper Yellow River in Qinghai. Within the Tibet Autonomous Region are a handful of medium-size dams. The 60 MW Jinhe Dam, located in Chamdo region on the Jinhe River (a Mekong tributary) sits at 10,700 feet in elevation. At 12,660 feet in elevation on the Lhasa River (Kyi Chu in the Tibetan language) is 100 MW Zhikong Dam. Further north on Lhasa River is Pando Hydroplant, also known as Pangduo, at 13,390 feet. Constructed by Sinohydro is Laohuzui Dam, located on the Ba River 210 miles east of Lhasa in the Kongpo area. The dam has a capacity of 102 MW and is 260 feet tall.

★ ★ ★

NEW POWER TRANSMISSION TECHNOLOGY IS RADICALLY ALTERING THE PICTURE FOR dam building in Tibet. In the early 2000s, German corporation Siemens Energy introduced ultra-high voltage (UHV) power transmission lines into China. Made from copper, these UHV lines can export hydropower over long distances. Previously, dams could only provide electricity for regions close by. Now it is possible to harness Tibet's immense hydropower and export it to power-hungry east coast China hubs. The same technology can be used to export power from Chinese-built dams in neighboring nations such as Burma into China.

China is currently building an 800 kV (kilovolt) supergrid that will connect all parts of the nation in the most sophisticated transmission system for electricity the world has ever seen. The new UHV lines can transfer power from the source up to 1,900 miles away. Nearly 80 percent of

China's water resources are in the southwest and Tibetan regions, and two-thirds of its coal is in three northern provinces, while demand centers for power are in coastal regions. In June 2010, China Southern Power Grid, in a joint venture with Siemens Energy, announced the opening of a UHV 800 kV transmission line approximately 930 miles in length. This link takes power from several hydroelectric plants in Yunnan Province and transports the energy to Guangdong Province, with its megacities Guangzhou (population over 13 million) and Shenzhen (over 10 million).

Tibet holds the world's greatest hydro potential, with rivers cascading wildly from 16,400 feet down to 5,000 feet and coursing through the deepest canyons in the world. The Yarlung Tsangpo River carries a volume of water greater than the combined flow of the 20 largest rivers in Europe—a volume greater than any river in the world bar the Congo and the Amazon. Up to two-thirds of China's exploitable hydro potential is thought to be located on the Tibetan plateau. China has a rolling development plan. Hooking Tibet up to a national grid changes the entire focus of damming on the Tibetan Plateau. Currently the focus for dam building is at the edges of the plateau, but the dam builders are working their way steadily toward Tibet with dam cascades. All the major rivers of Tibet will see dam activity on a large scale in the near future. Dam-building companies have saturated their efforts on the rivers of mainland China, leaving a load of dead rivers in their wake.

★   ★   ★

CHINA HAS FAR AND AWAY THE GREATEST NUMBER OF BIG DAMS IN THE WORLD. How did it become the world's number-one dam builder? It acquired foreign technology. The leading dam builder back in the 1930s was the United States, which boasted the mighty Hoover Dam. When completed in 1936, Hoover Dam was the largest dam ever built, at 725 feet in wall height and 2 GW capacity. It is odd to think that today the Three Gorges Dam dwarfs Hoover Dam, with ten times greater capacity at 22.5 GW. Until a few decades ago, China relied on technology from the Soviet Union and from Western companies to build projects. However, China required that those who did business with them had to manufacture half their turbines and electrical generators in China, with the participation of local hydro-engineers and technical staff. This was a cost-effective way of transferring dam-building technology from the West to China in a short time.

Dr. Ngo The Vinh, a Vietnamese physician and the author most recently of *Mekong: The Occluding River*, a Vietnamese-language best-seller, is deeply concerned with the impact of Chinese dams on Vietnam. He picks up the story: "Lured by billions of dollars in profit, the big companies of the West like ABB, Alstom, General Electric, and Siemens agreed to those terms and by the same token facilitated the transfer of industrial production process to China. The young Chinese engineers did not let that opportunity slip through their fingers. They learned fast and mastered the science of dam building from their foreign colleagues. It did not take them long to design and manufacture all the machinery and equipment needed for the construction of dams in Mainland China. The end result: China, nowadays, has surpassed its teachers, controlling the market of dam construction and is now in charge of 19 of the 24 largest dam building projects in the world."[8]

★ ★ ★

THE EMPERORS OF IMPERIAL CHINA SOUGHT TO LEAVE THEIR MARK BY building grandiose projects like the Great Wall, which ultimately failed for its intended purpose (keeping out the Mongol barbarians) but has left a handy tourism legacy. China's modern politburo is doing the same thing: building on a gargantuan scale. In fact, they have revived one of the great imperial projects—the Grand Canal, in eastern China—as part of a water-diversion megaproject.

You could trace the Chinese preoccupation with hydropower to 1949, when Mao Zedong came to power. He envisaged the building of the Three

Gorges Dam, which he saw as a way of taming flooding on the Yangtse. Before 1949, there were just a handful of dams of any significant size in the People's Republic of China. Mao instigated damming in China on a grand scale.

The Mao Zedong mentality from the 1950s was that Mother Nature can—and should—be defeated and overcome. The slogan "Humans must conquer nature" was widespread under Chairman Mao. Traditional Taoist philosophy promoted harmony with the heavens and respect for nature. But Mao ushered in an era of battling with Mother Nature. In the early days of the Mao era, taking on Mother Nature had mixed results. The consequences of tampering with the environment could be deadly. The Great Sparrow Campaign, initiated by Mao Zedong in the late 1950s, was launched because sparrows ate grain seeds and were thought to be detrimental to agriculture. It was decided that all peasants in China would bang pots and pans and run around to make sparrows fly away in fear. Sparrows were killed with slingshots, nests were destroyed, nestlings were killed. In early 1960, China's National Academy of Science found that sparrows ate insects more than seeds. By this time, however, it was too late. With no sparrows to eat them, the locust population exploded, swarming the country and compounding the problems already caused by the Great Leap Forward. A great famine followed and millions died of starvation.

Hydroprojects got under way in earnest in 1958 when Mao initiated the Great Leap Forward. In 1958 alone, more than double the amount of earth was moved for hydroprojects than in the whole of the previous decade. In an interview with dissident Dai Qing, Jonathan Watts sums up the havoc wreaked by hastily built dams: "Scrappily built and inadequately checked, many collapsed with deadly consequences. The first big dam to go was at Fushan, which lasted just four months before bursting and drowning 10,000 people downstream. By 1980, 2,796 dams had failed with a combined death toll of 240,000. This was not made public until many years later."[9]

Mao's arrogant legacy lingers today with the leadership of the military-industrial complex that rules China. In the 1990s and early 2000s, China's leadership was dominated by engineers-turned-politicians, with vested interests in large engineering companies that need megaprojects to keep going. Against fierce opposition, in 1992, Premier Li Peng, a Soviet-trained hydropower engineer, pushed through the Three Gorges Dam, with work starting in 1994. But the award for the world's most dangerous hydro-engineer must go to Hu Jintao, who was president of the People's Republic of China from March 2003 to March 2013. Apart from building his reputation for quashing Tibetans while governor there, Hu Jintao laid the groundwork for a massive expansion of dam building. He oversaw the construction of the Lhasa railway, completed in 2006, and the construction of the Three Gorges Dam, completed in 2012. He approved the building of megadams all over China and in the Tibetan highlands.

★   ★   ★

BUT NOBODY BOTHERED TO ASK THE APPROVAL OF THE TIBETANS WHEN BUILDING megadams in their homeland. Tibetans never requested the building of these dams, nor do they benefit from them. They are never consulted about the use of their resources. Chinese officials often claim that these dams are being built to help Tibetans, but you don't build a 2,000 MW dam so a few Tibetan villagers can turn on their TVs and watch Chinese propaganda. It is not Tibetans who benefit from the dams—the power is generated for mining and Chinese industry in Tibet, and eventually the power from dams will be exported to distant Chinese cities on a national grid.

Why should Tibetans have to sacrifice their resources to supply energy needs for China? Tibetans have burned yak dung as a source of fuel for centuries. They can easily get by using solar panels, as there is intense solar radiation on the Tibetan Plateau. Outside of the Sahara, the

Tibetan plateau has the greatest potential on the planet for harnessing solar energy. Due to Tibet's high altitude, the sun is very intense: with clear skies and large areas of desert, solar energy is most effective on the Tibetan Plateau. It has been used effectively in Ladakh, which is on the plateau on the Indian side. China has embarked on an ambitious program of dominating global production of solar panels, with more than 400 solar panel companies. It is also the biggest manufacturer and user of solar water heaters.

Can solar power compete in scale with hydropower? Recent developments in technology show that it can. In a desert in Arizona, a megaplant composed of more than 5 million solar panels was completed in early 2014. The solar megaplant cranks out 290 MW of sunshine power, raising the bar considerably for solar power as a competitive energy resource.[10] China is slated to become the world leader in manufacturing technology for harnessing wind power. Wind power and solar power do not require any water consumption. In Tibet, there is also tremendous potential for harnessing wind power and geothermal energy on the plateau. However, these forms of energy are very expensive to generate when compared with hydropower. The energy needs of Tibetans are minimal: the entire Tibetan population of 6 million would easily fit into a Chinese city like Chengdu. China refers to Tibet as "Water Tower Number One." Essentially, China is stealing Tibet's hydropower to save its own skin.

★   ★   ★

TIBET IS NEVER FAR FROM THE HEARTS OF TIBETANS IN EXILE—WHETHER JUST across the border in India, or across the globe. In Vancouver, Canada, at a demonstration staged by Tibetans, I meet Tashi Tsering, who is working on his doctorate on the impact of climate change on Himalayan water resources. A Tibetan in exile who is knowledgeable about megadams, water issues, and their impact on Tibetans, Tashi is a rare individual indeed. Tashi was born in India; he has never been to Tibet, but his fieldwork takes place just across the border in Ladakh, northwest India.

We talk at length about the situation in Tibet. Tashi is able to tap into Tibetan sources and Tibetan bloggers. He tells me that the crux of Tibetan grievance with China's policies is that they do not have platforms to have a say in the policies that shape their future. Tashi says there has been a lot of protest by Tibetans concerned about what the government is doing to the environment. These protests take different forms—some are just in simple but daring street songs, showing appreciation for the environment and hinting at the destruction that development is causing.[11]

The more I talk to Tashi, the more I realize how complex the environmental situation is in Tibet—and how little information about this is reaching the outside world. He fills me in on Tibetan beliefs in water spirits and mountain spirits, and the taboos associated with damage to sacred lakes and mountains. He tells me that not only is dam building proceeding in Tibet without local consultation, it is being done in complete secrecy, with police and military sealing off the construction zones—and with military or paramilitary manpower involved in the actual building. A trademark of Chinese dam builders is their amazing speed. Migrant workers flood the construction area, and the dam is often completed ahead of schedule. Speed and secrecy go hand in hand: the aim is to dodge protest by having the dam up and running as soon as possible.

There is one sure way that Tibetans will know what is happening: land grabs. A large area of land is required for flooding the zone of the reservoir of a megadam. That land is acquired by forcibly relocating Tibetan herders and villagers. In early 2008, thousands of Tibetan residents of Tawu and Nyagchu counties in Ganzi Prefecture (western Sichuan) were told they had to move from their ancestral lands to make way for the construction of a megadam in the area. The plan was vehemently opposed by the Tibetans, who refused to move, saying the land belonged to them. The Chinese government ignores questions of land ownership when it comes to dam building or mining in Tibet, claiming that all land belongs to the

People's Republic of China. In May 2009, a large number of armed police was dispatched to the region to destroy family homes. On May 24, 2009, a group of Tibetans gathered in Tawu County to vent their anger against the forceful relocation. The Public Security Bureau and the People's Armed Police fired indiscriminately on the crowd, seriously injuring six women.[12]

In April 2012, five nomadic villages in Tongde County, Qinghai, were called to a meeting convened by Chinese government officials. The residents of Setong, Dragmar, Seru, Machu, and Goekar villages were told they would have to give up 60 percent of their land and get rid of more than 50 percent of their animals. The villagers were advised to reduce the number of animals by selling them to slaughterhouses. But villagers cannot survive without their livestock: they unanimously refused to accept the government proposal. The government response was to force the villagers to surrender all their land so that a new town could be built to house 30,000 Chinese migrant workers who would construct two new megadam projects. That number was expected to rise to 100,000 migrant workers.[13]

At great personal risk, Tibetans have protested megadam construction, with a number killed, injured, or arrested. News of these protests is hard to come by as Chinese sources rarely report them, resulting in a virtual blackout. The news only travels via Tibetans themselves. One readily available source in English is Radio Free Asia.

★ ★ ★

IN 2006, KARMA SAMDRUP, A WEALTHY TIBETAN ART COLLECTOR, WAS NAMED philanthropist of the year by state broadcaster China Central Television for "creating harmony between men and nature." Along with his two brothers, Karma Samdrup ran an award-winning organization called Snowlands Great Rivers Environmental Protection Association. The group educated children in environmental protection and engaged local villagers in initiatives such as collecting litter, planting thousands of trees, and monitoring illegal hunting in the Chamdo area of northeast Tibet. Villagers sang as they worked—the brothers used tree planting as a time to come together as a community and have fun. The group won several prestigious awards for its work, including the Earth Prize, which is jointly administered by Friends of the Earth Hong Kong and the Ford Motor Company. The group also received an award from Jet Li's One World Foundation. Chinese conservationists regarded the work of the Samdrup brothers as an important initiative because the brothers' village lies in the Yangtse River watershed, which desperately needs trees to prevent soil erosion.

On June 24, 2010, Karma Samdrup was sentenced to 15 years' imprisonment on charges of dealing in illegal antiques, a charge that had been previously dropped against him in 1998. In court, Samdrup exposed the appalling torture he was subjected to during six months of detention in efforts to extract a confession (making that confession inadmissible by Chinese law), but this plea was overturned by the judge. It seems that Samdrup's sentence was in retaliation for his efforts to secure the release of his brothers, arrested after they publicly denounced a local police chief for illegal hunting of endangered animals in a nature reserve. Samdrup was one of the wealthiest businessmen in Tibet: his imprisonment is seen by human rights advocates as part of a crackdown on Tibetan artists and intellectuals that has intensified since March 2008, when extensive rioting across Tibet stunned the Chinese leadership.[14]

Karma Samdrup's brother Chime Namgyal was sentenced to 21 months in a labor camp for "endangering state security" because he did not register a new environmental group and unofficially organized litter collection, tree planting, and patrols to stop the hunting of endangered animals. Karma, who visited Chime in prison before his own arrest, said that Chime was tortured so badly that he was permanently disabled; he can no longer walk or eat without assistance. Karma's older brother, Rinchen Samdrup, was sentenced in July to five years imprisonment for "inciting subversion." Their mother, in her seventies, was beaten unconscious when armed police detained Rinchen from their family home.

This could have been a chance for Beijing to demonstrate progress in the implementation of environmental protection measures. Instead, Chinese authorities chose to use the courts and trumped-up charges to subvert justice. Chinese environmental NGOs and activism are tolerated, it seems, as long as they don't become too strong or too critical. But Tibetan activism is viewed as subversion.

★   ★   ★

TIBETANS ARE NOT ALONE IN THEIR CONCERNS ABOUT MEGADAMS. THE HEAVIEST dam-building activity has been in southwest China, in the provinces of Yunnan and Sichuan, where ethnic Tibetan areas overlap with other ethnic groups like Yi and Miao, and with Han Chinese farmers. There has been fierce resistance to megadam building by Chinese environmental activists and by farmers whose land has been forcibly taken from them.

In 2003, a region known as the Three Parallel Rivers was inscribed to the UNESCO World Heritage List. According to the UNESCO assessment, "Northwest Yunnan is the area of richest biodiversity in China and may be the most biologically diverse temperate region on earth. The property encompasses most of the natural habitats in the Hengduan Mountains, one of the world's most important remaining areas for the conservation of the earth's biodiversity."[15]

It's a region with myriad species of plants and rare or endangered animals and fish. The three rivers referred to are the Yangtse, Mekong, and Salween. Running close together, they roar through deep furrows in the Hengduan mountain range at the eastern edge of the Tibetan Plateau. The microclimates in these mountains host a huge range of flora, depending on altitude. Many ornamental plants in the West today derive from this species-rich region—species like azaleas, primroses, and rhododendrons collected there by Western plant hunters.

An odd sentence appears in the UNESCO assessment: "While large sections of the three rivers lie just outside the property boundaries, the river gorges are nevertheless the dominant scenic element in the area."[16] The Three Parallel Rivers World Heritage Site is protected, but the rivers that give the site its name are not protected, nor are the canyons that provide the most spectacular scenery. The powerful Salween River is among the last wild rivers left in Asia. It flows over 1,740 miles from source to sea, rising in the Tanggula Mountain region on the Tibetan Plateau, and coursing through Tibet, Yunnan, and Burma (which shares a border with Thailand) before emptying into the Andaman Sea. From Tibet, running through northwest Yunnan, the river carves a majestic grand canyon over 190 miles in length. Rushing between 13,000-foot peaks, it is one of the longest gorges in the world—and one of the most dazzling. And it runs right alongside zones set aside for the World Heritage Site.

No sooner was this World Heritage Site confirmed than Chinese engineering companies announced plans for building large dams on the Salween. In April 2004, plans were announced for construction of a cascade of 13 large dams on the river, ranging from wall heights of 110 feet to a whopping 1,007 feet. Half these dams would be constructed in the Salween River Gorge. The fact that some of these dams would be built in the region of a protected UNESCO World Heritage Site does not appear to be a contradiction to China's ruling powers. There are rumblings from international observers to place the Three Parallel Rivers region on the World Heritage in Danger list, since the dams could seriously impact local ecosystems.

"Why can't China have just one river that isn't destroyed by humans?" asked Wang Yongchen, a well-known environmentalist in Beijing. The river she refers to is the Salween. She has visited the area a dozen times in recent years.[17] Wang Yongchen is the cofounder of Green Earth Volunteers, which led an unprecedented campaign to save the Salween. It became a cause célèbre among Chinese environmental activists, and the campaign appeared to work. In 2004, when Premier Wen Jiabao announced a suspension of the dam cascade on the Salween, activists were jubilant. But the victory turned out to be a hollow one: ten years later, plans for damming the Salween were again resumed.

There have been a few success stories to counter dam building in Sichuan, where many of China's new dams are under way. At Tiger Leaping Gorge, on the upper Yangtse, a proposal was in place to construct a dam 912 feet high, with a reservoir stretching back 120 miles that would flood much of the breathtaking Tiger Leaping Gorge scenic region, and would displace 100,000 Naxi people. Work was actually proceeding on the dam illegally, without approval from the central government and without informing locals. After mass protest, in December 2007, it was announced that the project would be suspended. However, it appears that the same project has been re-launched upstream in an ethnic-Tibetan area, which would displace 20,000 Tibetans.

The movement to halt the dam at Tiger Leaping Gorge was spear-headed by Yu Xiaogang, who founded the Kunming-based environmental group Green Watershed in 2002 to educate local communities about the negative effects of dams and other development projects. Yu grew up in Yunnan, surrounded by a rich landscape of mountains and rivers. He completed postgraduate research on the environmental impact of Manwan Dam on the Mekong. Yu was involved with the campaign against damming the Salween River, and he worked to rebuild an area around Lashi Lake in southwest Yunnan after a dam destroyed the local ecosystem. Since then, he has helped locals oppose a number of big dam projects across China, and has won some prestigious international awards for his contributions. The fate of Tibet's rivers lies with courageous figures like Yu Xiaogang, triggering change from within China.

★ ★ ★

CHINESE STATE-RUN DAM BUILDERS HAVE GROWN WARY OF PROTESTERS AND ARE adopting devious tactics to get around them. Dam building proceeds under a shroud of secrecy: the idea appears to be to get the dam up and running before protest can slow the pace.

To avoid possible protest, megadam projects in southwest China are being pushed through without any environmental impact assessment (EIA), and without bothering to inform the locals. The two facets are related, in that an EIA would reveal to the locals what mega-impact such a megadam project would have—including massive relocation of people. There is a significant military and paramilitary presence in towns where protest is likely to erupt, in a blatant attempt to intimidate locals.

Following the introduction of a 2003 law, dams in China are required to have EIAs completed and officially approved, but there are ways around this, and there is corruption. Dam construction is being done in secret, and local residents are kept in total darkness regarding their own future. Work on Ahai Dam, in the upper Yangtse region, was carried out in secret by Sinohydro Corporation. Signs declaring the site a "military zone" were erected to discourage visitors. There was no EIA at Ahai Dam: authorities planning to visit the dam to approve the project were presented with a dam that was practically completed. No EIAs have been completed for other dams under construction in the upper Yangtse, at Ludila Dam (where a mudslide killed eight people in August 2008) and at Jinganqiao Dam.

★   ★   ★

THE BUILDING OF DAMS AND THE CREATION OF HUGE RESERVOIRS HAS BEEN FIRMLY linked to landslides and mudslides. More difficult to prove is a link to earthquakes. The colossal weight and size of a reservoir behind a dam has been linked to triggering seismic activity, in a phenomenon known as reservoir-induced seismicity.

The mountainous parts of Sichuan and Yunnan provinces are known to be very seismically active areas. On the basis of his surveys, Fan Xiao, chief engineer at the Sichuan Geology and Mineral Bureau, warned against the construction of Zipingpu Dam on the Min River, a Yangtse tributary in Sichuan, due to seismic risk. Construction of the 510-foot-high Zipingpu Dam went ahead anyway: it was completed in 2006, with its massive reservoir—holding 315 million tons of water—lying directly on a major seismic fault zone. The megadam has been implicated in the great Sichuan earthquake of May 12, 2008, which toppled thousands of buildings—with over 85,000 people killed or missing, and a further 5 million left homeless. The dam lies just 3.5 miles from the earthquake's epicenter: the weight of the reservoir and the subterranean seepage (lubricating faultlines) may have either triggered the earthquake or may have magnified what could have been a minor earthquake. Chinese official sources, however, deny there is any connection between Zipingpu Dam and the Sichuan earthquake.

In a report published in April 2012 by Canadian NGO Probe International, researchers overlaid maps of seismic hazard zones with known locations of large dams constructed, under construction, or proposed for the Yarlung Tsangpo, Parlong Tsangpo, Salween, Mekong, Yangtse, Yalong, Dadu, Min, and Yellow river headwaters. The researchers found that 48.2 percent of the dam locations are sited in zones of high to very high seismic activity, while 50.4 percent are located in zones of moderate seismic activity. Only 1.4 percent are found in zones of low seismic activity. The report concluded: "By constructing more than 130 large dams in a region of known high seismicity, China is embarking on a major experiment with potentially disastrous consequences for its economy and its citizens."[18]

Regardless of whether Zipingpu's reservoir triggered the Sichuan earthquake, a frightening scenario is raised here: What if one of these megadams were to suddenly burst due to an earthquake? All in the path of the dam would be swept away in a wall of water. Even scarier: Chinese engineers favor the building of dam cascades at the edges of the Tibetan Plateau. On the upper Yangtse, a cascade of 15 megadams is under way; along the Yalong River (a Yangtse tributary) 21 dams are planned, and on the upper Mekong, a cascade of 26 dams is projected. If an upper dam were to burst, the wall of water would inevitably take out other dams in the cascade, like an inland tsunami.

China Daily interviewed Cao Guangjing, the general manager of the Three Gorges Dam, who reassured readers: "The [Sichuan] earthquake has not damaged the dam or other parts of the project. The earthquake-proof capability of the Three Gorges Project is higher than national standards. The project is designed to withstand a 7-magnitude quake and is able to withstand an 8-magnitude quake for a short time."[19]

Simple calculations expose a crucial weakness in Chinese dam building. Cao Guangjing says the Three Gorges Dam was built to withstand a 7-magnitude quake on the Richter Scale, which is a higher earthquake-proof standard than other dams. But the quake in Sichuan measured 7.9 on the Richter Scale: it cracked Zipingpu Dam and caused damage to more than 60 other smaller dams in the region. Dam personnel and the military rushed to empty water from scores of dams in areas close to Zipingpu, causing considerable flooding downstream. If those dams had breached, millions downstream would have been killed. On April 14, 2010, a 7.1-magnitude earthquake hit the Tibetan town of Jyekundo in Yushu, Qinghai, killing over 2,000 people. When cracks appeared in nearby Changu Dam, soldiers rushed to empty reservoirs at three dams in the region.

The scenario of one dam taking out another dam has actually happened in China, leading to the world's worst dam disaster. In August 1975, a typhoon struck 400-foot-high Banqiao Dam on the Ru River in Henan, central China. The operators of the dam thought there was nothing to fear because the dam was engineered to withstand strong flooding. However, at midnight, a dam upstream burst, sending a huge volume of water down the river—which caused Banqiao Dam to collapse, unleashing a wall of water that hit the town of Huaibin like a tsunami. Flooding took out scores of other dams like dominos. The official death toll from flooding (released many years later) was 26,000, though the real figure is probably far higher.

It is thought that another 145,000 people died from epidemics and famine that followed the flooding.[20]

★ ★ ★

IN SICHUAN, AS IN TIBET, WHAT INITIALLY SPARKS DAM PROTESTS IS LAND grabbing—the forced eviction of farmers from productive land. Pubugou Dam on the Dadu River (a Yangtse tributary) became the flashpoint for some of the largest protests against dam construction ever seen in China. In late 2004, as work commenced on the dam, the construction site was over-run by thousands of farmers—a crowd estimated to be 10,000 strong—incensed about evictions stemming from planned flooding of the region. Thousands of protesters were jailed, and some killed. Local government officials were convicted of corruption. Dam construction was delayed by a year. Violence flared up again in early 2010 when farmers were forc-ibly evicted from their homes to make way for reservoir flooding. In all, about 100,000 people were displaced by the project. The dam reservoir has destroyed some of the best farmland in China.

Meantime, the Three Gorges Project Corporation carries on relentlessly, building Great Walls of Concrete all the way up the Yangtse. A dam corporation like this needs new megaprojects to keep going, regardless of whether the dams are actually needed or not. This fully state-owned company is given special protection, so in the past it has run practically free of supervision and regulations. That has allowed for bribery and corruption at the highest levels. Back in 2000, six years before the Three Gorges Dam started initial operations, authorities busted a ring of officials who siphoned off hundreds of millions of yuan intended for settlement funds for those relocated by dam con-struction. A report issued by the Chinese Communist Party's antigraft watchdog in February 2014 found that some officials involved in the Three Gorges Dam were guilty of nepotism, shady property deals, and dodgy bidding procedures. In one case, a company bidding for a construction project related to the dam area was told to pay a bribe of 1 million yuan ($163,200) by members of the hydropower giant's bidding evaluation panel.[21]

The second-biggest dam in China after the Three Gorges Dam is under way on the upper Yangtse. Xiluodu Dam, straddling the Yunnan-Sichuan border, is a concrete colossus standing around 920 feet tall, with a generating capacity estimated at 12.6 GW. Coming online in 2015, its construction was halted several times due to the lack of an EIA. Not far off, the third-biggest dam in China, Xiangjiaba, has started running generators, with a capacity of 6.4 GW. Also under construction by the Three Gorges Project Corporation are two more monster dams in this cascade on the Jinsha River: Beihaitan (capacity 12.6 GW, wall height 990 feet) and Wudongde (capacity 7.4 GW, wall height 770 feet)—both scheduled for completion by 2020.

What does this cascade of megadams mean for the upper Yangtse River? Death by dams, basically. Liu Jianqiang, an environmental journalist and campaigner, puts it this way: "[The Jinsha] is big and beautiful. But if you have 25 dams and every 100 kilometres [60 miles] there is a dam, then you don't have a river. You will never have a river again. It means you won't have fish, you will lose a lot of land and many people have to lose their homes. We call that a dead river."

What does a cascade of megadams mean for fish? Well, since the Three Gorges Dam was built, the downstream population of carp has fallen by 90 percent, according to Guo Qiaoyu of the Nature Conservancy in Beijing.[22] The Yangtse River is China's biggest freshwater fishery, believed to produce the best quality black, silver, grass, and bighead carp—the big four that have been farmed for hundreds of years and provide protein for millions of Chinese. The carp are under threat from overfishing, pollution, land reclamation, poor water management, and dam construction. Fish are key to the Yangtse River's ecosystem. Without them, the biodiversity of the river will disappear and the ecosystem will face collapse.

In the 1990s, the Upper Yangtse Rare and Endemic Fish Nature Reserve was created specifically to protect species threatened by the construction of the Three Gorges Dam. Among the hundreds of species protected are the four wild carp types that provide genetic stock upon which fish farms depend for breeding. This 250-mile-long reserve is the last stand for highly endangered endemic species like the Chinese sturgeon. The Chinese paddlefish may already be extinct, joining the *baiji*, a freshwater dolphin.

Disregarding all the warning signs, the Three Gorges Project Corporation presented plans for building Xiaonanhai, a 1,760 MW dam located inside the Fish Nature Reserve. The corporation's way around this inconvenient obstacle was to arrange to have the reserve's boundaries redrawn to reduce its size so that the dam would lie outside the "protected" area. In December 2011, official sanction was given to shrinking the boundaries of the reserve. Preliminary construction for Xiaonanhai Dam began in March 2012: its reservoir will likely flood part of the fish reserve and thus eliminate its boundaries.[23]

Construction of these dams on the upper Yangtse have been plagued by corruption, technical problems, human rights problems, and profound environmental impact. People are incensed about losing homes and valuable farmland. There have been outbreaks of unrest along the Jinsha. In 2011, riot police quelled a "mass disturbance" in Suijiang town, where 60,000 people were being forcibly relocated to make way for Xiangjiaba Dam. In a country where there is scarcely any arable land left, these farmers would at best be offered low-grade land as compensation, forcing them to scratch out a subsistence living.

★   ★   ★

IN AUGUST 2010, CHINA SURPASSED THE LEVEL OF 200 GW GENERATED IN TOTAL hydro output, roughly equivalent to a fifth of the total hydropower in the world. It took them 60 years of intensive damming to reach that level. Then in early 2011 came an astonishing report from *Shanghai Daily* saying that the aim is to *double* that output within the next decade and generate 430 GW of hydropower by the year 2020. In hydro terms, that is the equivalent of adding a Three Gorges Dam every single year from 2011 until 2020. The rationale behind this is that hydropower is clean, and this will reduce carbon emissions and dependency on coal-fired power plants. However, coal production will still expand annually until 2020 before tapering off around 2022. In other reports, massive dam building is also cited as a way to contain flooding—including flooding from glacial meltdown.

The following report appeared in *Shanghai Daily*, January 6, 2011: "With 2020 clean-energy targets to meet, China is set to accelerate the building of hydroelectric dams, reversing a long halt caused by environmental concerns and the social upheaval of relocating people living in the shadow of dam sites. The trend will create a 'golden decade' for the nation's hydropower sector, analysts say, as high fuel prices continue to squeeze margins of coal-fired power plants that comprise the bulk of China's electricity-generating capacity. Renewable energy sources like solar power have been slow to come on line on a big scale because of high costs and grid-configuration problems."

Is this a golden decade for hydropower, or is it a major catastrophe in the making? China's engineers are embarking on a reckless megadam-building spree that is without precedent in human history. The 2011–2015 energy sector blueprint, released by China's State Council in February 2013, confirmed plans to push forward with hydropower development, with a frenzy of dam building in the upper Salween, upper Mekong, upper Yangtse, and Yarlung Tsangpo river basins. Three of those rivers are transboundary, shared internationally. According to the plan, some 120 GW of new hydropower will begin construction by 2015 nationwide.

These plans mark a distinct shift in government policy, away from a more cautious approach to dam building over the previous decade in reaction to protesters who lobbied for cancellation of dams in ecologically sensitive regions or regions of seismic activity. Particularly shocking to Chinese environmental NGOs is the revival of plans for dams on the virgin Salween River. Following widespread protest, Premier Wen Jiabao suspended plans for a 13-dam cascade in 2004. But that suspension appears to be tied to his personal guarantee: as his term of office came to a close in 2013, the pro-hydro lobby surfaced again.

In February 2011, four Chinese geologists warned that the Salween runs through "an active fault zone, with frequent earthquakes, and in a landslide-prone area subject to frequent downpours. Due to high seismic and geological risks, large dams should not be built here."[24] Despite the warnings, dam builder China Huadian Corporation continued surveying for five megadams on the upper Salween—Songta, Maji, Yabiluo, Liuku, and Saige—and successfully lobbied to have these included in the 2011–2015 energy plans. Only one EIA has been completed for these dams on the Salween. For Liuku Dam, a brief summary of an EIA was posted, but the full version was never released because it was deemed a "state secret." Ignoring vigorous local objection, resettlement of the entire village of Liuku proceeded. Together, the five dams approved for the river would displace as many as 60,000 people, destroy the Salween's aquatic ecosystem, and flood the scenic gorges for which the area is known. Li Bo, director of China's longest-running environmental NGO, Friends of Nature, said in an interview, "There were signs during the past year that megadams were staging a comeback after being put on hold for years, but I'm still shocked by the lack of transparency in the decision-making process behind this."[25]

★ ★ ★

MORE THAN 26,000 LARGE DAMS, HALF THE WORLD'S TOTAL, ARE SITUATED WITHIN the borders of China. It has more large dams than the rest of the world combined. And it is going after the rest of the world, too. China is engaged in financing and building large dams on the same rivers sourced in Tibet, but also further downstream in the nations of Pakistan, Nepal, Burma, Laos, and Cambodia. In several cases—Burma and Laos particularly—the intent is to export the hydropower generated back to China via transmission lines.

China exports its megadam engineering expertise and financial backing to impoverished nations in Asia, Africa, and elsewhere—initiating projects with very little impact assessment, if any. These projects are potentially devastating to indigenous people, who are rarely consulted about the proposed dam. How has China achieved its dam dominancy of third-world countries in such a short period of time? The answer lies with the words *human rights*. Western companies routinely conduct EIAs, mindful of social and environmental impacts and wary of the rights of indigenous groups. Chinese dam-building consortiums have no such qualms: they often proceed without EIAs, even in secrecy, and regardless of ecological criteria set by the international community.

The Power Construction Corporation of China (PowerChina) has 148 branches in 71 countries, including 54 branches in Africa and 74 in Asia. It is the biggest dam-building consortium in the world, throwing up Great Walls of Concrete all over the map, particularly through its subsidiary Sinohydro. Chinese state-owned banks often provide the financing to enable these deals to proceed. Chinese engineers are supervising construction of more than 300 large dams in over 60 countries, particularly in Africa and Southeast Asia. A number of these are highly controversial. Local indigenous groups—the ones most impacted by large dam building—are rarely consulted about these projects. The Chinese engineering style is to sneak in and proceed with rapid construction before objections can be raised. Here is PowerChina's philosophy, taken from its website: "Harmony in humanity and harmony with nature, the core of traditional Chinese wisdom, are deeply embedded in PowerChina's business philosophy."[26]

But that ancient Chinese wisdom does not prevent PowerChina from destroying the forests of Sarawak and decimating the lives of the indigenous people. The Bruno Manser Fund has accused Chinese dam builders of causing cultural genocide in Sarawak, in Malaysian Borneo. The indigenous people of Sarawak—the Kayan, Penan, Kelabit, Iban, and Bisaya—are never consulted about dam building, and in some instances have no idea what a dam is. Some tribes have dismissed the idea of a powerful river being blocked, thinking this to be impossible. Sinohydro (a division of PowerChina), along with the Three Gorges Project Corporation, is building all over Sarawak, often in secret.

After decades of delay with a series of dam builders, Sinohydro took over the construction of Bakun Dam in Sarawak: it was completed in 2011. At 670 feet tall and 2,400 MW capacity, it is one of the largest dams in Asia (outside of China, of course). But currently the dam is not generating at full capacity. Mired by corruption and poor planning, the dam was originally slated to send 90 percent of its energy to peninsular Malaysia through undersea cables, but this proved too expensive and the idea was scrapped. In the end, this dam—which displaced 10,000 people and flooded 270 square miles of land—is a white elephant. It did not need to be built, since the whole of Sarawak only has 970 MW of demand. The Sarawak government is still looking for ways to sell surplus electricity. There were plans to power up an aluminum smelter run by mining giant Rio Tinto, but that venture fell through. Despite the huge surplus of electricity, there are plans for 50 more dams in Sarawak to be built by Sinohydro.[27]

In 2007, at the United Nations, China voted in favor of the UN Declaration on the Rights of Indigenous Peoples. This document stipulates that indigenous peoples have the right of consent regarding "any project affecting their lands." But from Tibet to the Sudan to Sarawak, this principle has been flagrantly violated by Chinese commercial interests, particularly Chinese dam-building consortiums.

CHAPTER FOUR

Stealing Water

Where Is the Thirsty Dragon Going to Guzzle Next?

Megacities, megadams, and megadeltas all go together. China has more megacities than any other nation on the planet, and the water to support its rapidly growing urban population and burgeoning industry has to come from somewhere.

Cheng Xiaotao, deputy chief engineer at the China Institute of Water Resources and Hydropower Research, explains: "China's population has increased by 700 or 800 million in the past few decades, and people have also been flowing into the cities with unprecedented speed. Urban industry is also rapidly expanding. This is something no other country has experienced. The water those people need just isn't available locally."[1]

China's population rocketed from a mere 560 million in 1950 to 1.4 billion in 2014. In a matter of six decades, the population has more than doubled. That has placed enormous pressure on food and water demands, especially in big cities. Here's what happens: first, urban centers appropriate water from agriculture, then they go after groundwater, and when those avenues have been exhausted or if local water is polluted, water-diversion projects start up. Fan Xiao, chief engineer at the Sichuan Geology and Mineral Bureau, says: "We need to ask why is there a water shortage? Inefficient water use is still a major issue."[2] Fan Xiao is referring to irrigation. It is estimated that up to two-thirds of water withdrawals in China are for agriculture, but half of that water may never reach the crops—lost through evaporation and antiquated irrigation systems. And perhaps 20 percent of urban water consumption is lost through leaky pipes.[3]

China has gone into the business of stealing from its rivers to solve problems like drought; in just a few decades, the nation has turned into the world's chief diverter of water. Around the country, huge water-diversion projects are under way, or under consideration. Siphoning off as much as 30 percent of water from the Yellow River for irrigation or to supply cities means that the river now often fails to meet the sea. There are water-diversion projects from the Yellow River to the Jin River. There are massive water-diversion schemes under way even in water-rich areas, like Yunnan Province, and in areas where there is abundant rainfall, like the Pearl River Delta in Guangzhou.

Saltwater diversions are under consideration as well: the Bohai Pipeline proposes dropping a pipe into the Bohai Sea, drawing more than 340,000 cubic meters (90 million gallons) of saltwater a day into a complex of coastal desalination plants, and then pumping the processed water uphill for more than 370 miles to Xilinhot in Mongolia for use in coal-mining operations. Mining and water-diversion go hand in hand.

Environment expert Keith Schneider notes: "Government analysts project that China's energy companies will need to produce an additional billion metric tons of coal annually by 2020, representing a 30 percent increase. Fresh water needed for mining, processing, and consuming coal accounts for the largest share of industrial water use in China, or roughly 120 billion cubic meters a year, a fifth of all the water consumed nationally."[4]

The regions of northern China are particularly hard up for water due to intensified desertification and increased industrial pollution. It is estimated that up to 70 percent of China's rivers are contaminated—to the point where the water is not drinkable, or even usable. At a conference in 1999, Wen Jiabao, then vice premier, noted dramatically: "The survival of the Chinese nation is threatened by its shortage of water."[5] Wang Shucheng, former minister of Water Resources, puts it even more extremely: "To fight for every drop of water or die: that is the challenge facing China."[6]

China is facing an unprecedented water crisis. Half of China's major cities experience water shortages. And half of its rivers seem to have disappeared. A three-year study by the Ministry of Water Resources and the National Bureau of Statistics compiled the first national water census for China. The results were released in 2013. Here's what they found: more than 27,000 rivers have disappeared from China's state maps.[7] Only 22,909 rivers were located by surveyors, compared with the more than 50,000 in the 1990s. Officials blamed the loss on climate change and on mistakes by earlier cartographers, but environmentalists blame it on poor development strategies and on pollution.

China is rising, but at what cost? Here's what dissident Dai Qing says, in an interview with Toronto's *Globe and Mail*: "The cost includes environmental devastation on a massive scale. Eighty per cent of the country's rivers and lakes are drying up. Sixty per cent of the water in seven major river systems is unsuitable for human contact. A third of the land is contaminated by acid rain. Two-thirds of the grassland have become desertified, and most of the forest is gone. Forty percent of the arable land has been degraded by fertilizers and pesticides. Of the world's 20 most polluted cities, 16 are in China."[8]

The old standby in times of crisis, groundwater, can no longer be relied on. It has been overused, causing wells to be sunk deeper and deeper to find water. While groundwater is a renewable source, it is extremely slow to replenish reserves. But much worse news: the groundwater is being contaminated from industrial dumping that causes chemicals to seep into soil. Textile, printing, and dyeing industries—all huge water consumers— dig wells to secretly dump their wastewater.

The Chinese solution to the water problem in the north is a mega-water-diversion project. *Mega* here means of a magnitude that has never before been attempted in recorded history. First proposed by Mao Zedong in 1952, the South-to-North Water Diversion project got under way in 2002 and is expected to take more than 30 years to complete, at a cost of over $62 billion. The plan is to divert up to 45 billion cubic meters (11.88 trillion gallons) of water every year from the Yangtse River Basin northward to water-starved regions.[9] This would involve a complex system of 1,800 miles of canals, tunnels, and pipes.

The environmental consequences of such a colossal water-diversion project are potentially enormous. In Central Asia, the Aral Sea was once the world's fourth-largest inland lake. In the 1960s and 1970s, after Soviet managers diverted two main feeder rivers for cotton production, the wetland ecosystem of the Aral Sea became a disaster area. The lake has almost disappeared; the remaining portions are too salty to support fish, leading to the abandonment of large-scale commercial fishing.

Under the South-to-North Water Diversion scheme are three diversion routes: eastern, central, and western. The Eastern Route is partly a revival of the imperial Grand Canal and is nearing completion. Depending on seasonal flows, there are plans to divert up to 13 billion cubic meters (3.4 trillion gallons) of water through the Eastern Route to Tianjin. But a problem has surfaced: by the time water in the Yangtse gets closer to the sea, it becomes heavily polluted, so what is being diverted, essentially, is polluted water that needs to undergo expensive treatment before it's usable. The Central Route got under way in 2004 and calls for up to 14 billion cubic meters (3.7 trillion gallons) of water to be diverted northward from Danjiangkou Reservoir toward Beijing.

The Western Route is in the planning stages, with a projected diversion of up to 18 billion cubic meters (4.75 trillion gallons) of water. This targets the Tibetan Plateau, with plans to divert water from upper Yangtse and two Yangtse tributaries (Yalong and Dadu rivers) to the upper Yellow River, reengineering the flow of rivers to help the parched provinces of northern China, and with an eye to supplying water for mining operations. Exact plans are not known, but it appears the Western Route involves the building of three megadams to intercept major rivers (with wall heights of 575 feet, 990 feet, and 970 feet) and a system of tunnels stretching some 250 miles. This is designed to divert water from the Yangtse River headwaters across mountains to the Yellow River headwaters. The proposed 990-foot-high Tongjia Dam, in Yushu County, is under consideration as the starting point of the Western Route.

If you've never heard of this South-to-North Water Diversion project, you have lots of company. Over a billion Chinese are completely in the dark about project details too. Although China publicizes the water diversion as a national triumph, Chinese authorities and engineering planners have neglected to offer specific details of this grand pipe dream will work—and the dangers involved if it does not work. Ma Jun, China's best-known environmental activist, says the government's obsession with giant engineering projects only makes matters worse, "causing us to hit the limits of our water resources."[10]

This mega-water-diversion project does not involve transboundary rivers, but other plans under consideration do. The official website for the South-to-North Water Diversion project says of the Western Route: "In 1950s and 1960s, it was considered to divert water from Tongtianhe [Yangtse], Yalongjiang, Daduhe, Lancangjiang [Mekong], Nujiang [Salween] Rivers. But these considerations could be the long-range plans due to the large projects' engineering scale."[11] That is, at that point in time it was not considered technically feasible.

Those long-range plans may be back on the drawing board. There is talk of a pharaonic scheme that would divert water eastward from the Mekong, Salween, and Yarlung Tsangpo rivers. In February 2013, a proposal surfaced on the website of the Yellow River Conservancy Commission of the Chinese Ministry of Water Resources. This is a feasibility study for a project called the Yellow River Waterway Corridor, a diversion of 150 billion cubic meters (39.6 trillion gallons) of water from six rivers on the

Tibetan Plateau. Unusually, the website gives details—for the proposed diversion of "50 billion cubic meters [13.2 trillion gallons] of water from the Yarlung Tsangpo (about 30 percent of the average annual run-off), 24 billion cubic meters [6.34 trillion gallons] from the Salween (35 percent of the average annual run-off) and 26 billion cubic meters [6.86 trillion gallons] from the Mekong (about 35 percent of the average annual run-off)."[12] A diversion of such magnitude would be utterly catastrophic for the nations downstream. If Chinese engineers can master methods of diverting water on a grand scale, then the whole of Asia is under severe threat.

The details for this feasibility study point to massive water diversion not only to China's northeast, but about half the water would go to the northwest—to the Tsaidam, Tarim, Turpan, and Junggar basins, which are all desert regions. Why divert large amounts of water to desert regions with such low populations? The answer involves mining and oil extraction, as well as irrigation. The Chinese mining dragon is a very thirsty one. The Tsaidam Basin is a heavy mining, oil extraction, and industrial area; these operations all need huge amounts of water. China intends to implement oil shale and oil sands extraction technologies in the Tsaidam Basin, which will require exponentially more water. Likewise, the Tarim Basin is an emerging oil and gas energy base. Both the Tarim and Junggar basins in the far northwest are potential sites for shale gas and oil sands extraction. Elsewhere across China, major water diversion is used for processing of coal. And in Tibet, diversion of river water for mining operations has caused major conflict with nomads and farmers.

★　★　★

NONE OF THE CHINESE DIVERSION OR DAMMING PROJECTS SEEM TO INCLUDE ANY Tibetan engineers or even Tibetan workers. That's because Tibetans are excluded from the whole process. It would also be very difficult for a Tibetan to qualify as an engineer under the Chinese educational system. Tibetans would most likely not be adverse to small-scale, well-managed hydro projects with proven benefits for themselves. In fact, the first dam operating in Tibet was set up by a Tibetan engineer.

In the 1920s, a Tibetan called Ringang pulled off a remarkable feat. He started up a hydroelectric plant near Lhasa. Ringang was sent to England in 1913 as part of an educational experiment. Four Tibetans, known as "the Rugby Boys," were sent to Rugby School and then on to other higher education institutions. Of the four, Ringang benefited the most.[13]

Ringang studied electrical engineering at London and Birmingham universities. He returned to Tibet fired up with a fantastic dream: to harness the plateau's mighty hydropower. With Herculean resolve, Ringang arranged for hydroelectric components from Birmingham to be shipped to Asia and then carried over the Himalayas to Tibet. Because porters were not enamored of their heavy loads, some loads disappeared over cliffs "by accident"—leaving the project with missing parts. But eventually in 1928, Ringang got the hydroelectric plant functioning at the foot of a mountain stream. Except for the winter months, when the stream was frozen, this provided Lhasa with some electric lighting. But as time wore on and parts wore down—and replacement parts did not arrive—the plant fell into disarray, and eventually yielded only enough power to drive the machines at the mint, which produced coins, banknotes, rifles, and cartridges.

Another of the Rugby Boys, Mondo, trained in geology, hoping to become a mining engineer. He returned to Tibet bent on fossicking for precious metals, particularly gold. But he ran up against Tibet's conservative clergy, who claimed he would disturb the spirits of the earth by digging, and this would cause the crops to fail. Mondo was blocked from mining at a number of locations. He finally gave up on his mining ambitions and instead held some minor administrative posts. And the other two Rugby Boys, Ghonkar and Kyipup, fared no better when it came to modernizing of Tibet. After graduating from Rugby, Ghonkar was sent to Woolwich Military Academy to prepare him to modernize the Tibetan army. Ghonkar got more than he bargained for. World War I broke out, and he got to see the fabulous machines of the West used for purposes of mass destruction. On his return to Tibet, the idea of modernizing the army was soundly rebuffed by conservative forces, and Ghonkar was dispatched to a frontier station. This was a major oversight, as modernization of the Tibetan army could have stymied invasion by Chinese troops in 1950.

Kyipup, after finishing at Rugby, took surveying courses. On his return to Tibet, he was assigned to the task of developing the telegraph line for a planned extension from Gyantse to Lhasa in the early 1920s. The idea was to modernize Tibet's communication system by at least introducing a few telephones in the Potala Palace in Lhasa. However, Tibetans kept stealing wire along the route for their own construction projects. After a short stint as superintendent of telegraphs, Kyipup turned to other administrative posts. Sadly, any gains that the Rugby Boys were able to make were wiped out by the conservative Tibetan clergy. However, Ringang's experiment with hydropower seems to have proved a hit. Unfortunately, without maintenance, Ringang's hydroplant slowly fell apart. In 1947, by which time Ringang had passed away, his small hydroplant was out of commission.

Enter Peter Aufschnaiter, an Austrian who escaped from a prisoner-of-war camp in British India in 1944 and trekked across Tibet with fellow Austrian Heinrich Harrer. Upon reaching Lhasa, Aufschnaiter found himself in an unusual position: he was the sole trained engineer in a land of zero engineering. Starting in December 1946, he became the first foreigner ever employed in the service of the Tibetan government. He joked about becoming Chief Digger and Minister of Agriculture (he trained as an agricultural engineer). The chief digger soon discovered some unusual problems. He was asked to dig several drainage canals around Lhasa in 1947, but Tibetan workers were afraid of digging because they believed it would disturb wrathful demons dwelling in the earth. Diggers would run away screaming when a worm surfaced: all sentient creatures are considered to be reincarnated beings and had to be given a safe home.

Most of the wealthy in Lhasa used their own diesel generators, imported from India, for power. Aufschnaiter proposed construction of a hydroelectric plant to supply the whole of Lhasa. The plan was to import three 125 kW (kilowatt) hydroelectric generating plants from England and set them up on the Kyi Chu River. In 1948, Aufschnaiter moved to Perong, five miles east of Lhasa, to be closer to the new hydroelectric project. Mr. J. Reid from General Electric in India arrived to plan street lighting in Lhasa. But the entire project was doomed. It was abandoned when China invaded from the east of Tibet in October 1950.

★   ★   ★

ONE THING THE CONSERVATIVE TIBETAN CLERGY OF PRE-1950 INDEPENDENT TIBET would never have allowed is meddling with sacred lakes. The Tibetan Plateau is dotted with over 1,500 lakes ranging from small to huge, mostly glacial-fed—part of the region's immense water resources. But the lakes are under siege due to climate change, encroaching desertification, and human interference. Wetlands are drying up and receding—most likely due to permafrost melting that causes loss of soil moisture for grass and plants. There are a handful of sacred lakes in Tibet that pilgrims make great efforts to get to. They may attempt to walk around the entire lake, such as Manasarovar near Mount Kailash, or Namtso to the north of Lhasa, or Lhamo Lhatso, famed as the site where signs are sought by diviners to indicate where the next Dalai Lama will be reincarnated. This is done by interpreting mirages appearing on the lake's surface—and was the method used to locate the current, fourteenth Dalai Lama.

Heading from Lhasa to Gyantse, you crest Khamba La, a pass with a magnificent view of Lake Yamdrok Tso, among the most revered in Tibet. Fed by glacial meltwater, the lake acts as a huge natural reservoir: its surface area is about 450 square miles in extent. The lake is an important habitat for migrating birds, such as the black-necked crane. Yamdrok Tso is regarded as a great talisman for Tibet, a "life-power lake." It attracts Tibetans on pilgrimage, with several monasteries in the vicinity. If its waters dry up, legend has it, Tibet will no longer be habitable. The lake is a stunning shade of turquoise, with Himalayan snowcaps bordering Bhutan in the backdrop. But that turquoise color may be changing, and the lake itself is in danger of significantly dropping in level, or just plain disappearing. Winding down from Khamba La toward Gyantse, you pass a hydropower plant with four German-made turbines sitting by the side of the lake. The sacred waters of Yamdrok Tso have been exploited in a highly controversial hydroproject.

Chinese disregard for the sacred nature of Yamdrok Tso started in the 1960s when commercial fishermen set about exploiting the lake, even using explosives to net the fish. Tibetans leave sacred lakes alone because they are thought to be the dwelling place of serpent-spirits, known as *nagas*. The nagas are greatly offended by pollution and impurity of any kind. They possess an energy that can be a source of wealth and good fortune—or the energy can be poisonous, inflicting a horrible skin disease for life. Nagas are also thought to create the rains, making them very important to placate for crop production. That's one reason Tibetans avoid eating fish.

Right from the start of the Yamdrok Tso hydroproject in 1985, opposition was very vocal. Tibetans were furious that their sacred lake was being defiled. The Panchen Lama, the highest ranking religious figure in Tibet at the time, managed to get work on the project stopped in 1986, but after his death in early 1989, work resumed. German firm JM Voith AG supplied four turbines as well as pumps and steering systems for the Yamdrok Tso project, and Austrian company ELIN supplied on-site engineers. The contracts were worth over $40 million. Both companies have been criticized in the past for their involvement in third-world dam projects where local populations have been forcibly removed from their land.[14] In 1991, an estimated 4,000 to 5,000 cadres of the People's Armed Police moved into the Yamdrok Tso area to build the project under a shroud of secrecy while China's propaganda machine launched a campaign glorifying the hydroproject as benefiting all Tibetans.

In 1993, freshwater wells in the vicinity of the lake suddenly started drying up, forcing villagers to rely on the lake itself for water supply. In 1996, there was talk of the collapse of a tunnel leading from the lake to the turbines. The 90 MW plant started generating power in 1996. Yamdrok Tso Power Station was designed as a pumped storage system to provide electricity for Lhasa in times of peak demand. The idea seems to be to drain water out of Yamdrok Tso to provide hydropower, and then replenish the lake water levels by pumping water back in from the nearby Yarlung Tsangpo River. But this means snow-fed lake water would be replaced with muddy river flow, with uncertain results for the ecosystem around the lake. One result is certain: the lake will lose its natural deep turquoise hue. And the sacred lake is in danger of receding substantially.

The battle to save Yamdrok Tso was lost, but east across the plateau in Ganzi Prefecture (western Sichuan) a project to dam Megoe Tso Lake was scrapped due to pressure from local and international NGO groups. Tibet environmental expert Tashi Tsering was a key member of a campaign to stop this dam project. He told me that when he showed up at a conference as part of a US delegation, his Chinese counterparts were stunned to find themselves facing a Tibetan activist for the first time. The cancellation of the dam project at Megoe Tso was achieved on the basis that the lake is sacred to the Tibetans and a key tourism attraction—and that its natural beauty should be preserved. On that basis, it could be argued that many sites in Tibet should be preserved from damming.

★ ★ ★

Lhasa, September 2010: An unusual minivan passes me on the street. It is a moving billboard, both sides plastered with a photo-collage promoting a new brand of bottled water from Tibet. The collage shows the plastic bottles with the brand name in Chinese characters, backed by crystal ice–like peaks and a Tibetan nomad in a sheepskin cloak. Later inside a shop I come across a brand called Tibetan Magic Water. In fact, this shop displays half a dozen brands of bottled water from Tibet that I have not seen on previous trips, including Himalaya Natural Mineral Water and Shigatse Spring Water. Clearly, selling Tibet in little bottles is big business. Companies sell the myth that Tibet's water is somehow magical and pure. One company even implies that it is selling Everest in little bottles. Close to Tingri, in western Tibet, is a water-bottling factory that claims to bottle Qomolangma (Mount Everest) meltwater from a glacial source. As the north face of Everest is an iconic symbol for Tibet, it's not clear whether the source of this bottled water is right at Everest, or whether the company is just using the mountain as a branding device. Certainly there's a lot of competition for using the north face of Everest for branding by other water-bottling companies in Tibet.

Why this proliferation of bottled water from Tibet? Fingers point at the Lhasa train, starting up for commerce in 2006, enabling bottled water to be shipped economically to Shanghai and Beijing for the first time. Unlike China, where groundwater is either depleted or severely polluted, Tibet has massive groundwater reserves, which are mostly untouched. More than a hundred spring sites have been identified across the Tibetan Plateau.

The most prestigious brand of bottled water is 5100 Tibet Glacier Spring Water. This brand is served up in first class and business class on Air China flights. The brand has been heavily promoted. It is handed out on high-speed trains (China Railway Express) and is the official bottled water at high-level Chinese Communist Party events, such as important anniversaries. A sort of high-altitude tonic, 5100 comes from a spring at Damshung, about 105 miles north of Lhasa. The brand 5100 supposedly derives from the elevation of the spring (given in meters). The processing plant is only 13 miles from the rail line, which is key to its success as the bottled water is destined for export to east-coast cities. Without the railway, the venture would simply not work.

Established in 2005 as a joint venture with Canadian Chinese entrepreneur Wallace Yu, the company is headquartered in Hong Kong but incorporated offshore in the tax havens of the Cayman Islands and British Virgin Islands. In 2009, Tibet 5100 Water Resources Holdings Ltd. produced almost 2 million gallons of bottled water, which was shipped out of Tibet by train in a business estimated to be worth over $100 million a year. The water collected would otherwise flow through wetlands where yaks and sheep graze. It is not known how the factory's siphoning of water has impacted the ecosystem. What is certain is a proliferation of plastic bottles from this venture. As water activist Maude Barlow puts it, "The bottled water industry is one of the most polluting industries on Earth, and one of the least regulated."[15]

A single 11-ounce bottle of 5100 Tibet Glacier Spring Water sells in Shanghai or Beijing at about five times the price of an 18.5-ounce bottle from a nonpremium company. So the 5100 brand appears to be aimed at China's rich. Recent years have seen a meteoric rise in consumption of bottled water in China, particularly the high-end brands. With distribution assistance from Danish companies Carlsberg and Alectia, the venture hopes to establish 5100 as a world-class brand, a sort of Asian equivalent of Evian or Perrier. However, in Europe, brand 5100 may run into some resistance from Tibet support groups that depict it as tainted water, or water stolen from Tibet.

★　★　★

EXITING TIBET ON THE OVERLAND RUN TOWARD THE NEPALESE BORDER AT Zhangmu, you get a spectacular send-off from a raging river, the Bhote Kosi. The river rises in the foothills of Mount Shishapangma: it is narrow, but stunning for its staggering drop in elevation, cascading through tremendous gorges, replete with waterfalls and rapids. At certain points on the road to the border, you get a free car wash courtesy of the Bhote Kosi. Due to lower elevations, these gorges are much lusher and greener than in Tibet, with abundant vegetation clinging to cliff-sides. After the dry, rarefied air of Tibet, all is suddenly moist, with lots of spray suffusing the habitat and nourishing ferns, bushes, vines, flowers. The river is a magical living thing—brooding, gushing, hurtling along with power and majesty. The Friendship Bridge, which forms the actual Tibet-Nepal border, straddles the Bhote Kosi. Looking down at the river from the bridge, I marvel to think that this river from Tibet will course all the way through Nepal, providing the steepest rafting in the nation. It then joins forces with the Sun Kosi and feeds into the Ganges, traveling all the way to the sea. That's a pretty wild ride. Standing on the bridge, I wave good-bye to Tibet, and the Bhote Kosi carries on, thundering into Nepal. Along the way, Lamosangu Dam blocks part of the rafting run in Nepal. With more hydro projects in the works, the Bhote Kosi may become even less accessible to rafters. Perhaps this river is trying to tell me something. Do rivers have rights? Do they have the right to run to the sea without being blocked or diverted? Do they have the right to remain wild and free?

Back in Canada, I could find no documentary about China's ruthless exploitation of Tibet's water resources, so I set about making one myself. The tools for documentary-making have become a lot more democratic since the switch to digital filmmaking in the early 2000s. All you need is a camera, a laptop, a large monitor, and tons of time and patience to master video-editing programs. The main obstacles for making the film were technical, as in getting visual material like footage. Here I had to scramble. I finally managed to get some good river footage from my kayak contacts and completed a 40-minute documentary called *Meltdown in Tibet*, blowing the lid off dam building in Tibet.

The documentary was shown at film festivals and at independent film screening venues hosted by various NGOs and Tibet-support groups. I showed up at some events for Q&A sessions with the audience. Screening venues ranged from a simultaneous viewing on six LCD screens at the Foreign Correspondents' Club in Bangkok, Thailand, to a presentation from a laptop hooked to a projector inside a tent at the Kalachakra 2012 in Bodhgaya, India.

Questions from the audience were often the disturbing kind: I had trouble answering them.

"If coal burning is bad for the environment and if dams are damaging for the rivers, where is China's energy going to come from?" That question threw me for a loop, but on further reflection, this is really about China's double-digit growth rate over the last few decades—a success story that comes with a huge environmental cost. Why should pristine Tibet be sacrificed to pay for China's excesses? Destroying Tibet to provide energy fixes for factories thousands of miles away in Shanghai or Shenzhen will only lead to greater environmental problems in the future—not only for China, but for the nations downstream from Tibet.

"What can be done to stop China's building of megadams on shared rivers?" No answer for that one, either. As far as I can tell, very little is being done, either by the countries downstream or internationally. Various NGOs, such as International Rivers, have taken China to task and petitions have been circulated, but it is clear that China has absolutely no intention of sharing transboundary rivers and has never acknowledged the principle that they should be shared. Neither have they acknowledged that building a megadam on a transboundary river should require consultation with the nations downstream, though UN guidelines call for this. Even the Mekong River Commission, established to start dialogue on transboundary issues for the Mekong, has failed to make any headway. That's largely because China and Burma refused to join the commission. Southeast Asian nations have rallied to stop China from claiming the entire South China Sea and all its resources, but that is with the backing of American naval might, and with the backing of the UN Convention on the Law of the Sea. The South China Sea is rich in oil and gas deposits: China wants to monopolize those resources through force, employing its expanding naval power. This has led to fierce disputes with Vietnam and the Philippines. Chinese maps claim 90 percent of the 3.5 million-square-kilometer (1.35 million square-mile) South China Sea. China has bullied the maritime nations of Taiwan, Malaysia, Brunei, the Philippines, and Vietnam over its ridiculous territorial claims.

That led to another question—a rhetorical one. A man in the front row at a screening looked at me and said, "We're all doomed, aren't we?" He appeared to be shell-shocked, with a look of horror written on his face as the implications of all this started to sink in. And the dam documentary shows only part of the environmental horror. It barely touches on rampant mining in Tibet, or the forcible removal of nomads from their grassland habitat.

CHAPTER FIVE

Vanishing Nomads, Vanishing Grasslands

Why Are Tibet's Grasslands Being Usurped by Desert?

China has a term for those Tibetans displaced by dam construction: they are called ecological migrants. But *outcasts* would be closer to the truth—these people are refugees from China's greed in its reckless exploitation of Tibet's resources. Tibetans have become refugees in their own land. *Ecological migrants* is a euphemism for people in limbo, with few opportunities to make a decent living, people deprived of their sustainable lifestyle, people with no future. A significant portion of the displaced are Tibetan nomads.

Between 1995 and 2015, official Chinese policy has mandated the forcible removal of more than 2 million Tibetan nomads from their traditional grassland habitat for settlement in "new socialist villages." The relocation and forced settlement of the nomads may at first appear to be a human rights issue. But if you look deeper, this is ultimately an environmental issue. That's because Tibetan nomads have acted as the stewards of Tibet's grasslands for 4,000 years, with their livelihood dependent on yak herding. This is a sustainable lifestyle: the nomads depend on the grasslands, and they have to keep the grasslands in good shape to survive. If the nomads go, there is nobody left to preserve the grasslands. The vast grasslands of Tibet protect wetlands—and they form an important carbon sink. Alpine grasslands are not much discussed as a factor influencing climate change, but as grasslands degrade and turn to desert, this means whole regions are less able to absorb moisture—and more likely to radiate heat. The degradation of the grasslands in Tibet is partly caused by climate change—but mostly due to the shortsighted Chinese policy of shifting out the nomads and using fertile valleys of grasslands for extensive mining and damming, which can only harm regional ecosystems and degrade the grasslands. Pollution from mining in particular affects nomads, as it kills livestock by poisoning the water supply.

Snuffing out the Tibetan nomad way of life is tantamount to cultural genocide. Chinese officialdom refuses to see nomads as part of the solution for the grasslands. China views nomads as a problem, claiming they are backward and uneducated. In fact, on the slimmest of pretexts, all nomads within China have been targeted for resettlement, including the Mongolian, Kazakh, and Kirghiz nomads.

★　★　★

LITANG, JULY 2010: I TRAVEL TO EASTERN TIBET TO SEE A RENOWNED HORSE-racing festival. I am not going as a tourist exactly: I plan to film Tibetan nomads undercover in order to make a short documentary about what is happening to their culture. Every summer, nomads gather at various grassland sites across the Tibetan Plateau for festivals—to get together and exchange news, party, and show off their equestrian skills. Litang is the largest horse-racing festival in the region of Kham, eastern Tibet.

After changing planes three times and taking a Land Cruiser overland from Zhongdian, I reach Litang in time for the start of the festival, which always takes place on August 1. Nomads don't do anything according to the regular calendar; their activities are based on a lunar calendar, with last-minute get-togethers. But the Litang horse-racing festival was actually organized by Chinese authorities as a tourist attraction for Chinese visitors, so they set a fixed date for an annual weeklong event, August 1 to 7. I prepare all my gear for filming at the festival. Then, at the last minute, word reaches the hotel that the Litang horse-racing festival had been canceled by Chinese authorities. No reason given. Kham is home to the former warrior clans of the Khampas—tall, brawny, proud, headstrong, and with allegiance to no master. They are not above stealing yaks. When throngs of exuberant Khampa nomads get together, there is potential for trouble. Maybe this is why the festival has been canceled.

What to do? I team up with a photographer and we hire a jeep and driver to try to locate other festivals where nomads gather in summer. After a few false starts, we stumble into a festival area, but only a few nomad tents are visible. Are we too late? Too early? Inquiries reveal the tents have all migrated to the next valley over. We jump back into the jeep and head over the hills to the base of a sacred peak, where an extraordinary consecration ceremony is under way. Scores of monks are chanting, with several monks blasting away on longhorns. Smoke from burning juniper and incense billows into the air. Maniacal horsemen with unkempt hair and sheepskin jackets are racing their steeds around a set of prayer flags, whooping and hooting and hollering for all they're worth. They're throwing paper squares into the air, embossed with the mythical wind horse, a symbol of good fortune.

Then the prayer ceremony abruptly draws to a close, and in a matter of minutes, the tents are collapsed and put on horses or on jeep roofs to be moved back to the main horse-racing venue. Through the driver, we acquire a tent that will be our home for the next few days. The place is a sea of white tents, magically lit up at night by the flicker of lamps.

Morning: I peer out of the tent, searching for sunshine after a freezing night. Now it looks like a full-blown horse-racing festival. Horses and riders are streaming in from all directions. Tents stretch to the horizon. Lots of action out there. Crowds split into two sides that form the actual barriers of the racetrack. At the far end of the track is a large contingent of monks in maroon robes and, opposite them, a cluster of nomad women with long dresses and puffy orange headgear. The women are out to impress—dressed in their finest robes with a fantastic array of jewelry, and hair woven in 108 braids. Horse-racing festivals present an opportunity for matchmaking. Tough-looking Khampa men with Stetsons and bowler hats form most of the onlookers. Armed Chinese police on patrol keep a close eye on proceedings.

Finally, the riders take up starter positions with their trusty horses, whose manes and tails are decorated with streams of ribbons. Some horses appear to be spooked by the prospect of running the gauntlet between the lines of people. The festival launch develops into a kind of rodeo. The crowd is in high spirits, cheering on the riders—and on occasion dodging wayward horses. Warm-ups for races feature individual stunt riders, who show off their equestrian skills—like leaning off the horse to pick up white scarves laid out on the ground. Brash, swaggering Khampa cowboys parade around, performing daredevil equestrian tricks.

A horse throws his rider and barrels into the crowd. The rider captures his horse, mounts again with others restraining the horse—and is thrown off again. The horse bolts, with onlookers giving chase. In the mayhem, I am hit in the shoulder by another horse and thrown to the ground. The spectators laugh. They find this funny. Dusting myself off, I get back to photographing races. A rider is stomped by a horse and carried off the field. There are some qualifying races, limited to groups of three riders, as otherwise it could be too dangerous for the crowd. Burly monks push back the crowds as they press forward for a better view of the riders. The chaotic events go on for several days, a mix of stunt-riding, racing, dancing, eating, drinking, and socializing. This is what I came to see: a breathtaking spectacle full of action and excitement—a gathering of nomad clans.

Despite being entirely dependent on yaks for survival and placing great store on these remarkable animals, the real passion of nomad men is horses. Horses provide little in practical terms, but they embody freedom, providing transport in rugged mountain terrain. Tibetan horse breeds are distinctive: a high-spirited, stocky horse, well adapted to high altitude. There's a long tradition of nomad summer get-togethers and competitions on the high grasslands, all centered on horses.

The driver ushers us into a tent, where we are hosted by entrancing nomad women—most likely his relatives. They chow down on dried yak meat, which they offer us. In one corner is a freshly slaughtered yak carcass. And we are offered yak butter tea from a large kettle. Yak butter tea is definitely an acquired taste—I sip slowly, knowing that as soon as the cup is drained, it will be instantly refilled. Not having sugar, Tibetans instead use salt and yak butter for their version of tea. Yak butter, high in fat and protein, helps the body counter cold conditions at high altitude, while salt assists in hydration.

Tibetans are addicted to tea—and this is directly related to horses. How so? Well, these small stock horses bred at altitude are thought to be a distinct bloodline. They are very strong, and are famed for their endurance and stamina. In centuries past, they were highly valued by the Chinese as war horses. In exchange for buying Tibetan horses, Chinese capitalized on the Tibetan love of tea. Dating back to the Tang Dynasty, the "Tea-Horse Road" developed as a network of trails from tea-producing regions of Yunnan and Sichuan all the way to Lhasa. Sometimes up to 500 yaks would gather at trading-post-like Kangding to pick up loads of tea. Tea bricks were even used as a form of currency in the Land of Snows. That trade no longer continues—but Tibetan nomads continue to breed horses. A strong, fast horse is a status symbol in the backcountry.

Coming back from the horse festival, about 15 miles short of Litang our jeep passes some new construction: a housing settlement for nomads. Chinese laborers are hammering away: the wooden housing is shoddy, with only a few windows in the design. I get out to film the construction. And I have a very hard time imagining how proud, self-reliant nomads would be able to adjust to semi-urban life in a settlement like this. Nomads are used to wild open spaces by day—and a canopy of stars by night.

★ ★ ★

OVER 60 PERCENT OF TIBET'S LAND AREA COMPRISES GRASSLANDS, WHICH SUPPORT the grazing of yaks, sheep, and goats, and wild animals like the Tibetan antelope. Around the town of Litang lie some of the biggest and lushest grasslands on the Tibetan Plateau. We hire a car and driver to film nomads in these areas. We're filming a way of life that is under threat of extinction at the hands of Chinese authorities.

Sonam, our driver, is a Tibetan educated in India, so he can act as translator. Nomads are known in Tibetan as *drokpas*, or dwellers of the black tent. Woven from yak hair, the sturdy tent keeps out wind and rain and is easily collapsed for moving. We watch a nomad clan arrive with a herd of yaks. They have shifted locations and are unpacking yak hair tents to set up. Yaks are employed as beasts of burden, carrying tents, household goods, and sacks of barley flour when shifting camp.

We join a nomad herder urging his yaks to feed on the grass high in the mountains. Out on the grasslands, herders keep wayward yaks from wandering from the herd by firing warning stones from a sling—made from yak hair, of course. The sling is wielded with astonishing accuracy at great distance. Returning to the camp, we are invited into a yak hair tent where a fire illuminates the space—a fire from burning yak dung. A nomad woman is combing yak hair, the first step for weaving ropes, bags, and indeed the material for the tent itself. Two children look at us, wide-eyed with curiosity. We are offered yak butter tea, piping hot.

Through Sonam, I inquire about the future of life on the grasslands. The patriarch of this tent is worried. There has been a lot of pressure to sell their animals and settle, but he says he would not know what to do if he was not a nomad. Being a nomad, he tells us, is not a job you apply for: it's a job you are born into. And that's why he is worried about his son and daughter—whether they will be able to carry on the nomad traditional way of life or not. He says he will stay on the grasslands as long as he can, because he has talked to others that settled and they were very disappointed with their new lives. They were no longer free. Everything suddenly came down to a question of money and having to buy food and clothing. Here, he says, he has his freedom—and he never pays for his food or water. And he likes his animals—his horses, his dogs, his yaks. If he moves to a row of houses, he won't be able to keep them. The yaks would most likely have to be slaughtered if he settled—and he doesn't have the heart to do that.

Ingenuity and toughness: Tibetan nomads have developed a way of life that rests entirely on their yaks for survival. Nomads have figured out myriad ways to utilize the gifts the mighty yak provides. Burning yak dung is the main source of fuel for nomads on a largely treeless plateau. Milk from the *dri*, the female of the species, is processed into butter, yogurt, and cheese. In English, as in most other languages that have borrowed the Tibetan word, *yak* generally refers to both sexes, as in yak cheese.

Yak butter is the yak's greatest contribution to the Tibetan lifestyle. It is used in tea and for lamps in temples. In pre-1950 Tibet, tax was collected from nomads in the form of sheepwool and yak butter. Nomads believed that this tax of yak butter went to Lhasa to light up the main temple with yak butter lamps, and to provide the monks with yak butter tea. Yak butter is also used as a kind of cosmetic by nomad women, who smear their faces with the stuff to counter strong wind and sun. Yak bone is used for making rosaries. Yak skulls, carved with sacred symbols, are left at shrines. Yak hair is used to make tents, rope, bags, blankets, and clothing. Yak hide is used for making boots. Yak hide is also ingeniously used to make small boats for river crossings. Yak tails are sold as souvenirs: they have found a niche as theatrical props, used for opera wigs, Santa Claus beards, and sewn into Chinese lion-dance costumes.

Nomads pride themselves on their self-reliance and sustainability. The intimate connection between the nomads of Tibet and the grasslands of the plateau is a relationship that has been ongoing for millennia.

Tibetans are pastoral nomads, roving around in a constant quest to find the best grass for their herds of yaks, sheep, and goats, and for their horses. The nomads have a profound knowledge of the grasslands, gained through expertise passed down from generation to generation. This knowledge extends to considerable skills in dealing with animals: yaks, horses, cashmere goats, sheep, and Tibetan mastiffs.

The yak, domesticated from the wild yak thousands of years ago, is the main beast of burden on the Tibetan Plateau. Wild yaks are still around, though rarely sighted today. Yaks are superbly adapted to their high-altitude environment and can withstand subzero temperatures. They handle snow conditions with ease, and unlike horses, they can easily walk through deeper snow. Crossing high passes, yaks tend to move in single file, carefully stepping in the footprints of the lead yak. The yak's long shaggy coat keeps it toasty in cold conditions—a kind of cow with dreadlocks. In summer, the yak's shaggy coat may cause it to overheat, so it loves standing in freezing rivers to cool off. Yaks can be quite temperamental: it takes a lot of skill to deal with their innate stubbornness. Yaks can be ridden, but they are unpredictable in such situations, and in any case, they are slow. Tibetans may buy leather saddles for horses, but they also improvise by throwing a saddle rug over a wooden saddle. Saddle rugs are often handwoven from wool, similar in form to carpets. Self-sufficiency at work: nomad women spin their own wool from their own sheep to make the saddle rugs.

Sheep and cashmere goats are part of the nomad herder's flock; they are raised for milk, wool, and meat. Before 1950 Tibet had a large international wool trade. But China has turned its back on the nomads and now buys its wool from places like Australia. These days in Tibet the focus is more on cashmere, which is the fine underwool grown by the goats in severe weather, as in fierce biting winds and freezing cold. Cashmere wool, woven into shawls and scarves, is highly valued in the fashion industry because it is light yet very warm.

Guarding all of the preceding from attack from poachers and predators is the Tibetan mastiff, a dog about the size of a Saint Bernard and just as slobbery. Nomad tents cannot be closed or locked: the security system is a fierce, 130-pound mastiff. The Tibetan mastiff is thought to be the oldest guard dog and hunting dog in existence, with a bloodline going back thousands of years. The dog has been known to take on predators like snow leopards or Tibetan wolves that go after baby yaks.

★   ★   ★

BACK IN A LITANG RESTAURANT, I DISCOVER YAK BURGERS ON THE MENU, PRESENTED fast-food style with French fries. Tough and chewy, but high in protein. The diet of Chinese consumers has become more meat-centric over the last few decades as they have greater income to buy meat products. China's meat consumption (particularly of beef) has risen from being unnoticeable to being among the largest in the world. Dried yak jerky is sold in packets in places like Litang and Zhongdian. There are also traditional Chinese medicine variations: yak penis is consumed in soup, supposedly to boost male potency.

I find something very strange in the markets of Litang: Chinese butchers selling yak meat to Tibetans and Chinese customers. These are urban Tibetans, possibly former nomads. Tibetans will not butcher yaks themselves. Attempts to get Tibetan nomads to provide meat for Chinese consumers have largely failed because of the Tibetan concept of *nor*, which translates roughly as wealth on the hoof. Tibetans highly value live yaks, which produce milk and hair over many years and can transport goods. Killing a yak is considered bad karma. Other yak products have a small market within China. Yak cheese is produced by nomads but mostly for barter. Tibetan cheese-making technology is very basic. When Swiss technology is applied to yak milk to make cheese, the results are far better: excellent, nutty-flavored yak cheese is made this way in Bhutan, and in parts of Nepal. Chinese consumers buy little in the way of dairy products like milk or cheese, but yogurt is finding its way onto the menu. The yogurt is more likely to be imported from places like Australia or New Zealand, although yak yogurt is sold in some western provinces.

★　★　★

AT THE END OF THIS TRIP, IN NEPAL, I FOUND OUT WHY THE LITANG HORSE-RACING festival had been canceled. I went into an Internet café in Kathmandu and Googled "Litang festival problems." Up came a video about a nomad called Rungye Adak. In August 2007, Rungye Adak took the microphone onstage at Litang and addressed the crowd. He talked about problems created by Chinese officials, causing nomads to fight over land and water rights. Chief among these problems is the Chinese policy of fencing traditional herding land. Adak also called for the release of the missing Panchen Lama, and for the return of the Dalai Lama. He was arrested as he left the stage. For his short speech, the 57-year-old nomad was sentenced to eight years in jail for "provocation to subvert state power." Three friends of Adak, who tried to pass along photos and information to foreign media, were given sentences of ten years, nine years, and three years for "endangering national security." The severity of those sentences reveals just how ruthless Chinese authorities are in suppressing any news. China's way of dealing with criticism is to silence the critics.

In 2008, a protest that started in Lhasa—initiated by monks from Sera and Drepung monasteries—spread across the entire plateau, involving Tibetans from all walks of life—urban dwellers, farmers, and nomads. It was the biggest mass protest by Tibetans since the 1959 uprising after the Dalai Lama fled Tibet. A vicious crackdown ensued in the wake of the 2008 protests, with over a thousand Tibetans believed killed and many more missing or imprisoned. After the events of 2008, it appears the attitude of Chinese officials toward nomads hardened. They view the nomads as having too much freedom and being too independent—living on remote grasslands, far from the arm of the law. Since then, nomad settlement has shifted into high gear. Settlements are easily accessed by police and military vehicles so that former nomads can be closely watched. There is definitely a political agenda in the drive to settle the nomads. The real intent of this resettlement policy is to wipe out nomad culture and its strong connections to traditional Tibetan values.

★　★　★

HOPING TO INTERVIEW SOME NOMADS WHO HAVE RECENTLY ESCAPED FROM TIBET, I venture to the foothills of the Himalayas, to the small town of McLeod Ganj, in Dharamsala, northwest India. Dharamsala is a former British hill station and the seat of the Tibetan government in exile. Nestled high up in the mountains, it is a long drop down from the splendor of Lhasa's temples. But Dharamsala has some precious aspects that Tibet does not have: teachers from Tibetan Buddhist lineages, and freedom of speech. The town is tiny, with Tibetans numbering in the thousands. India does not want Tibetans gathering in large numbers in one spot, so they are scattered in different settlements, with big groups residing in southern India.

With the help of a translator, I arrange to meet some former nomads, but some major obstacles pop up. The first is that you need half a dozen specialized translators because nomads from different regions speak thick dialects that Tibetans from central Tibet cannot comprehend. But the main obstacle is that these nomads are not willing to be interviewed on video for fear of endangering relatives back in Tibet. The long arm of China threatens them here too.

Nonetheless, there are transcripts of interviews translated into English that I can access from the Environment and Development Desk in Dharamsala. Leafing through these interviews, my eye is caught by testimony from a Golok nomad called Dhondup, from Pema County in Amdo. I have seen Golok nomads on pilgrimage at Labrang Monastery in Gansu—wild-looking people dressed in greasy sheepskin cloaks and yak hide boots. They are the toughest of the nomads. Their name means "head on backward." They have a reputation for being obstinate, aggressive, and fearless, and have historically been quick to repel outsiders, staving off occupation by Chinese, Mongolian, or central Tibetan forces. And yet even the Golok nomads were convinced to move to concrete settlements, or maybe forced to do so.

Dhondup's interview dates from 2006. There are six counties in Golok: Matoe, Machen, Pema, Gade, Darlag, and Chigdril. Dhondup talks about a series of disasters—snowstorms that killed livestock, and lack of rain in summer that resulted in livestock going hungry due to reduced grass growth. The government blamed this on pikas and ordered the nomads to take part in a campaign to kill these rodents, but nomads believe that taking life is a sin. The government built highways on the grassland, introduced a fencing policy, and started removing nomads to towns, claiming that animal grazing was destroying the grasslands. Matoe County, Dhondup said, once had livestock in abundance, but numbers dwindled due to reduction through sales to slaughterhouses. The interview reads: "The nomads of Darlag County have been reduced to begging. Damkar used to be the richest in Pema County but due to excessive mining, that has resulted in a change of climate which has brought nomads into poverty." Dhondup adds, "An area of Machen County contains all the nomads that have settled in the lowland. Now these nomads have neither land nor livestock."

Failing to set up interviews with former nomads in exile, I settle instead for an in-depth interview with Tenzin Norbu, head of the Environment and Development Desk. Tenzin was born in India. He is a graduate of the Asian Institute of Technology in Thailand, where he studied environmental technology and management, and later worked as a senior researcher in the environmental engineering program. He is thus a rare researcher among Tibetans—a trained environmental expert. Tenzin Norbu is not only willing to talk, he is outspoken and opinionated, which is refreshing.

I start with a simple question: Why do the Chinese authorities want to remove nomads from the grasslands? Tenzin Norbu reflects for a moment and answers. "Now these Chinese policies, what they did was, they first removed the nomads from the grassland, blaming them for degrading the grassland. On one side, they are saying these nomads have a backward lifestyle. They want to educate the nomads. Educate the nomads for what? Because this is the life that they want to live—the life that they have been living for thousands of years. Are they successful in educating the nomads in this concrete housing? Do we see any retraining programs before the nomads are moved? We see nothing. What we see in the end is that these nomads are forcefully displaced from their grasslands. Now the nomads have nothing to offer. Whatever they have known from their generations of traditional knowledge, everything is gone. Even if they want to pass it to their grandchildren, granddaughters, there is nothing. It is not too late to give the nomads what they actually want—to give the nomads the pride that they had when they used to live happily with their herds."[1]

Tenzin Norbu explains that nomads' sustainable lifestyle relies on their yaks—live yaks. They are not willing to raise yaks for meat to sell to Chinese buyers. "Earlier, the Chinese considered Tibet as a meat factory, to get a whole supply of meat for the Chinese population. Since the nomads have their own religious beliefs, they restrain themselves from killing the animals. They always want their wealth on the hoof. They are not concerned about any profits or cash demands. They want to live simply and successfully on this Tibetan Plateau."

Tenzin Norbu explains that nomads have suffered from a series of disastrous policies. From 1958 to 1979 they were stripped of their livestock and possessions and forced into the commune system. In the 1980s, their animals were given back to them, but land was not. Later, nomads were given longer land leases. But starting in 2003, Norbu says, "There is this new policy which says, 'Abandon livestock to restore the grasslands.' That means in a way they want the nomads to get rid of their livestock: yaks and sheep. So without the yaks, the nomads have nothing to do. And some nomads have to sell their yaks at a much lesser price. So in the end, these yaks end up in the slaughterhouse."

Chinese authorities in many Tibetan areas have enforced strict limits on the number of animals that each nomad family can have, and then steadily reduce that number. If nomads become settled, they must either sell their yaks to other herders or send the animals to the slaughterhouse. The slaughter of yaks, especially on a large scale, is offensive to Tibetan Buddhist belief. Yaks are normally only slaughtered out of necessity. Tibetans have protested the construction of slaughterhouses, which are run by Chinese entrepreneurs. Religious leaders have spoken out against the slaughter of yaks for their meat. In February 2014, three senior monks in Pema County in Qinghai were arrested for purchasing 300 yaks from a slaughterhouse to save them as an act of merit.[2] Selling yaks to slaughterhouses ensures that settled nomads cannot return to their previous way of life, as they cannot survive without their animals. Slaughterhouses sell to Chinese consumers, for whom yak meat is an exotic eating experience. After seeing yak burgers and yak jerky for sale, it occurs to me that there's an easy way for China to deal with any surplus of yaks: they can eat them.

Tenzin Norbu tells me that Chinese policy is to blame for the degradation of the grasslands: "Once a huge herd is fenced, so automatically the pasture inside the fence will be degraded." In the 1990s, Chinese authorities started dividing nomad pasture land with wire fencing, particularly in the Amdo region of northeast Tibet. The nomads thus lost their mobility and access to rotational grazing, which led to serious disputes over who owned the land. In the end, because ownership of land is vague under Chinese law, promises over leases are often ignored, and land grabs have become common for the purposes of mining and dam building.

★　★　★

CHINA'S GRASSLANDS ACCOUNT FOR OVER A THIRD OF ITS TERRITORY AND LIE PRIMARILY in Inner Mongolia, Xinjiang, and on the Tibetan Plateau. These grasslands have suffered from mild to severe degradation over the last few decades. In 2005, the China Geological Survey Bureau concluded a milestone five-year survey of the Tibetan Plateau. Some snippets from the report: desert on the Tibetan Plateau expanded to 193,500 square miles, representing 19.5 percent of the total area. Grasslands decreased by 24.3 percent from the 1970s to 2002. Many lakes dried up. And glacial areas shrank by 56 square miles each year.[3]

There is little doubt that the grasslands of Tibet have seen degradation. The question is the cause of that degradation. Wang Yongchen, founder of the NGO Green Earth Volunteers in Beijing and a frequent visitor to the Tibetan Plateau, points out that the grasslands have not improved since nomad herders have been removed, and in her opinion, climate change and mining have had a bigger impact.[4] As large-scale mining gets under way in Tibet, the grasslands are being steadily encroached upon and turned into wastelands.

Colorado State University professor Julia Klein and others who have conducted field research on how traditional nomadic grazing system works with the Tibetan Plateau environment, found that grazing provides nutrients for the top soil, which helps with the regeneration of grass. She also suggests that grazing may mitigate the effects of climate change and may prevent invasive plant species from taking hold.[5] The Tibetan Plateau "is a system that has evolved with grazing; the removal of grazing from the system could have profound ecological consequences," says Klein.[6]

American rangeland expert Dan Miller, who has explored grasslands across Asia, claims, "The Chinese policy of settling the nomads goes against state-of-the-art information and analyses for livestock production in pastoral areas. This body of scientific knowledge champions the mobility of herds as a way to sustain the grazing lands and nomads' livelihood. Decades of experience with livestock development in other pastoral areas of the world and considerable recent research in Asia, including Tibetan areas, all lead to the conclusion that settling nomads is not appropriate. Livestock mobility should be encouraged instead of eliminated and nomads should be empowered to manage their own rangelands."[7]

Miller points out that nomads possess a great body of knowledge about the environment in which they live and about the animals they raise. They are highly familiar with local climatic conditions and key grazing areas: they know which plants have special nutritive value, which plants are useful for medicinal purposes, and which plants are poisonous. Says Miller, "Settling the nomads will erode their unique body of ecological knowledge of the grazing lands and how to use them....Who will pass this indigenous knowledge of the grasslands on to the next generation if nomads are settled in towns?"[8]

It is more likely that China's tampering with the grasslands and its experimental policies have been the cause of severe degradation. Starting in the 1950s, millions of acres of grassland in Tibet and Inner Mongolia were converted to irrigated croplands by state-owned farms and enterprises in order to boost China's domestic grain production.

In 1959, when the Dalai Lama fled to India, the Chinese enforced new approaches to agriculture in Tibet. They started up communes on a mass scale and ordered wheat to be planted instead of barley. No arable land was to be left idle; teams embarked on massive irrigation projects, built dams and reservoirs, and collected waste matter for fertilizer. Propaganda posters from the 1960s show happy, smiling Tibetans with bumper harvests, enthusiastically parading around wheatfields with Mao Zedong pictures. But the reality was very different: tens of thousands of Tibetans starved to death. China's disastrous agricultural policies led to severe famine in Tibet. No sooner was Tibet's crop harvested than it was taken by the army or shipped to China. The whole intent of forming communes was to create a breadbasket for the starving People's Republic, which was suffering its own catastrophic famine due to similar disastrous policies. From 1959 to 1962, the Great Famine in China itself claimed tens of millions of lives.

Chinese incursions have upset the natural balance on the grasslands of Tibet. In the 1960s and 1970s, Chinese settlers and military decimated the population of raptors, foxes, wolves, and bears of the Tibetan Plateau. With no natural predators to keep them in check, there was an explosion of pikas, gerbils, and other rodents. These rodents eat grass and dig burrows. Pikas, which are relatives of rabbits, are blamed for deteriorating grassland quality, but there is no proof of this. In actual fact, pikas may prove to be an essential part of the plateau ecosystem. Digging by pikas brings up minerals that help plants grow, and their burrows offer shelter to insects that pollinate flowers, as well as offering homes as nesting sites to various birds. Chinese authorities decided the pikas were pests and set about poisoning them. The pika poisoning program has been going on for 30 years. In Qinghai alone, roughly 116,000 square miles has been targeted for eradicating pikas through use of poison. That's an area the size of Italy.

★   ★   ★

EXACT FIGURES ARE HARD TO COME BY, BUT IT WOULD APPEAR THAT BY 2014, over a million nomads have been forcibly settled in Tibet, and a comparable number of farmers have been moved off their land. Farmers must be relocated when mining and dam-building operations start up. In an era where sustainability is the mantra, the Chinese policy of settling the nomads makes no sense. Vague reasons given for settling the nomads cite their lack of access to medical and educational facilities. What China is doing is parking the nomads, condemning them to a life in limbo—in what amounts to reservations on the fringes of remote towns. In these settlement camps, nomads live in dreary wooden or concrete structures hastily built by Chinese contractors. These former nomads are marginalized and have little chance of making a decent living or finding a new profession. Previously, when grazing yaks, they were self-sufficient and lived in an entirely sustainable way. Now, they are unemployed and dependent on the Chinese government for handouts—and for food.

Tenzin Norbu talks about the nomads using their surplus of yak butter, milk, and cheese to barter with farmers for grains—the source of the food staple of *tsampa* (roasted barley flour) and for making bread: "The nomads never fell short of their daily basic needs…like yak meat, butter, cheese, milk. They have plenty of these things. Now in the concrete resettled areas, the removed nomads, once they live in those camps, they have to adjust to urban life. They are wholly dependent on state aid. Since these nomads have been removed to these concrete blocks, it is affecting the traditional economy in Tibet, which we have for thousands of years. The nomads used to get grain from the farmers, and in return they used to give yak meat, butter, and cheese. So now the nomads are removed, even if they want to get some grain, they have no money, they have no jobs, they are not trained."

Former nomads face a crisis as their traditional food sources have dried up. Settled nomads are given a government spiel about the promised land to coerce them into resettling, but the promised land turns out to be far from the truth. Settled nomads get an annual government subsidy, but it is a fixed amount and does not account for the rising cost of food. Items that the nomads had in abundance before—yak milk, butter, meat, and yak dung—are items they simply cannot afford to buy. Items they could easily barter for before, like tea and *tsampa*, are now hard for them to obtain or priced out of their reach. In some regions, Tibetans report that it is very sad to see proud ex-nomads scavenging for metal scraps, or begging for food. Some nomad women have drifted into prostitution. Men have taken to drinking alcohol. The nomads have become beggars in their own land, starving and deprived of their food sources.

Following his mission to China in December 2010 where he saw the conditions of newly settled nomads in concrete camps, Olivier de Schutter, the UN Special Rapporteur on the Right to Food, publicly opposed the resettlement policy. In a UN report issued in January 2012, he sums up the situation: "The International Covenant on Economic, Social and Cultural Rights prohibits depriving any people from its means of subsistence, and the Convention on Biological Biodiversity (1992) acknowledges the importance of indigenous communities as guarantors and protectors of biodiversity. China has ratified both these instruments. The Special Rapporteur urges the Chinese authorities to immediately halt non-voluntary resettlement of nomadic herders from their traditional lands. . . . He calls on the Chinese authorities to engage in meaningful consultations with herding communities."[9]

The UN Special Rapporteur cited many factors against resettlement, including loss of economic independence, relocation to areas unsuitable to agriculture, increased cost of living following resettlement near urban areas, and disruption of traditional patterns of livelihood. The Chinese government rejected the findings and maintained that resettlement to "new socialist villages" is very popular, while declining to respond to specific issues raised by the UN Special Rapporteur.

In the settlement areas, the promised schools and medical facilities often fail to materialize. And if there are schools, they fly the Chinese flag and teach only in Chinese, with the main subject likely to be "Love the Motherland." There is a high rate of depression in these settlements as former nomads drift into alcoholism—which may lead to suicide.

Completely missing in the settlements are temples—very important for devout Tibetans. Intrepid blogger and activist Tsering Woeser visited a village of "ecological migrants" on two occasions, five years apart, in 2007 and 2012. The migrants were former herding families, forcibly removed from Sanjiangyuan National Nature Reserve. Their bleak village is located on the outskirts of Golmud in Qinghai. Woeser writes: "When I was in the newly built migrants' village back then, what made me feel particularly desolate was that in this place there was not a single Mani Lhakhang [temple] or stupa for Tibetans to practice Buddhism; neither were there any resident monks who could have helped these Tibetan migrants overcome the emptiness in their hearts."[10]

Returning five years later, Woeser found the migrants had built a small reddish-colored temple from their own funds and decorated their surroundings with sacred banners and prayer flags. Tibetans usually make small cairns out of mani stones (stones carved with sacred text) near stupas.

But the cairn they built here was bizarre: "When I was leaving the migrants village, I once more looked at the field of sacred banners and was surprised to see that underneath them there were large mani stones; but they were not real stones, they were turned-over pool tables on which there had been engraved the six words of truth (Om Mani Padme Hum). I suddenly understood what had been going on. The migrants, facing the difficulty of having endless time but not knowing what to do, spent their time drinking, gambling and playing pool and then the pool table had somehow turned into a mani stone."[11]

★ ★ ★

NO SCHOOLS, NO TEMPLES, NO CLINICS, NO NEWS, AND NO JOB RETRAINING. ONCE moved to settlements, nomads are unemployed. There has been no attempt on the part of the Chinese government to retrain nomads to adjust to living in a semi-urban environment. Ex-nomads are marginalized because they cannot speak Chinese, a key requirement for getting a decent job. Nomads cannot read Chinese; they most likely cannot even read Tibetan. They have gone from being self-sufficient as nomads to being unemployed—and dependent on government handouts.

The Chinese assault on the traditional way of life in Tibet specifically targets the Tibetan language with its elegant script, which originally derives from Sanskrit. In towns across the plateau, Chinese characters are written large for signs and billboards. Tibetan script appears at a much smaller size—if there is any script at all. In large towns, where schools are likely to be found, the Tibetan language has all but disappeared as a medium of instruction—everything is taught in Mandarin. The result is that Tibetan youth are increasingly mixing Chinese words and phrases into their conversation—a form of language dubbed "Chibetan." Mandarin has become the lingua franca of Tibet, replacing Tibetan language in many spheres of public life. In hospitals, diagnosis and testing are conducted only in Chinese. Reports, even from monasteries, must be done in Chinese.

Letters addressed in Tibetan script have no chance of being delivered. Language and culture are intimately linked: separating Tibetans from their language has inevitably led to profound loss of identity.

Speaking precious little Chinese, and without any formal education, options for retraining or employment of adult nomads shifted off the grasslands are severely limited. They can get work as manual laborers, from road construction to dish-washing. Or washing cars. In Litang, the local constabulary has discovered a devious way to collect extra income: by fining anyone driving a dirty car. After being fined, a driver is directed to an impromptu car wash place, which is invariably funded by the same constabulary. Litang has a number of these small street-side car wash operations. With so much dust around Litang, car-washing is a growth industry. The police, of course, drive immaculately clean cars to press the point home.

Tibetans at the eastern side of the plateau can make real money from picking medicinal herbs and exotic mushrooms high up in the mountains. If they work hard enough in the spring, they could get enough money to last through the rest of the year. Varieties like the cuckoo mushroom are exported to Europe and Japan, but the biggest market by far is east coast China. Valued for its medicinal properties—said to counter altitude sickness, arthritis, and colds—is the snow lotus (aka *Saussurea*). This rare plant grows at elevations of 11,500 to 16,500 feet across the Himalayas. Varieties range from a tall thistlelike plant to a dwarf alpine species. The snow lotus is dried for several months after collection before being put on sale.

The Holy Grail for traditional medicine purposes is the Chinese caterpillar fungus (*Cordyceps siniensis*), known in Tibetan as *yartsa gunbu*. Is it an insect? Is it a plant? Well, halfway in between. Like something out of the *X-Files*, yartsa gunbu is a parasitic fungus that grows on the larva (caterpillar) of the ghost moth over the winter season and takes it over, killing it in the process. The resulting specimen "grows" in surface soil at more than 13,000 feet and is highly valued in Tibetan and Chinese traditional medicine as a general health enhancer and tonic. Among other miraculous properties touted by Chinese medicinal practitioners are its ability to enhance longevity and its aphrodisiacal properties—a kind of Himalayan Viagra. Top-quality specimens of this wormlike fungus can be worth more than their weight in gold. Chinese caterpillar fungus is often added to soup to make a kind of medicinal brew. That medicinal broth may be consumed by Chinese athletes, supposedly to enhance their performance. It is fed to racehorses. Special gift-boxes containing dried Chinese caterpillar fungus specimens are given to officials as bribes (no money changes hands, just lots of fungus).

According to German mushroom expert Dan Winkler, collection in the Tibet Autonomous Region rakes in around 30 to 50 tons of this bizarre fungus each year.[12] When you consider that a ton is equivalent to roughly 3 million *Cordyceps* specimens, that's an awful lot of fungal worms being traded. Annual collection of yartsa gunbu in the spring months provides significant income for Tibetan nomads or former nomads. Because of the high value of the fungus, there are fights over collection permits and territories. Poachers move in, without permits. Bags of yartsa gunbu are stolen. People are involved in shoot-outs over fungus collection. Poachers are killed. In recent years, competition over collecting the fungus has heated up because the number of fungus specimens found has been dwindling, possibly due to climate change. Others cite the fact that the fungus is being collected too rapidly and that the annual harvest is not sustainable.

There is one trade where former nomads stand to make significant income. About 55 miles from Lhasa, near Gongkar Airport, I notice a large billboard featuring dogs and tell the guide to detour in our Land Cruiser. The dogs on the billboard are Tibetan mastiffs. This turns out to be a breeding center: the place has long rows of cages and harbors about 300 Tibetan mastiffs. Why so many dogs?

Here's the short answer. In March 2011, a red-haired Tibetan mastiff sold for the jaw-dropping sum of $1.5 million to a coal baron in northern China. The purebred male was, he said, "an investment" to be loaned out for stud duties. For Chinese, red is a lucky color. The dog was christened

Big Splash. Prior to that sale, the record price for a Tibetan mastiff was set in 2009 when a wealthy woman from Xian bought one for $586,000—and sent a convoy of 30 Mercedes-Benz cars to the airport to pick up her new dog. Those extraordinary sales figures make the Tibetan mastiff the most expensive dog in the world. In March 2014, a red-haired Tibetan mastiff reportedly sold for $1.9 million in Zhejiang. Due to its lionlike mane, the dog has become the ultimate status symbol among China's ultrarich. The lion is a lucky symbol in China, and red is a lucky color, so a red-coated Tibetan mastiff is the ultimate pet.

Xinhua News Agency has reported that among the must-haves for the ultrarich in north China are: a beautiful young wife, a Lamborghini, and a Tibetan mastiff—the bigger, the better. That puts the Tibetan mastiff into a similar status class as Chihuahuas among socialites in Hollywood. But the Tibetan mastiff is not the sort of dog you carry with one arm. It can grow to more than 160 pounds and is known for fierce loyalty to its master.

I am filming some mastiffs at the breeding center when one without a leash comes toward us, sniffing the air. Our Tibetan driver instinctively jumps back in fear. If that dog was unchained outside a nomad tent, it would probably sink its teeth into you. But the dogs at the breeding center will never take on a wolf or a snow leopard. Although they are being bred for guard duties, these caged dogs seem quite docile to me—a temperament more suited for patrolling the home of a millionaire. There is not a Tibetan in sight at this breeding center: Chinese entrepreneurs run the entire operation. However, Tibetans are involved in lucrative mastiff breeding in Yushu Prefecture in Qinghai—making the transition from yak herders to dog breeders.

CHAPTER SIX

Paper Parks, Theme Parks

Why Is China Snuffing Out Tibetan Nomad Culture?

TINGRI, WESTERN TIBET, AUGUST 2005: I SPOT A SIGN FOR QOMOLANGMA National Nature Preserve. *Qomolangma* is the Chinese pinyin spelling of the Tibetan name for Mount Everest. In Tibetan, Jolmolangma is the Goddess of the Snows—a female deity thought to reside at the summit. "That's great," I say, pointing at the sign, "preserving the environment." My guide, Dorje (not his real name), breaks into a laugh and says, "That's not what the sign means. It's just an excuse to get rid of the nomads."

That sentence takes a long time to digest. With further clarification, Dorje reveals that this park exists on paper only—and that by creating the park, Chinese officials have the leverage to seize traditional grazing land from nomad herders and remove them from the region. "Tibetans have no need for national parks," Dorje tells me. "They had their own sanctuaries centuries ago."

This could be the ultimate form of greenwashing—declaring areas as national parks when their real purpose is land grabbing. Later, we pass another sign in Chinese and Tibetan characters proclaiming the urgent need to preserve wildlife, with visuals of a wild yak and black-necked cranes. And yet this sign was put up by the same brutal regime that allowed the decimation of Tibet's wildlife in less than 20 years, from the 1960s to 1970s.

Paper parks: they look good on paper, but without patrols, monitoring, and enforcement, this is all show. There are no rangers in uniform to be seen anywhere in this nature reserve at Everest. There are several checkpoints where papers are scrutinized—and where you cough up an exorbitant entry fee. But nobody is checking for bad behavior—like Chinese tourists throwing glass bottles out the windows of moving vehicles, deliberately smashing them. Or Chinese tourists dumping garbage. At Rongbuk, closer to Everest, I notice some ingenious recycling of tourist garbage: a Tibetan-run guesthouse has built an entire wall from discarded Snow Beer and Lhasa Beer bottles—though how you could drink this much beer at this altitude is beyond me. Garbage accumulation from tourism is not a good thing in Tibetan eyes. Tibetans believe that Jolmolangma, the Goddess of the Snows, is greatly offended by pollution and by lack of respect. This deity has a wrathful aspect: she can trigger avalanches or whip up the winds and cause snowstorms.

Why is China not making use of extensive nomad knowledge to safeguard the grasslands and patrol national parks? It's a perfect match. They know the grasslands, they know the mountains, they know the wildlife. But putting Tibetans in uniform would give them quasi-policing powers, and China definitely does not want that. And Tibetans may be too good at their work in stopping poachers, as the case of the Samdrup brothers illustrates (recounted in chapter 3). On the other side of Everest, in Nepal, Sagarmartha National Park, which was inscribed as a UNESCO World Heritage Site in 1979, has park patrols—with strict controls over activity within the reserve. In an effort to clean up the mountain, climbers on the

Nepalese side have been told they not only have to take their own garbage out, but they have to carry other garbage back—or they will forfeit a hefty deposit.[1]

It seems that while China has an array of environmental protection laws, these exist largely on paper, with no punch when it comes to enforcement on the ground. According to official figures cited by *People's Online Daily*, in 1990 nature reserves accounted for 4 percent of the land area of the Tibet Autonomous Region. By 2012, that figure jumped to over 33 percent of total land area, with over 60 nature reserves established, encompassing 158,300 square miles.[2] And that is just the TAR. Outside the TAR, in Tibetan areas of Qinghai, Sichuan, and Yunnan, more vast nature reserves have been established, such as Sanjiangyuan National Nature Reserve, which covers 20 percent of the land area of Qinghai Province.

Why such a meteoric rise in the number of nature reserves? Why such big reserves? And why in Tibet? There's no clear answer, but the timing—from 1990 to 2012—coincides with large-scale removal of nomads from their grassland habitat. Along with the establishment of national parks come coercive laws that severely limit the rights of people in and around the designated areas—usually Tibetan nomads. Yet within the boundaries of these reserves, there seems to be very little in the way of protection going on: nomads are pushed out, grasslands are mismanaged, herbs are harvested unsustainably, wildlife is poached, trees are felled, and illegal mining takes place.

Environment writer Emily Yeh notes that reserve managers are more interested in generating revenue through exploiting the reserve than in protection: "Many protected areas are 'paper parks,' with at least one-third lacking staff, management and funding. The Nature Reserve Law of 1994 did nothing to remove control of the land under protection from the government that was managing it when it became a reserve. Moreover, except for national-level reserves, it failed to provide a guaranteed source of funding for reserve administration and staffing. This has led to a situation in which reserve managers' primary goal has become revenue generation rather than biodiversity conservation."[3]

Henan-based environmental activist Huo Daishan, quoted in an article by Radio Free Asia, claims that designation of national parks or nature reserves is tied up with vested interests that often propose the parks in the first place. He says that local governments are adept at retaining control over areas given nominal protection under central government laws. "According to what we are seeing on the ground, and from what the NGOs are able to observe, there is a huge gulf between [laws protecting parks and reserves] and the local government's implementation of them," Huo says. "There are always local interests bound up with protected areas. In the end, this entanglement…this conflict between the designation of a protected area and local development interests, destroys the protected area."[4]

Some of these parks do not cover a single area with clear boundaries: they are broken up into different zones, making protection vaguer. The Three Parallel Rivers region in Yunnan, declared a UNESCO World Heritage Site in 2003, consists of eight geographical clusters divided into protected nature zone areas and scenic areas. Just outside these areas lie the mighty rivers and canyons that give the site its name. Megadam building is proceeding on these same rivers, thus endangering the riverine ecosystem, not protecting it.

In Yushu, northeast Tibet, Sanjiangyuan National Nature Reserve was created in 2000, supposedly to protect the headwaters of the Yellow, Yangtse, and Mekong rivers. Sanjiangyuan covers an immense area of 58,800 square miles—the size of England and Wales combined. A map of Sanjiangyuan did not appear in any official source until early 2009. That's because the whole exercise appears designed to bamboozle not only Tibetan nomads but also watchful foreign outsiders. The official map of Sanjiangyuan that finally surfaced is a chaotic jumble of zones: core zones, buffer zones, and experimental zones. The latter two allow for "development" and "green industries." This seems to refer to options for mining and for building of hydropower stations (in Chinese references elsewhere, dams are considered "green"). In 2005, part of a core zone was adjusted to a buffer zone to allow gold-mining company Inter-Citic to start up operations. The company alluded to the region as being "uninhabited." What they failed to mention is that all the nomads of this region were forcibly shifted off the same grasslands to make way for mining exploitation, which caused extensive damage to the region. Over 300,000 nomads have been forcibly resettled in Qinghai, with a significant number of those coming from the Sanjiangyuan area. This is being done under the cloak of conservation.

In 2006, the US-based NGO Conservation International claims to have initiated a program for Tibetan nomadic families from Cuochi village to patrol and protect a small section of Sanjiangyuan, but little has been heard about this project since. What is clear is that state-run mining companies have moved into the nature reserve; also moving in are hydro consortiums building a bevy of small dams within the region. Sanjiangyuan may become the starting point for the ambitious water diversion of the Yangtse River headwaters to the Yellow River headwaters. Is this vast nature reserve protecting the headwaters of the rivers, or opening the door to their exploitation by state-run companies? In December 2013, it was announced that Sanjiangyuan's area would double in size to 152,500 square miles for the purposes of "rehabilitation" of the land. That size represents around 54 percent of the land area of Qinghai Province, and the real target of this "rehabilitation" appears to be the last remaining nomad strongholds. By more than coincidence, at the same time that expansion of Sanjiangyuan was announced, another official site said that 90 percent of nomads in Qinghai would be resettled by 2015.

In June 2008, a Reuters article reported from Lhasa on a proposed "ecological security plan" to counter the impact of receding glaciers and shrinking grasslands in Tibet.[5] The report quotes Zhang Yongze, director general of Tibet's Environmental Protection Bureau. According to

Reuters, the plan, which could initially cost 10 billion yuan ($1.5 billion), would involve turning grasslands into protected forests, restricting grazing, and creating "green jobs" for Tibetans that would ease pressure from population growth and development. "The solution to problems like global warming is out of our hands, but this document will give us a framework to work in," Zhang says. Tibet would also have to develop more hydroelectric power stations on the region's many rivers—an option opposed by some conservationists—to provide enough power, he says.

The rhetoric gives an idea of Chinese doublespeak on the environment. Creating green jobs for Tibetans? Chinese officials have taken away a million "green jobs" from Tibetans by removing nomads from the grasslands. If you want to save the grasslands and keep Tibet green, the nomads are best left alone. If you want to ease pressure from population growth and development, that's simple: stop waves of Chinese miners and immigrants from flooding into Tibet on the railway. Turning grasslands into forest? That's not feasible as large areas of the Tibetan Plateau lie above the tree line. The plan calls for building of dams to "provide enough power." Power for what exactly? Why is dam building mentioned in connection with environmental plans? Zhang Yongze goes on to cite the usual Chinese take that dams are green, and thus better for the environment than burning coal, but he fails to mention that Chinese mining and industry need power from megadams, not Tibetans. Meaningless eco-babble like this is regularly churned out by Chinese official sources to make everything sound clean and green in Tibet. Plans for establishing an "ecological security barrier" in Tibet speak about pouring billions of yuan into setting up more national parks and protected reserves—which may exist only on paper.

And that is the trouble with China's approach generally. The government has environmental laws that exist only on paper; they do not seem to be enforced. China signs international agreements protecting the rights of

MAJOR RIVERS
SOURCED IN TIBET

www.MeltdowninTibet.com © Michael Buckley

INDIAN OCEAN

(top) Sacred peak of Kawakarpo in Kham, east Tibet

(center) Sacred peak of Kailash, west Tibet, with monastery at left

(bottom) Highly revered Lake Yamdrok Tso, near Lhasa

(above) Chinese mega-dam under construction on the upper Yangtse

(below) A lone kayaker takes on a mighty river in east Tibet

(above) Nomad tents on the grasslands of east Tibet, with fencing visible

(below) Nomad woman milking a dri (female yak)

(above) Construction of large housing project, where nomads will be forcibly settled

(below) The yaks end up here: Chinese butcher selling yak meat in Litang market

(top) Chinese troops arriving in Tibet by train

(center) The train is flooding Tibet with Chinese tourists and migrant workers

(bottom) Chinese troops on patrol in the center of Lhasa

(top) A nomad yak-hair tent sits opposite a Chinese mining venture on the grasslands

(center) Bulldozers and heavy equipment are tearing up grassland areas for mining

(bottom) A highly toxic asbestos mine in northwest Qinghai province

(top) Girls helping to harvest grain, Ganges-Brahmaputra Delta, Bangladesh

(center) Floating market in the Mekong Delta, Vietnam

(bottom) Nepalese village crops here depend on a river sourced at the Tibetan border

indigenous peoples and then turns around and sets about snuffing out their culture by taking them off their traditional lands.

★ ★ ★

By far the largest of Tibet's parks is Changtang National Nature Reserve, with an area of 115,000 square miles, comprising grassland and desert. Established in 1993, this reserve is home to perhaps 70 percent of Tibet's population of the chiru, the Tibetan antelope. But within the park's boundaries, not enough has been done to prevent the poaching of the antelope, which is on China's highly endangered species list. The fleet-footed Tibetan antelope can outrun predators—with the possible exception of the Tibetan wolf—but it cannot outrun hunters with four-wheel-drive vehicles and high-powered rifles.

In the 1980s, there was a sudden explosion in demand for shawls and scarves made from *shahtoosh*, a special wool used by weavers in Kashmir. Shahtoosh shawls have long been a symbol of status—worn by the royalty of India and Central Asia, mostly men. In fact, translated from Persian, *shahtoosh* means the wool (*toosh*) of kings (*shah*). But which animal did the wool come from? It was a complete mystery. The secret of the wool's source was as closely guarded by Kashmiri weavers as the origin of silk was by the Chinese. Kashmiris variously claimed that the wondrous wool was picked off bushes in Tibet after the ibex (Tibetan wild goat) passed through, or that the ibex rubbed on rocks, leaving hair behind. Others claimed that shahtoosh came from the down of the "toosh bird," or the Siberian goose.

In 1991, American wildlife expert George Schaller received a letter from Michael Sautman, a Californian who was running cashmere-processing plants in Mongolia and Tibet. Sautman had received a request from a firm in Italy for 1,100 pounds of shahtoosh, from the Changtang region of north Tibet. George Schaller knew there were few ibex in the

Changtang region. However, he had seen a lot of Tibetan antelope carcasses at a nomad camp, and Michael Sautman had seen shahtoosh arriving in Lhasa ready for shipment to Kashmir. Comparing notes, the two men concluded that shahtoosh had to be the underwool of the Tibetan antelope.[6]

In the late 1980s, shahtoosh shawls and scarves became popular in fashion boutiques in the West, sold to socialites and movie stars for up to $5,000 apiece, with larger shawls fetching up to $20,000 each. Tibetan antelopes cannot be raised in captivity—attempts to do this have failed. To get this wool, Tibetan and Chinese hunters shoot the antelope and strip the underwool, leaving the carcass behind. Drop-dead gorgeous: the Tibetan antelopes were being shot in large numbers to feed a fashion craze in Milan, Hong Kong, Paris, London, and New York.

Recent research has revealed that shahtoosh is the finest animal fiber in the world—finer than the hair of the vicuña (South America) or the Arctic muskox. The Tibetan antelope's wool is a special adaptation that traps layers of warm air close to its body so it can tolerate freezing temperatures—the key to its survival in the extreme environment of Tibet. The wool is gossamer in weight and texture, soft as baby's skin, yet incredibly warm. Shahtoosh is so fine that even a large shawl can be pulled with ease through a finger ring.

Eventually, a specific DNA test was created to identify shahtoosh, even when mixed with other kinds of wool. George Schaller mounted a successful campaign to have the shahtoosh trade banned in Kashmir in 2000, and shipments of shawls were seized around the world. The solution to the trade in shahtoosh is very simple: just replace it with pashmina. Kashmiris weave fine shawls and scarves from pashmina, which is high-grade cashmere wool shorn from the underbelly of goats in Tibetan and Mongolian regions—a sustainable trade. With demand down, the killing of antelopes tapered off in the early 2000s. George Schaller calculated that in the 1990s, between 200,000 and 300,000 antelopes were killed. His calculation was based on annual sale figures for shahtoosh shawls in Kashmir; the weaving of a single shawl requires the underwool of three antelopes.[7]

Who are the poachers? Nomads, officials, truck drivers, miners, military, all out for quick profit. Well-equipped poachers drove jeeps into the Changtang and other regions from Golmud and Xining, hunting at night, freezing antelopes in their headlamps and gunning the confused animals down. Tibetan nomads hunted antelopes for centuries, but they used ancient muskets only capable of bringing down a few antelopes at a time. The game changer was the introduction of fast vehicles and high-powered automatic weapons that could mow down entire herds of antelopes. It is extremely unlikely that Tibetan nomads would be allowed to buy or use such weapons, or would have access to expensive vehicles. A more plausible explanation is that Chinese settlers and military looked upon the killing of antelopes as a way to boost their income. Significant population influx came from illegal gold mining. Adjacent to Changtang National Nature Reserve in Qinghai are two more reserves: Kekixili and Arjin Shan. The discovery of gold in 1984 in the Kekixili region caused some 30,000 Chinese miners to pour in; rampant poaching of antelopes followed. The same situation occurred when Arjin Shan Reserve was invaded illegally in the early 1990s by more than 50,000 gold miners. Poachers found the calving grounds of the chiru, where the antelopes gathered in large numbers.[8] The antelopes were being slaughtered at the rate of 20,000 a year in the 1990s, according to estimates by George Schaller. Poaching probably continues in Changtang National Nature Reserve, despite the ban on the shahtoosh trade, because of a lack of patrols and enforcement.

★ ★ ★

FROM PAPER PARKS TO THEME PARKS: HAVING DISPLACED NOMADS THROUGH LAND grabs for dam construction and mining ventures, and having shuffled them off to remote settlements, China is targeting what remains of Tibetan culture by flooding major monasteries and pilgrimage sites with millions of Chinese tourists. The tourists and their guides show little interest in Tibetan culture or religion. Their interest lies in scenery, fresh air, blue skies, photography, and shopping. And all this sends local prices through the roof.

In July 2010, before traveling on to Litang, I spent some time acclimatizing to altitude at the town christened Shangri-La, in upper Yunnan. The town was originally called Gyalthang in Tibetan, and Zhongdian in Chinese. There was an official name change to Shangri-La in 2002, a few years after Shangri-La Airport opened, catering to Boeing jets. I first visited this town in 2001 and witnessed its transformation over a decade from a quiet backwater town to a burgeoning Chinese tourist magnet. It transformed into a Tibet theme park for Shangri-La, based on a dubious link to British author James Hilton's novel *Lost Horizon*. The small old quarter of the town was pulled down; the sound of saws and hammers filled the air as carpenters put up new wooden structures and covered the roofs with moss. These became boutique hotels, restaurants, bars, and souvenir shops. Large fake-Tibetan-style hotels appeared: the architecture of the Holy Palace Hotel was partly inspired by the Potala in Lhasa. The five-star Paradise Hotel featured a central courtyard enclosed by a Plexiglas dome in case of bad weather. The hotel had its own hyperbaric chamber to deal with altitude sickness. Chinese tourists flocked in. Outside of town, at Sungtseling Monastery, a big parking lot was carved out so that Chinese tour buses could disgorge their loads of tourists.

To keep Chinese tourists busy at night, there were dinner shows at hotels with ethnic performers. More elaborate was a show called *Dynamic Shangri-La*, which took place in a large theater with fancy stage sets, lighting, and sound effects. This presented Tibet-themed choreography I had not seen before—like a dance number showing high-kicking Khampa nomad women in a can-can chorus line. I figured out that these could not be real Khampa women, as they would never show so much leg. They were Chinese performers in costume. Monks in ceremonial dress appeared on stage, but they stayed mute; they did not perform any throat singing or chanting, because they were Chinese, and throat singing requires years of training. There was a pathetic attempt at sacred Tibetan Cham dancing with heavy wooden masks of various deities and animals. About 20 dancers dressed in hairy yak costumes pranced around the stage in a conga line, with a herder chasing them around. The rest of the performance mixed in elements that seemed to be of Chinese origin, like a dance with swirling paper umbrellas—and another featuring men covered from head to toe in chicken feathers, performing acrobatic moves.

In December 2013, a blaze ripped through the wooden structures of Shangri-La town. News reports said it was tragic that an ancient Tibetan town burned down. Actually, it was a Chinese replica of an ancient Tibetan town that burned down—obviously one with little in the way of fire prevention measures.

★ ★ ★

French journalist Claude Arpi calls it "the Disneyland of Snows." He is referring to the theme park model being applied to Lhasa in central Tibet. The Land of Snows is being packaged and sold to Chinese tourists en masse. When I first arrived in Tibet in 1985, no Chinese tourism was evident at all. Tibet was considered backward and without facilities. Now Chinese tourists arrive at the rate of 10 to 15 million a year, and there are plans to boost that figure. When you consider China's population of 1.4 billion, that target would not be too difficult to achieve. Again, the Lhasa railway is the game changer. Prior to 2006, only wealthy Chinese tourists could make it to Tibet because of the high cost of airfares, so Lhasa was a trophy destination. But the railway brought the price down considerably and put Lhasa within a two-day overland journey from Beijing. The same train floods Tibet with migrant workers who come in for projects such as mining and dams. There are significant subsidies and tax breaks offered to Chinese who settle in Lhasa. The result is that the Chinese resident population in Lhasa easily outnumbers the Tibetan population.

* * *

LHASA, SEPTEMBER 2010: ACROSS FROM THE YAK HOTEL AT THE SHANGRI-LA Restaurant, a nightly dinner-dance show for Chinese tourists is staged. Here, nomads have been reduced to a curiosity. Performers present a medley of nomad folk songs accompanied by lutes and foot-stomping with boots to provide percussion—similar in concept to flamenco. The highlight of the evening is a yak dance, which is traditionally a welcome dance. Two Tibetans inside a yak costume take the stage, pursued by a herder cracking a whip. The yak suddenly charges off into the audience, harassing Chinese tourists seated at tables, drinking Lhasa Beer. The tourists are delighted, as this provides for the best photo opportunities.

Tibetan song-and-dance routines show up regularly on local TV stations: you get the idea that happy smiling nomads are like children living in a socialist paradise where all their educational and medical needs are taken care of. There's an endless replay of choreographed festivals on TV: the yogurt festival, the walnut festival, anniversary festivals.

Because of my guidebook writing, I know of certain hotels with rooftop vantage points over the Jokhang Temple and Barkhor Bazaar. Good places to take photos from. But clambering up to these rooftops, I find these perches occupied by men in full military regalia, with binoculars—and guns—trained on the Jokhang and Barkhor below—the launching point of many demonstrations in the past. These snipers looked like part of a SWAT team. On the ground, soldiers sit behind sandbag bunkers every block or so in the old quarter of town. There are lots of checkpoints where identification papers are checked. Five-man teams patrol the back alleys;

at least one of the men is armed with a machine gun. Video surveillance cameras are mounted at street corners. The core area of Lhasa looks like it is under military lockdown. And vigilance is tighter at monasteries like Drepung, which in the past has seen demonstrations led by monks. Visiting the monastery, I am surprised to find a new building inside the front gate. Looking up, I see it has surveillance cameras mounted on it. This turns out to be a Public Security Bureau office, cleverly disguised as a traditional Tibetan structure. The police are monitoring every single move the monks make.

★   ★   ★

THE JOKHANG TEMPLE IS THE SPIRITUAL HEART OF LHASA, BUT IT IS SO CROWDED with tourists that it is difficult to move through the chapels. The token monks pose for photos and seem to spend their time catering to Chinese tourists, serving up tea and Coca-Cola on the rooftop or selling fake *dzi* stones as good-luck trinkets. On the Jokhang rooftop, Chinese tourists are taking photos of each other and jabbering at high volume on cell-phone calls to Shanghai or Guangzhou. Some retreat to discrete corners of the rooftop to light up cigarettes. Signs throughout the temple indicate that smoking is not allowed anywhere on the grounds—this is a place of worship, supposedly, and in a wooden structure like this, smoking is a fire hazard. If any Chinese tourists attempted to make phone calls or smoke like this inside Mao Zedong's tomb in Beijing, they would most likely be dispatched to some gulag in Qinghai Province. But at the Jokhang Temple, they get away with it.

Nowhere are Chinese tourists more rude and arrogant than at the Potala Palace. It is the ultimate must-see destination for Lhasa: the palace has to be ticked off the list for a successful visit to Tibet. But a limited number of tickets are available for sale each day. Hence a lot of bad tempers are on display in the crush to get in, and noisy jostling is going on at the various chapels as Chinese tourists jockey for the best vantage points for photography. Once I get in, my Tibetan guide tries to move through at high speed, saying I have a 45-minute time limit for the entire tour. But there is no written rule about this. Interested in photography, I promptly lose the guide in a sea of people and take my time. The guide finds me a while later, looking quite upset about losing his client. I ask him a question about the Dalai Lama, which he brushes aside. He whispers that he cannot say anything about the Dalai Lama or he will lose his guide license and probably be thrown in jail. This is quite ironic when you consider that the Potala Palace is the former home of the Dalai Lamas.

What about future plans for the Disneyland of Snows? Well, it seems the concept is gathering momentum. In 2013, construction workers ripped up sturdy ancient buildings around Barkhor Bazaar and replaced them with modern Chinese replicas of Tibetan buildings, with better plumbing and better facilities for shopping. Demolishing the ancient Tibetan stone buildings has ripped the heart out of old Lhasa. Barkhor Bazaar is the main pilgrim circuit of the city, but Chinese authorities are only interested in the shopping aspect of the area, completely ignoring the spiritual significance.

Northeast of Lhasa, a mini Potala Palace has been constructed as a theater, providing regular nighttime entertainment in the form of a multimillion-dollar extravaganza with 600 performers. The show is the grand opera *Princess Wencheng*, about the life of the Chinese wife of Tibetan king Songtsen Gampo, who ruled in the seventh century AD. Princess Wencheng is often trotted out by the Chinese propaganda machine in efforts to stake an early Chinese claim on Tibet, saying that she had great influence over the king. In fact, he had a Nepalese wife and three Tibetan queens as well. All the actors seem to be Chinese who dress as Tibetans when required by the script. In fact, in today's Lhasa, there is no need for Tibetans. Chinese guides may pose as Tibetans when escorting for-eigners around. The ticket sellers at various attractions dress Tibetan-style.

Chinese saleswomen in big department stores dress up as Tibetans. It's like being on an elaborate movie set.

★   ★   ★

APART FROM VISITING THE POTALA PALACE, THE MUST-SEE LIST FOR CHINESE tourists comprises scenic attractions that are most likely to be Tibetan pilgrimage sites. Now these places are being flooded by rude Chinese tourists who have no respect for the sacred nature of the landscape.

One of the top scenic spots on the Chinese tour agenda is beautiful Lake Namtso, about 130 miles north of Lhasa. Thousands of lakes are scattered across Tibet, but half a dozen are highly revered and are thus major pilgrimage spots for Tibetans. Namtso is one of these—a vast sea backed by the sublime snowcaps of the Nyanchen Tanglha range. Back in the 1990s, reaching Namtso required a very rough journey over a dirt road. Nomad encampments were visible near the sacred lake. I stayed at a tiny guesthouse run by nuns. The place was imbued with a highly spiritual atmosphere: there were cave temples hewn into rock faces, shrines, and hermitages for contemplation.

Fast-forward to the summer of 2005: the same trip ten years later is a much faster journey on a smooth paved road. The location has been renamed Namtso Lake Nature Reserve. The edge of the lake looks like a parking lot, crammed with tour buses on day trips and 4WD overland vehicles. Annoying vendors hawk cheap jewelry. Other annoying vendors try and talk you into posing with a gaudily decorated yak—for an exorbitant fee. Chinese tourists—large numbers of them—are shouting, taking photos, drinking beer, tossing garbage. The spiritual atmosphere has gone: the pilgrimage site has been overrun. It is more of a circus atmosphere now than sacred site. The nomad encampments near the lake are thinning out, pushed back by the advancing tourists.

Close to Namtso, I spot a strange Chinese billboard slogan: "Environment First, Development Unlimited!" You don't have to tell Tibetans how to protect a sacred lake, but protecting the lake from the rush of Chinese tourism could be an entirely different matter. That's where the "Development Unlimited" part may come into play. Chinese tourists litter the landscape with empty noodle packets, discarded plastic water bottles, and empty oxygen bottles.

Development Unlimited: shifting to another famous pilgrimage site in western Tibet, I was appalled to learn that the pilgrimage path around sacred Mount Kailash would be paved so that Chinese tourists could drive around it in a matter of hours in tour buses instead of taking three days to trek the sacred circuit. A paved road around this top Tibetan pilgrimage site would remove its sacred significance. Pilgrimage is meant to be arduous—a difficult journey to achieve insight. There is nothing difficult about driving around the mountain in half a day.

★ ★ ★

WHAT KIND OF FUTURE IS IN STORE FOR THE GRASSLANDS OF TIBET? NOT A HAPPY one, it seems. Like the glaciers, grasslands are shrinking. Tibet has high peaks and deep gorges, and fertile valleys with large grasslands. And it has big deserts, which are expanding at a phenomenal rate. Reliable figures are hard to come by, but the United Nations Development Programme's 2002 *China Human Development Report* states that 965 square miles of China's land turns to desert each year, and that the capacity of the grasslands to support animal and human population is thus decreasing. China, the UNDP says, is "one of the most seriously eroded countries in the world. Nearly two fifths of the total land area suffers from various degrees of soil erosion, and more than two thirds of its grassland."[9]

Following on from this UNDP report, Tenzin Norbu sums up the broader implications for Tibet in an interview: "Millions of tons of carbon are trapped in these grasslands. So talking from a scientific point-of-view, these grasslands are very important to maintain the whole carbon balance on the Tibetan Plateau. . . . And now with the nomads being removed, there is nobody there to take care of these grasslands—to restore the grasslands. And this rate of desertification will further increase—and in 2020 to 2035 you will see the whole grassland has been converted into desert. And on top of that, this desertification is hugely enhanced by climate change, global warming—and the desert storms that we get from the Taklamakan Desert, and from the whole of Mongolia. So this is a huge speed-up in the rate of desertification on the Tibetan plateau."

★ ★ ★

AND THEN THE CONVERSATION TURNS TO MONGOLIA, BECAUSE MONGOLIA IS A forerunner for what may come to pass on the grasslands of Tibet. China targeted settlement of Mongolian nomads much earlier than settling Tibetan nomads, so the longer-term fallout can be seen. Desertification of grasslands as a result of Chinese interference is clearly illustrated in Mongolia. Reading like one of Aesop's animal fables, the following brief report about Mongolia is a cautionary tale about greed and failure to protect the environment. It involves an animal prized for its wool: the cashmere goat. Cashmere, the goat's valuable underwool, is a runner-up to the undercoat of the Tibetan antelope for its superb insulation qualities. The Tibetan antelope is wild and cannot be raised in captivity. The cashmere goat is domestic: the animal is reared by both Tibetan and Mongolian nomads—and it relies on the grasslands of these regions for sustenance. But somewhere along the line in Mongolia, things went terribly wrong.

Since the early twentieth century, Mongolia has been divided into Inner Mongolia (under Chinese control) and Outer Mongolia (now an independent nation, previously under Soviet control). On the modern map, "Mongolia" designates only the independent nation, but the inner and outer names are retained here to differentiate the two regions.

Chinese officials have been trying to pin blame for erosion and desertification of Inner Mongolia on climate change and on overgrazing by Mongolian nomads. But for this one, the Chinese have only their disastrous experimental policies to blame—and their unbridled greed for cashmere.

Back in 1949, the ratio of Mongolians to Han Chinese in Inner Mongolia was estimated at 5 to 1. By 2010, the ratio was inverted, with an estimated six Han Chinese for every Mongolian. Estimates placed the Han Chinese population at 24 million, and the Mongolian population at just 4 million. That's a deliberate population transfer designed to dilute Mongolian nomad culture. And those Mongolians are no longer nomadic; they have largely been shifted off the grasslands into villages and cities as part of Chinese government policy. Along with the policy of overwhelming Mongolian culture with an influx of Han Chinese came new policies concerning land use. The Mongolians are traditionally nomadic—herding yaks, Bactrian camels, horses, sheep, and goats. The Han Chinese settlers introduced a more agrarian society, cultivating corn, oat, and potato fields, which resulted in erosion problems and sped up the degradation of the grasslands.

In the meantime, something quite catastrophic was taking place. By the 1990s, China had cornered the world market on cashmere, which derives from the soft undercoat of the cashmere goat. The cashmere goat only grows this underwool in harsh, cold, wind-swept conditions that are prevalent in Mongolia and Tibet. Catering to huge demand from Western buyers, Chinese officials in Inner Mongolia decided to greatly increase herds of cashmere goats.[10] The wool was processed in Chinese factories and shipped at enormous profits to places like Italy, where it was turned into shawls, sweaters, and luxury clothing items.

One unforeseen problem: cashmere goats are definitely not grasslands-friendly. Unlike yaks, which nibble the grass and graze lightly with minimal impact, cashmere goats graze voraciously—consuming all greenery and ripping grass out by the roots. The sharp hooves of cashmere goats pierce the soil surface—a crust composed of fungi, mosses, lichens, and bacteria that help retain moisture. Once the crust is torn, strong winds in Mongolia can carry away the sand underneath in dust storms.

The end result was that large swaths of Inner Mongolia turned into wasteland, stripped of grass by the increased numbers of cashmere goats— and destroyed by the greed of Chinese entrepreneurs selling cashmere. When Gobi Desert dust started raining down on Beijing, Chinese officials got the message: something disastrous was going on. Officials backtracked and ordered the decimation of cashmere goat herds and ordered more rotational farming. Meantime, a particularly harsh winter in 2010 killed off large numbers of goats.

With a sudden drop in cashmere production from Inner Mongolia, China's cashmere buyers turned their attention to independent Outer Mongolia for supplies. Outer Mongolia's population of cashmere goats soared. According to one report, the number of goats in Outer Mongolia increased from 25 million in 1993 to 40 million by 2007, by which time cashmere goats accounted for almost half of all livestock.[11] China is the largest buyer of Outer Mongolia's raw and washed cashmere, taking an estimated two-thirds of all exports—one-third legally, and one-third smuggled to avoid export taxes. And with this comes the same colossal cost: potentially turning the grasslands of Outer Mongolia into desert.

Another major cause of soil erosion in Mongolia, both inner and outer, is mining on a colossal scale. Inner Mongolia has seen an explosion of mining for much-valued rare earth elements, particularly around Baotou. China dominates the world trade in rare earths, producing around 95 percent of the global total. There are several dozen rare-earth elements, including erbium, gadolinium, dysprosium, neodymium, and yttrium. In very short supply globally, these are important components for high-tech systems, from cell phones and wind turbines to missile guidance systems and night-vision technology. China's 95 percent dominance of world trade in rare earths has come at a high price for the environment. The reason China has been so productive is that it is willing to do toxic and often radioactive work that the rest of the world has shied away from—holding out until safer methods of extraction can be devised.[12]

Inner Mongolia holds an estimated 26 percent of China's domestic coal reserves. Located on the Yellow River in Inner Mongolia, Wuhai City used to thrive on grape growing, wine making, and dairy farming. Back in 1998, there were four factories in Wuhai. In 2012, that number skyrocketed to more than 400 factories, mostly connected with coal production. Wuhai, a city of half a million, produced 38 million tons of coal in 2012. Chickens and other animals in the area have turned black from coal dust and pollution, as most of the coal processing takes place right in the city.[13]

Is environmental horror China's greatest export? Quite possibly, if you think about China's excessive coal burning and its global reach in other areas like deforestation and mining. Next door in independent Outer Mongolia, environmental havoc is being wreaked not only due to cashmere demand, but also due to China's voracious appetite for coal and copper. Mining is a severe threat to the pristine grasslands of Outer Mongolia, wiping out the nomads of the region. When I visited the Gobi Desert region of Outer Mongolia in the early 1990s, it was a great wilderness—home to a surprising amount of wildlife. I spotted gazelles, bighorn sheep, and various raptors. The only human inhabitants of this region were nomadic herders leading a traditional way of life as they had done for centuries, raising horses, sheep, and Bactrian camels. Not anymore. A vast mine has started up at Tavan Tolgoi, with estimated reserves of 6.4 billion tons of coal. Mining has led to dried-up wells, shrinking water holes, and clouds of black dust from 100-ton trucks that barrel through and blacken all within sight, including the animals of the nomads.[14]

Another massive mine is under way at Oyu Tolgoi, in the southern Gobi close to the Chinese border. Oyu Tolgoi is projected to produce large quantities of copper, as well as gold, over the next half century. The

Gobi Desert is a region that experiences very high water stress. Somehow the mine has been permitted the use of 20 million gallons of water daily over the coming decades, which is obviously not good news for the region's nomads. Foreign mining companies involved are British group Rio Tinto and Canadian-headquartered Turquoise Hill Resources (formerly Ivanhoe Mines). The main buyer of the copper and other resources will be China. Nomads out, miners in. Mining has become the main income source for Outer Mongolia, or "Minegolia," as some now call it. A scary preview of what will most likely come to pass in Tibet.

CHAPTER SEVEN

Plundering the Treasure House

How Much Can an Ecosystem Take before It Collapses?

O n March 29, 2013, a massive avalanche of mud, rock, and debris buried 83 miners. They were sleeping at a camp on a mountaintop location that is part of a copper and gold mine, about 45 miles east of Lhasa. There were no survivors. The official Chinese verdict is that the avalanche was a natural disaster, but evidence seems to point to a man-made disaster. Gyama mine is open-pit, and the walls of an open-pit mine are prone to collapse. Hasty mining without regard to safety is the signature here—and the miners paid the ultimate price. The world's worst mining safety record belongs to China. There are no unions for miners to lobby for safer conditions. Thousands of Chinese miners are killed each year. The exact figures are not known because details of disasters are generally obscured from the press.

Mining at Gyama is on a huge scale: the site is believed to hold reserves of 5 million tons of copper, 530,000 tons of molybdenum, 135 tons of gold,

---

6,600 tons of silver, and 580,000 tons of lead and zinc.[1] On August 30, 2012, seven months before the disaster at Gyama, China's national online news agency ran a story titled "A Mining Miracle." The article opened with the following paragraph: "In 2006, the landscape around Gyama Valley, located almost 70 km from Lhasa, capital of the Tibet Autonomous Region, could be described as post-apocalyptic. Photos released on websites around the world showed a portrait of devastation: large pools of murky water, dead wildlife strewn about and a natural environment almost completely destroyed by mining operations. The incident put the spotlight on the government: How had they allowed mining companies to strip the region of its resources while polluting the environment?"[2]

After this blunt opener, the article proceeded to praise Huatailong Mining Group for cleaning the place up and establishing "eco-friendly mining." In 2008, Huatailong acquired rights for mining at Gyama, replacing 15 smaller companies that "seriously damaged the region's fragile ecology with their haphazard operations." Snippets from the article reveal the damage: "Previous mining companies, using outdated techniques and equipment, left several ponds of tailings that allowed waste water to pollute local water sources. Copper levels in the waterways were far beyond the levels of national safety standard."[3]

The news story claims that after extensive cleanup by Huatailong "the scene has been transformed, replaced with a panorama of lush green trees and grasslands, new roads and infrastructure, and cleaner mining facilities, giving the local people a better life."[4] The article talks about benevolent Huatailong Mining Group compensating Tibetans for livestock lost from pollution, about employing Tibetans at the mining site with handsome salaries, and about social responsibility programs that sent Tibetan students to university.

Local Tibetans, both villagers and nomads, offer a very different perspective. They have vigorously protested against mining operations at Gyama. In 2009, Huatailong started construction of a water-diversion facility, redirecting water from a nearby river to the state-sponsored mine site.

On June 20, 2009, this led to clashes between Tibetans and Chinese miners. The locals rely on river water for crop irrigation and drinking water, and conditions were very dry. Many villagers were arrested by police.

Up until Gyama, Tibet had never seen a major mining disaster—in a history spanning four millennia. Why? Mining was on a very limited scale in pre-1950 Tibet. Tibetans mined for gold, silver, and lead for use in temple construction, but extraction was done without chemicals or explosives. Gold was obtained not by digging but by sluicing alluvial gold flecks from streambeds. Though there were fine gold- and silversmiths in Lhasa, metalworking and blacksmithing were regarded as lowly occupations, forbidden to monks. Mining was frowned upon: Tibetans believe that digging would scar the surface of the earth, disturbing malicious spirits dwelling within, with dire consequences. This largely derives from Bon, a much older Tibetan animist faith—with belief in spirits dwelling in the mountains, trees, rocks, and earth. Digging of any kind—from digging a well to ploughing the fields—would require special "permission" from the deities, approached through prayers.

For Tibetans, mining hits home harder than damming. Mining may take place at the site of a sacred mountain; many villages in Tibet regard local mountains as the abodes of protector deities. Mining is seen as polluting the home of these deities and destroying the beauty associated with the sacred mountain. Disturbing these mountain deities is regarded not only as sacrilege, but as a very bad omen. While dams tend to have long-term negative impact, the damage from mining is immediately apparent. Grassland areas are eroded, drinking water is poisoned, herd animals are killed.

A prime source of information about Gyama from the Tibetan point of view is Tsering Woeser, who has visited the site several times and conducted interviews with locals, taken photographs, and written about the situation. Tibetans who protest against mining are quickly silenced—beaten, arrested, or jailed on trumped-up charges. Tsering Woeser is a courageous Tibetan who breaks the silence. She is our woman on the ground in Tibet—the voice of Tibet, a rare Tibetan eyewitness who relays news while managing to stay out of prison.

Woeser was born in Lhasa to a Tibetan mother and half-Tibetan, half-Han Chinese father who was a high-ranking officer in the PLA. Her family's impeccable revolutionary credentials count a lot: they are most likely what have kept her from being arrested. She was raised and educated entirely in the Chinese language, studying literature in Chengdu, Sichuan, and never learned to read or write in her native Tibetan. Ironically, this is what has enabled her to be such an influential voice: she is thought to be the first Tibetan to have played the role of a public intellectual in China, through her command of public media. Woeser describes herself as "a one-person online news station"—battling the powerful Chinese propaganda machine. She is a historian, human rights advocate, author, poet, and blogger.

Although she visits Tibet frequently, she is mostly based in Beijing, where she lives with husband, Wang Lixiong, with whom she has coauthored several books about Tibet. Her books and blogs are banned in China, but she manages to get published in translation in the West, with pieces appearing on Radio Free Asia and via her Facebook account and Twitter feed. In December 2007, Woeser was awarded the Norwegian Authors' Union Freedom of Expression Award for "bravely choosing to publish her books, despite content deemed controversial by the Chinese authorities." She was unable to attend the award ceremony in Oslo because the Chinese government denied her a passport. Her request was denied on the grounds of "national security," a common accusation against dissidents. She has received numerous international awards for her courageous writing but has been unable to accept them in person because of the refusal of Chinese authorities to issue her a passport. When she was honored with the Prince Claus Award in 2011, she was placed under house arrest to prevent her from receiving the prize at the Dutch embassy in Beijing.

Woeser's e-mail, blog, and Skype accounts have been hacked, and she has periodically been placed under house arrest. But she continues to write fearlessly about issues in Tibet, from loss of identity to self-immolations. And she writes about environmental destruction. In this post from 2009, she talks about the quality of drinking water: "The water of the Qinghai-Tibet plateau in particular is really deteriorating. Originally, as noted in the classic works, the Buddhist master Atisha uses graceful poetry to praise: 'taste a mouthful of the water of the Land of Snows, it is ice-cold and tasty, fresh and pure, clear and fragrant; when one drinks it, it will not hurt one's spleen or stomach, but it will moisten one's heart. This is Tibetan water with its eight virtues.' But what about today? Nyima Tsering, a monk from Jokhang Temple, once said when interviewed by journalists, that in the past when he became a monk he could drink the water from the Lhasa River and it was absolutely not toxic, but now it was really a pity that one could not drink the river water anymore."[5]

How has such clean water turned into dirty water? One ugly explanation: upstream from Lhasa lies the mining site of Gyama, where toxins from ore washing flow directly into the Lhasa River. Woeser writes: "Over the past few years, when I went to Gyama village, I learned that because in some mining areas there was none or no adequate sewage systems in place, this has caused dirty water polluted with chemicals to flow all over the place. It not only led to the nearby villages' loss of drinking water but also forced them to gain access to drinking water through a primitive pipeline connected to the isolated and rugged area at the back of the mountain. The harvest of highland barley in the fields decreased massively and forage grass on the pasture land was also poisoned."[6]

In response to strong Tibetan protest over pollution, Woeser writes in her blog in 2010: "The Huatailong mining industry has caused most severe pollution, many livestock have died, many villagers have fallen ill but the compensation is not much. Last year, due to a drought, Huatailong used the villagers' water, causing serious conflicts. Reportedly, Huatailong had approximately up to 10,000 workers at their disposal, most of them Han Chinese, while there were only a few thousand villagers. Yet, immediately, a great number of military police, including special police forces, were sent from Lhasa patrolling through Gyama with armored vehicles for many days arresting villagers. Up to the present day there are three villagers (one of them the village head) who are still imprisoned awaiting their sentence."[7]

In another post from 2013, Woeser talks about the continued threat that pollution from Gyama will have on Lhasa River: "Such severe contamination of water supply does not only threaten the local population. The Gyama mining area has been active for many years and it is situated on the upper reaches of Lhasa stream. According to what local Tibetans revealed, Huatailong Mining Development Company, a subsidiary of the China Gold Group, placed their washing plant on the land where the farmers of Gyama used to cultivate their fields in the past and from there, thick water and drainage pipes lead straight into Lhasa stream. The water pipe extracts water from Lhasa stream, whereas the drainage pipe pumps sewage from the washing plant back into the river. This has been going on for five years, which represents an acute threat to the water resources of Tibet's most sacred city, Lhasa."[8]

★　★　★

WHAT'S ON THE HORIZON FOR THE ENVIRONMENT IN TIBET? WELL, AS FAR AS THE eye can see, ruthless exploitation of Tibet's mineral, oil, and gas resources. China did not have the technology and the transportation in place to embark on large-scale mining in Tibet until the 2006 opening of the Lhasa railway. The railway changed everything.

In March 2010, the Chinese government announced plans for exploiting over 110 proven varieties of minerals (with 3,000 potential mining sites) on the Tibetan Plateau, worth more than $125 billion. But the real value could be up to ten times more. There are huge reserves of copper, chromium, gold, and lithium, to mention a few minerals, as well as large oil and gas reserves. It is estimated that 80 million tons of copper, 2,000 tons of gold, and 30 million tons of lead and zinc could be extractable from the Tibetan Plateau.

And what share of this tremendous wealth do Tibetans stand to get? Nothing in the way of royalties, compensation, jobs, or community outreach projects. Tibetan environmental NGOs are forbidden. Tibetans have become mute spectators as their land is exploited and their sacred mountains are savaged. What they get in the end is pollution and poisoning of their water resources.

Australia-based environment expert Gabriel Lafitte brings up some important points when talking about Chinese corporate responsibility. He says that mining companies like Zijin, China's largest gold producer, follow a very different approach in places like Peru versus Tibet. In Tibet, Zijin can rely on the state to silence Tibetans, and there is no need to compensate them or provide community outreach projects: "When Zijin bought its Peruvian copper mine, it announced it would spend $80 million on helping local peasant communities with projects chosen by the communities. In Tibet, there is no such corporate social responsibility, nor do Chinese mining companies belong to industry bodies such as International Council on Mining and Minerals (ICMM), which promote high standards of local community and indigenous involvement in how mining is done and who benefits. Although ICMM publishes Chinese language manuals on human rights in mining, no Chinese miner has joined. At a time when indigenous community protests and environmental protests have largely persuaded the global mining giants that ignoring environmental and social harm is bad for business, a new generation of Chinese mining corporations, in Tibet and in Africa, are obeying the party-state's directive (and subsidies) to 'go out,' establishing new standards of corporate behavior that pay little heed to the environment or social impacts."[9]

China has an insatiable appetite for Tibet's minerals and oil reserves to feed its industrial base. The Chinese term for central Tibet (TAR) is *Xizang*, which means "Western Storehouse" or "Western Treasure House." The term dates from the nineteenth century, when Tibet was regarded as an important repository of Buddhist manuscripts. During the 1965–1975 Cultural Revolution, large amounts of Buddhist statuary and manuscripts

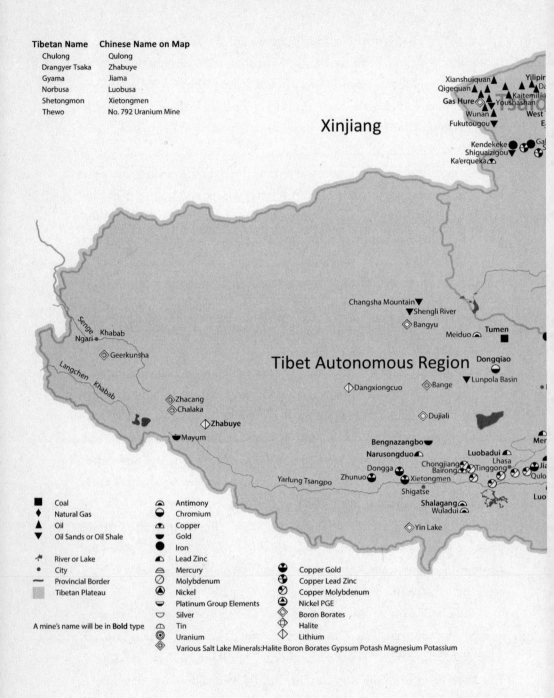

Tibetan Name	Chinese Name on Map
Chulong	Qulong
Drangyer Tsaka	Zhabuye
Gyama	Jiama
Norbusa	Luobusa
Shetongmon	Xietongmen
Thewo	No. 792 Uranium Mine

Xinjiang

Xianshuiquan
Qigequan
Gas Hure
Wunan
Fukutougou

Yilipin
Da
Kaitemiliki
Youshashan
West E

Kendekeke
Shiguaizigou
Ka'erqueka

Gal

Changsha Mountain
Shengli River
Bangyu
Meiduo
Tumen

Tibet Autonomous Region

Senge
Khabab
Ngari
Geerkunsha

Langchen
Khabab

Zhacang
Chalaka
Zhabuye
Mayum

Dangxiongcuo

Dongqiao
Bange
Lunpola Basin

Dujiali

Mer

Bengnazangbo
Narusongduo
Zhunuo
Dongga
Chongjiang
Bairong
Luobadui
Lhasa
Tinggong
Jia
Quo
Yarlung Tsangpo
Shigatse
Xietongmen
Luo

Shalagang
Wuladui

Yin Lake

	Coal		Antimony		Copper Gold
	Natural Gas		Chromium		Copper Lead Zinc
	Oil		Copper		Copper Molybdenum
	Oil Sands or Oil Shale		Gold		Nickel PGE
			Iron		Boron Borates
	River or Lake		Lead Zinc		Halite
	City		Mercury		Lithium
	Provincial Border		Molybdenum		
	Tibetan Plateau		Nickel		
			Platinum Group Elements		
			Silver		
A mine's name will be in **Bold** type			Tin		
			Uranium		
			Various Salt Lake Minerals:Halite Boron Borates Gypsum Potash Magnesium Potassium		

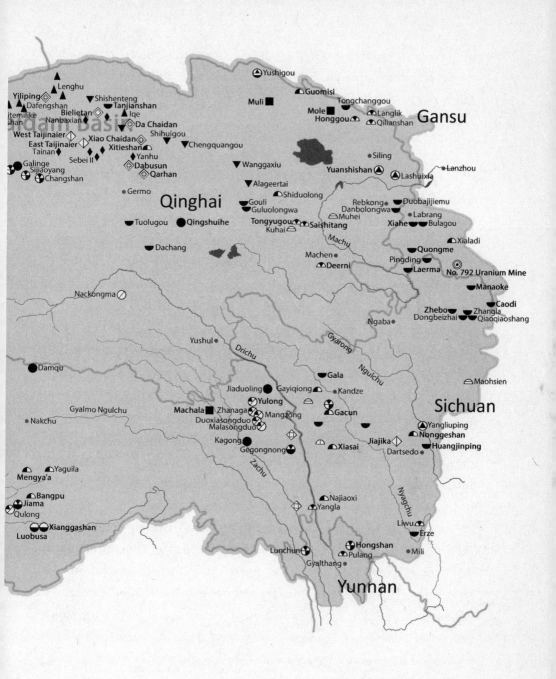

Oil, Gas & Mineral Resources
of the Tibetan Plateau

were taken from Tibet and sold on the international market. Xizang today alludes to something quite different in the way of treasure: mineral wealth and hydropower.

★ ★ ★

GREEDY CANADIAN CORPORATIONS ARE FACILITATING THE TREASURE HUNT IN TIBET. China needs advanced Canadian mining knowledge and technology to extract minerals. The needless destruction of Tibet's pristine environment must be agonizing for Tibetans to witness. Tibet is not my native country—yet I am incensed when I see what Chinese engineers are doing to this pristine land. But Canada *is* my country—and it makes my blood boil to learn that Canadian companies are complicit in this travesty.

Headquartered in Vancouver, Canada, China Gold International Resources took over operation of Gyama in December 2010; it considerably expanded operations. Canadian mining safety standards are obviously not in force at this site. China Gold is essentially owned by the Chinese Communist Party, so it is actually more of a Chinese company masquerading as Canadian. The China National Gold Group, which has its senior people assigned their positions by the CCP, owns 40 percent of China Gold International Resources. China Gold is using Canadian financial markets to raise money to exploit the already dire situation in Tibet.

In 2010, Bill C-300—known as the Corporate Accountability Act or Responsible Mining Bill—was introduced in Canadian Parliament, but it was defeated due to the powerful mining lobby. If passed, the Bill would have enforced political and financial sanctions against mining companies operating in foreign countries without the consent of local indigenous peoples. Tibetan rights groups have protested at company shareholder meetings and investors' conferences to put pressure on Canadian mining companies operating in Tibet to focus on safety.

Canada is the foreign nation with the greatest number of investments in Tibet, particularly in the railway and mining sectors. The Canadian corporations turn a blind eye to human rights abuses in Tibet, ignoring the forced resettlement of Tibetan nomads to make way for mining projects.

There seems to be a recurring pattern for Canadian joint-venture mining operations on the Tibetan Plateau. Chinese companies use Canadian technical expertise for mining exploration and development. Along the way, Chinese engineers acquire expertise with this technology. Then the Chinese government stonewalls on permits to actually launch the mine (stonewalling can go on for years), and finally the Canadian company is bought out for low prices by a large Chinese mining company, usually state-run. Half a dozen Canadian mining companies have suffered this fate in Tibet, including Sterling, Inter-Citic Minerals, Lara Exploration, and Continental Minerals. Putting considerable pressure on these companies within Canada were Tibetan human rights groups like Students for a Free Tibet and Canada Tibet Committee.

On June 24, 2009, I put my covert video skills to good use by crashing the annual general meeting (AGM) for shareholders of Continental Minerals Corporation, held at a hotel in downtown Vancouver. Since 2005, Continental Minerals, a subsidiary of Hunter-Dickinson Inc., had been engaged in exploration at Xietongmen copper-gold mine near Shigatse, central Tibet. The mine is located near the Yarlung Tsangpo River, and its operation will inevitably pollute the river. Tasked with getting video footage, I cued up two friends who would sit in at the AGM, each holding a compact camera hidden under a newspaper, while I waited outside in the hallway with a larger camera.

When it came around to question time at the AGM, things got lively. Tsering Lama from Students for a Free Tibet stood up and berated Continental's CEOs for their unethical involvement in Tibet and presented them with a thousand letters protesting the mining operation. Meantime, one CEO spotted a compact camera in use and demanded that its operator be ejected. He was ejected, but he kept the video running—as he headed for the exit downstairs, he recorded other protests in progress. He stepped over three students staging a "die-in" near the elevators, prone on the floor with Tibetan flags draped over them. A CTV News cameraman, invited for the occasion, was filming the die-in protesters; hotel security staff demanded that he leave. It was only then that they noticed me also shooting this scene. Eventually, we all got thrown out—and joined a raucous street protest outside, waving placards and being quite vocal about the need for Continental to get out of Tibet. The Continental CEOs were rattled by the action, which generated negative publicity on CTV News and on YouTube. In April 2011, Continental's mining operation in Tibet was bought out by Chinese state-run Jinchuan Group for $431 million. I like to think that the protest actions had something to do with Continental's retreat from Tibet—such as convincing investors to pull funds from the corporation.

Why is Canada home to more than 70 percent of the world's mining companies? That is the question that investigative reporters Alain Deneault and William Sacher set out to answer in a book published in Montreal in 2008. The book drew the ire of two Canadian mining companies, which sued the publisher for a total of $11 million in a blatant attempt to silence the authors. The book was withdrawn, but it was revamped and published again in 2012, this time in English, under the title *Imperial Canada Inc.: Legal Haven of Choice for the World's Mining Industries.* Litigation is ongoing. The book focuses on Canada's immense global mining reach, but has nothing on the situation in Tibet.

★　★　★

TRAVELING OVERLAND BY LAND CRUISER IN TIBET, I WOULD OCCASIONALLY STRAY across an entire town that was not there on my previous visits and did not show up on any Chinese map. One such mystery town popped up west of Gyantse when I passed through in 2005. It was a sea of shiny tin roofing and it was brimming with Chinese migrant workers. They were involved in water diversion and some sort of exploratory mining survey. Water and mining go together. Water is needed to process minerals, and hydropower is needed to power mining operations.

That's as close as I could get to mining operations on the ground in Tibet, but I found another way to have a look. I managed to drop in and visit mines in remote locations in Tibet from 250 miles overhead—taking a ride on the Landsat-8 satellite, used by Google Earth. Even if you were on the ground, you wouldn't be able to see what is going on at mining sites. But satellite views show a lot: they show ore-processing plants, pollution discoloration, and tailings storage ponds with toxic sludge. I enlisted the help of Agent Griffon, who prefers to remain anonymous. He generated the map that goes with this chapter, and from that map was able to pinpoint the coordinates of various mine sites in Google Earth. You can hide mines on the ground, but you can't hide them from Google Earth. According to Wikileaks, China in fact once complained about Google Earth, demanding that details on "strategic sites" should be made blurrier. But Google, having been booted out of China, ignored the request.

* * *

YOU MAY KNOW MORE ABOUT THE MOVIE *AVATAR* THAN YOU DO ABOUT MINING IN Tibet, but the film offers uncanny parallels to the situation on the Roof of the World. Tibet is the largest colony in the world. Tibet is under military occupation by Chinese troops. Tibet is being ruthlessly exploited for its valuable minerals, against the wishes of the inhabitants, who deeply resent what is happening to their land. In *Avatar*, the action takes place some 150 years into the future, on a distant moon called Pandora. Here, rapacious foreign CEOs and military figures seek a mineral of astronomical value called "unobtanium." The only thing stopping them in this endeavor is the blue-skinned Na'vi, who refuse to allow mining on their sacred ground. Tibetans have, throughout their history, prevented mining of their land— which they regard as sacred.

Today, there are many valuable minerals being extracted in Tibet by Chinese and foreign companies. And one alone would qualify for the status of unobtanium. That's lithium. Lithium is the metal of the moment: used for making batteries for computers, cell phones, and many other gadgets. And lithium is a very rare mineral, in very short global supply. Tibet has emerged as one of the world's largest sources for the making of lithium carbonate, a process involving extraction from Tibet's salt lakes. In fact, if your laptop, iPad, or cell phone was assembled in southwest China, you probably carry a tiny piece of Tibetan lithium around in the battery for the device.

Demand for lithium will soar as electric vehicles with lithium-ion powered batteries hit the market. Tesla Motors makes several innovative car models using lithium-ion batteries. The futuristic Nissan Leaf hatchback, a pricey all-electric car, runs on a 550-pound lithium-ion battery. China's Great Wall Motors plans to market all-electric cars in a joint venture with a Californian company. Chinese car-battery maker BYD has a 20-year option for lithium extraction at Zhabuye Lake in western Tibet. The corporation even convinced top American investor Warren Buffet to purchase stock. A YouTube clip from 2011 shows Warren Buffet and Bill Gates in China giving a thumbs-up at the launch of a new BYD electric car, under a banner that reads: "BYD Green Technology Lights up Tibet."[10] Buffet and Gates are presented with *khatas* (ceremonial scarves) by Tibetan women in full costume, but how does BYD's lithium venture benefit Tibetans? BYD stands for "Build Your Dreams." The Chinese dream, it would seem, is to get wealthy. Tibetans do not dream about driving cars powered on huge lithium batteries. They dream about the return of the Dalai Lama to Tibet.

★ ★ ★

ZHABUYE LAKE LIES IN A REMOTE REGION OF FAR WESTERN TIBET. IT IS ONE OF the many lakes in Tibet where salt can be harvested. In old Tibet, salt was loaded onto yaks and transported over high passes to Nepal to barter for grain. But Chinese miners are not interested in harvesting salt. They're interested in extracting lithium carbonate from this lake, which has a very high concentration of lithium salts. These lithium lakes look eerily serene on Google Earth, with patterns of salt evaporation ponds. But extracting lithium is a dirty business, with toxic chemicals seeping into air, soil, and water, far from the eyes of any monitoring.

Between salt lakes in western Tibet and in Qinghai, Tibet is reckoned to have more than 2.4 million tons of lithium deposits, making it the world's third-largest source of this precious element. And that's just a fraction of Tibet's mineral wealth. Starting basically from the 1990s, geologists are finding a lot more as they explore for mineral and oil deposits in central Tibet.

Tibetans have a lot to fear from Chinese mining companies, which have the world's worst safety record. Along with that goes complete disregard for environmental impact and for impact on local communities. These mining companies are only interested in one thing: generating large profits quickly. For a graphic illustration of this, you only need to look at Mangya mine in the Tsaidam Basin in northwest Qinghai. You don't want to be on the ground here. The fine white powder visible in satellite images of this site is not snow. It is asbestos dust. This is a mine for white asbestos. Airborne asbestos dust has such deadly links to cancer that its use has been banned in a number of other countries. China is the world's largest consumer of white asbestos, and though there are strict rules on its use, the rules are often ignored. Parts using asbestos have turned up in Chinese products sold abroad, such as low-cost cars made by Great Wall Motors.

A Google Earth image of the Xitieshan lead-zinc mine in the Tsaidam Basin reveals black coal dust coating one area, and red chemical dust in another zone. Mined rock containing lead and zinc is sitting next to the town of Xitieshan. This implies that state-controlled Western Mining Company, which owns the site, is not concerned with environmental or health issues. A disaster of biblical proportions is unfolding in

Tibet: so big you can see it happening on Google Earth—the mining, the pollution, the destruction.

★ ★ ★

THE TSAIDAM BASIN IS PART OF A HUGE GULAG IN QINGHAI PROVINCE WHERE political prisoners are banished to labor camps—some related to dirty mining. And as the area transformed into an industrial wasteland, Tibetan nomads were pushed out. They may be the lucky ones.

Back in the 1950s, the mineral of greatest interest to China was not lithium or gold or copper. It was uranium—to be used in making nuclear weapons. Qinghai Province proved to be a valuable source for uranium extraction. At the town of Xihai, to the northeast of Qinghai Lake, lies "Atomic City," where Chinese researchers designed and developed China's first hydrogen and atomic bombs. That led to the detonation of its first A-bomb in 1964, catching the world by surprise. Testing and research continued at Xihai from the 1960s to the 1980s.

A bunker-style museum in Xihai has become a prime tourist attraction. Visitors shuffle through to look at nuclear missiles (mock-ups, of course, although real ones are deployed around Qinghai Province), models of the original H-bomb and A-bomb developed here, and murals of the scientists who were part of the top-secret Ninth Academy, which designed all of China's nuclear weapons until the mid-1970s. But entry to the museum is forbidden to foreigners. Even though the research facility closed down decades ago, secrecy is still in place. Officials have a blasé attitude to the lingering effects of radiation in this area. The surrounding Jinyintan grasslands, where radioactive waste is thought to be buried, have turned into a recreation spot for tourists. Most residents seem content with the local government's reassurance that there is no danger associated with living here. The local government claims that there have been no signs of environmental or health problems related to A-bomb testing.

But a vet tells a different story. In an interview reported by Toronto's *Globe and Mail*, one herder said he took his sick sheep to the veterinarian and was told their teeth were turning black from the radiation. Once their teeth turn black and break, the sheep will be unable to chew grass. The shepherd mentioned that they have a year to raise sheep before their teeth turn black, and they usually sell the sick ones to butchers—but have no idea where the meat ends up.[11]

China's secrecy in developing an A-bomb is one thing: secrecy over the dangers of radiation is quite another. Tibetans in exile say scores of herders have died from illnesses linked to radiation in Qinghai Province. There seems to be scant regard for informing locals about potential health hazards—like whether they should be drinking groundwater that may be in the vicinity of buried radioactive waste. Because of secrecy involved, little is known about the mining of uranium on the Tibetan Plateau, but dozens of sites are thought to be in operation. Dumping of radioactive waste has resulted in premature deaths of Tibetan nomads and their livestock. In mainland China, dumping of toxins in rivers at midnight is a practice used by chemical and other factories. This has led to the horrendous phenomenon of more than a hundred "cancer villages" in China, where incidences of cancer run exceptionally high. There could be as many as 400 villages like this. Tibet seems to be the next victim on the horizon.

★ ★ ★

THE TSAIDAM BASIN IN QINGHAI HAS BEEN ACCESSIBLE BY EITHER ROAD OR RAIL OR both for around 50 years, and it offers a scary preview of what can happen to Tibet when it comes to pollution. If you want to see dirty mining, the Tsaidam Basin has it in spades. The region holds enormous reserves of zinc, lead, lithium, natural gas, and crude oil. Gasikule Oilfield in Qinghai has been pumping out a million tons of oil a year for decades. Dirtier extraction methods are under way. China intends to use both oil shale and tar sands oil extraction technologies in the Tsaidam Basin. Large quantities of oil shale and oil sands have been discovered on the Tibetan plateau. To acquire the technology for highly destructive tar sands oil extraction, China has simply bought out some large Canadian mining companies, with particular interest in those operating in Alberta's tar sands region. A large problem remains in the Tsaidam. It takes 2 tons of mined oil sand to produce just one barrel of synthetic crude oil. And it takes about three or four barrels of water to generate one barrel of oil from oil sands. The Tsaidam is essentially a desert: it will be necessary to divert enormous quantities of water to the Tsaidam and other potential oil sands regions like the Junggar and Tarim basins for mining extraction to go ahead. That water diversion could come from the Tsangpo, Mekong, and Salween rivers. Also on the horizon is shale-gas extraction (fracking), which uses huge amounts of water, but may pollute groundwater because of the chemicals used. China's shale-gas deposits are thought to be among the largest in world. In 2013, Anglo-Dutch corporation Shell signed a billion-dollar deal for exploiting shale-gas in the Sichuan Basin.

★ ★ ★

MINES NEED LARGE QUANTITIES OF TWO THINGS: WATER AND POWER. TIBET'S cascading rivers supply both. Significant dam construction has been implemented across the plateau to power mines. More large-scale mining in Tibet means the building of more megadams—and that means more obstruction downstream on major rivers from Tibet.

Yulong Copper Mine in Chamdo is slated to become China's largest copper source with an estimated 7 million tons, one of the largest deposits in Asia. Under construction near Yulong on the upper Mekong River is Guoduo, a large dam with a capacity of 165 MW. Guoduo Dam is slated for completion in 2015 as the key power source for Yulong Copper Mine. And copper is the key element for ultra-high voltage lines, which are capable of transferring hydropower from dams on the Tibetan Plateau all the way to the power-hungry megacities of eastern China.

Entire mountains may disappear under large-scale mining extraction of copper. Big corporate miners do not go looking for nuggets of a particular metal: they seek out mountains that have a significant concentration locked in their bedrock. For copper, the concentration is often less than 1 percent, which means 99 percent is waste rock. If the concentration of the metal looks economically recoverable, the corporate miners dismantle these mountains, crush the rock, and treat it with solvents that leach out the metal. The metal is then recovered from the solvent using chemicals and electricity.

★　★　★

LARGE-SCALE MINING HAS STARTED UP IN TIBET, BUT IT IS WIDESPREAD, smaller-scale, illegal gold mining that has caused the most damage so far. A gold rush started in various parts of the Tibetan Plateau in the 1980s and continued through the 1990s and early 2000s. Poor Chinese immigrant miners used mercury and cyanide for the extraction of flakes of alluvial gold from streambeds. Those toxic minerals found their way back into the rivers—along with arsenic, which is naturally present in rock where Tibetan gold is found. Local officials assembled much larger dredges to chew through riverbeds for placer gold, destroying pastures and river banks. All this blasting, sluicing, and digging has had major impact on the grasslands of Tibet.

Tsering Woeser paints a picture of what happened to the grasslands of Mato County, Qinghai: "In the 1980s, hundreds of thousands of outsiders poured into Mato county looking for gold. Outsiders flooded into this Tibetan area, engaged in mining and gold-digging, grasslands were destroyed, the river-bed dried up, wild animals were hunted, and caterpillar fungus as well as other precious medicinal herbs were dug out; all these various factors came together, and, taken as a whole, finally led to what we see today. Online surveys reveal that between the 1980s and the 1990s, excessive and uncontrolled gold digging has not only damaged the gold resources, but also severely devastated grasslands and destroyed the ecosystem and virtuous cycle, leading to the disappearance of fertile soil and the desertification of the land. In 1999, 47.8 percent of the entire county area was covered in desert and sand or bare ground and the percentage of wild animals dropped to 31 percent."[12]

★ ★ ★

On a research trip to Dharamsala, northwest India, I arrange to interview Tsering Tsomo, executive director of the Tibetan Centre for Human Rights and Democracy. The center puts out an annual report documenting protest and abuse in Tibet, painstakingly piecing together information from eyewitnesses who have arrived in exile, and from reports smuggled out of Tibet. It is a thick tome. When I ask her what the biggest environmental issue is in Tibet, she replies, without hesitation, "Land grabs!"

"From the interviews and from the testimonies that we have collected from new Tibetan refugees arriving into exile," she tells me, "we have actually observed that a lot of Tibetans—Tibetan families—are being forcibly taken off their land, off their ancestral lands—lands where they have lived for generations. The Tibetan people should have the rights to manage their own land and resources. Now the ownership of land is not very clear and that's why the government can, anytime—without any conditions, without consulting the local people—grab lands for mining purposes. Or sometimes they can grab lands to build hydropower projects, which, if you look at the past experiences, we can see that it has caused a lot of suffering to the local people."[13]

I ask her how Tibetans feel about mining. She responds, "Given that the Tibetans are so religious, and they care about their religion deeply, especially against the background of all the repression that is going on in Tibet, they feel like mining is sacrilegious. They feel it's almost like you are destroying the home or the abode of their gods and goddesses."

I can hear Tsering Tsomo's voice cracking with anger and outrage, as she tries to hold her emotions back. She regains her composure and continues talking. Sacred mountains under siege, rivers being poisoned, and grasslands turning to dust—this is how Tsering Tsomo sees it: "Many local Tibetans complain that the grasslands have actually degraded thanks to the mining activities because you have all this digging going on and disposal of chemical waste, and it also poisons the river systems of Tibet. And as many of us know, the drinking water source of the majority of Tibetans in Tibet are the rivers and the lakes. So when that gets poisoned, it not only affects the health of the local Tibetans but also their animals, their herds. And when we talk about the herds of Tibetan nomads getting killed, it also means they are going bankrupt. Because their animals are their only source of wealth, their livelihood. And when these get killed, it's almost like your bank balance is being robbed—by the government."

★ ★ ★

DECAPITATING OF SACRED MOUNTAINS BY CHINESE MINING CONSORTIUMS IS abhorrent to devout Tibetans. The more daring express their feelings on blogs. The following poem, translated from a longer piece written in Tibetan, was originally posted to a blogsite in Tibet in 2011, and was quickly censored:

> On the top of the mountain, people with metal fangs
> Tear off the skeleton of the mountain, Blue sheep
> Start on the hillside, hawks hover in the sky
> Unable find a rock to stay on, feathers
> Shed in the wind
>
> On the silent grasslands, those
> Tracks of wheels, like a scar on a young girl's face
> Oppress the vessel of the mountain, while those
> Irrelevant rocks, exposed
> Shapeless blood, whiter than milk

Drop by drop, flows along
With the wound of the hillside[14]

★ ★ ★

THE MOST EXTREME FORM OF TIBETAN PROTEST AGAINST CHINESE REPRESSION—
and against desecration of their land—is self-immolation. On November
20, 2012, a farmer called Tsering Dhondup set himself on fire at the gate
of a gold-mining site in Amchok, Amdo, northeast Tibet. A week later,
there was another self-immolation at the same gold-mining site by a young
nomad, Kunchok Tsering. These are the first known self-immolations that
specifically protest against mining. Since 2009, over 130 Tibetans have set
themselves on fire in the ultimate form of protest. The self-immolation
protesters have been a diverse group from all walks of life and age groups.
Some have left statements behind giving reasons for self-immolation, ranging from the trauma of forced resettlement to lack of religious freedom.
Among the self-immolators a high proportion are monks and nuns.

Activist Tsering Woeser wrote a short book on the self-immolations,
which was published in France in 2013, with cover art by Beijing dissident
artist Ai Wei Wei. Woeser calls the self-immolations "earth-shattering." She
writes: "Self-immolation is the most hard-hitting thing that these isolated
protesters can do while still respecting principles of non-violence."[15]

Beijing condemns the self-immolation protests as acts of terrorism and
blames them on hostile forces, particularly the Dalai Lama. Military and
paramilitary patrols in places like Lhasa have taken to carrying fire extin-
guishers on their backs—not to save lives, but to prevent pictures of the
person on fire from being disseminated online. Such photos could damage
China's image abroad. In February 2014, Woeser tweeted a copy of dra-
conian new regulations that appeared in Zoige County, an ethnic-Tibet
region of Sichuan. The regulations are part of an aggressive drive to criminalize self-immolations by punishing the immolators' next of kin, their
monastic communities, and the towns where they set themselves alight.

Woeser called the regulations "absurd and terrifying." Under the regulations, villages where the self-immolation protests occur will be completely deprived of government assistance, and farmland or pasture registered in the name of the self-immolator taken by the authorities. Monasteries where self-immolations occur will have to pay a penalty of between 10,000 to 500,000 yuan ($1,650 to $81,978). Large rewards are offered to those who provide information on people who may be planning to self-immolate, or those that have occurred.[16]

In February 2013, the troubling Chinese policy that punishes friends, relatives, and associates of self-immolators resulted in the sentencing of nearly 90 Tibetans in Qinghai and Gansu provinces.[17] In April 2013, two monks from Beudo Monastery were each sentenced to three years in prison for offering religious rituals for self-immolator Wangchen Norbu. And in Ngaba, in August 2013, Dolma Kyab was sentenced to death in connection with the immolation of his wife, Kunchok Wangmo.

★ ★ ★

PARTICULARLY AT SACRED MOUNTAIN SITES, CHINESE MINING OPERATIONS HAVE LED to fierce protest by Tibetans. Several protests stand out.

In northern Yunnan, inside the Three Parallel Rivers UNESCO World Heritage Site, lies Mount Kawakarpo, a highly revered mountain with a pilgrim path around it. In February 2011, a Chinese gold-mining operation started up close to the pilgrim circuit. Infuriated Tibetans pushed equipment worth hundreds of thousands of dollars into a river far below.[18] The mining operation was shut down—a rare victory. But protests against dam construction on the rivers running close to this nature reserve have not been successful.

In mid-August 2013, Tibetans from Dzatoe County staged a three-day sit-in protest against an illegal mining operator in Sanjiangyuan National Nature Reserve. The operator's license to mine turned out to be fake: he obviously paid off corrupt officials. Protesters put up a gate flying

Chinese flags and bearing posters of President Xi Jinping, quoting from his May 2013 speech about the importance of guarding the environment for future generations. The protest in Dzatoe was broken up by over 400 military and paramilitary troops using tear gas and electric batons and firing machine guns in the air. At least one protester was killed. Fourteen protesters were hospitalized, and a large number arrested. Video footage of the protest was taken by Tibetans using smartphones: this was smuggled out of Tibet and posted to YouTube—confirming that gunfire was used against unarmed protesters. The video is a rare chance for the outside world to see what actually happens at a mining protest.[19]

Dartsedo County, Sichuan, October 13, 2013: a toxic spill from a mine contaminated a long stretch of river in an ethnic-Tibetan region in western Sichuan. The spill resulted in the death of livestock and fish. Tibetan villagers carried large quantities of dead fish to the township government offices in protest. The Chinese response was to cut off all cell phone and internet communication in the area and to send in Chinese troops to quell any protest.

In a posting from June 2013, blogger Woeser focuses on the region of Chamdo, northeastern Tibet, where megadam builders like PowerChina and big mining companies like Chinalco have moved in. Woeser writes: "In Markham County, Chamdo Prefecture, Tibetans have been resisting against the mining activities of the ZK Group for many years. Not only did the company mine in the sacred mountain, even worse is that the chemical elements utilized to clean the minerals have been discharged into the river water, poisoning local fish stocks, leading to cattle and residents being infected with strange diseases. Between 2005 and 2009, in Tsangshö Township, Markham County, 26 people and 2,442 cattle and sheep died from poisoned drinking water. In April 2009, 500 young Tibetans lay down on the street day and night, obstructing the mining activities of the ZK Group. When the local authorities sent in military police to disperse the protesters, 2,000 men and women, the young and the elderly, simultaneously went out to sleep on the streets."[20]

After a few months of protest, the ZK Group stopped mining, but resumed again later. In August 2012, as 2,000 locals gathered again to protest the mining, military police opened fire, killing one Tibetan and injuring six others. Penalties for Tibetan protesters are severe. In mid-2014, six Tibetans from Phondo County were given prison sentences of eight years each for taking part in anti-mining demonstrations. Arrested in April 2011, they disappeared for more than three years before their sentencing became public.

★　★　★

IN AUGUST 2014, THE GREENPEACE EAST ASIA WEBSITE REVEALED SHOCKING undercover photographs of a massive coal-mining operation in Qinghai on the Tibetan plateau. The main company involved is Kingho Group, chaired by well-connected billionaire Huo Qinghua. The open-pit Muli coalfield sits at around 14,000 feet in the Qilian mountains. The sheer scale of this mining operation is staggering. On its website, Kingho Group indicates 23 million tons of coal to be exploited. So much for China's grand plan to wean itself off heavy coal use. From what Greenpeace East Asia can determine, this coal-mining operation is illegal: it violates a number of water protection laws and local nature reserve regulations. The operation has cut off alpine meadows that channel water from glaciers and rainfall to the Yellow River. And here, the worst fears of environmentalists across China and Asia all come together: paper parks, removal of nomads, corruption, exploitative mining, grasslands degradation, river pollution. The location is right near the headwaters of the Yellow River—part of a region previously announced as a "nature reserve" to protect those same headwaters.

★　★　★

ANCIENT TIBETAN BELIEF HOLDS THAT DIGGING THE EARTH CAN CAUSE DISASTER, by disturbing wrathful demons that could unleash earthquakes, famine, drought, and epidemics. And they may yet be proven correct: wrathful demons *are* being unleashed, but not the kind they had in mind. The new demons are invisible but deadly. Toxins have no barriers—they are released into water, land, and air. Digging, even for wells, can release arsenic, which occurs naturally at varying soil-depths in the Himalayas. And large-scale mining activity could disturb shallower permafrost layers in Tibet, leading to the release of methane locked in the ice. Methane is a superpotent greenhouse gas: its sudden release could trigger accelerated climate change.

One of my guides in Tibet once confided, "The Chinese won't be happy until they have taken every last stone from Tibet"—until they have extracted the gold, the copper, the lithium, desecrated Tibet's sacred mountains, turned its grasslands into desert, destroyed the nomad culture, wiped out the Tibetan language, and yoked Tibet's mighty rivers, capturing the water behind megadams.

Mining accounted for just 3 percent of Tibet's economy in 2000: by some Chinese sources, it may rise to 30 percent by 2020, and 50 percent by 2050. Currently, processing of minerals and smelting is done after material is shipped to Chinese industrial centers, but to cut costs, the processing could be established on location in Tibet. It could lead to the Lhasa region becoming a new industrial base, which could result in complex new pollution problems. China's biggest aluminum company, Chinalco, has set up a Tibet subsidiary in Lhasa, presumably with the intention of starting up processing or smelter operations there. Chinalco has been implicated in major pollution in the Amdo region.

New technology under development will speed up mining in Tibet. Alarmingly, Chinese engineers are delving into the dark arts of mountaintop removal, using super heavy bulldozers and other customized machinery. China is moving mountains. In June 2014, the scientific journal *Nature* published a letter from three Chinese scientists in Xian warning about the implications of wide-scale mountaintop removal in central China.[21] The object is to fill valleys with the mountain debris to create flat land that will enable the expansion of cities and allow for more agriculture. Another

Chinese scientist says: "Land creation by cutting off hilltops and moving massive quantities of dirt is like performing major surgery on Earth's crust."[22] Mountaintop moving has been done before in strip mining, especially in the eastern United States, but it has never been carried out on this scale. In central China, dozens of hills 300 to 500 feet in height are being flattened over hundreds of miles. Such infill has never been used for urban construction. Plans of this scale are unprecedented: the scientists warn that earth moving on this scale without scientific support is sheer folly—and that high-rise buildings constructed on this new unstable land may topple. Added to this are the hazards of landslides, flooding, and altered watercourses. Near the city of Lanzhou, where mammoth earthmoving projects are under way for removal of scores of mountain-tops, researchers have estimated soil erosion will increase by 10 percent, and the concentration of dust particles in the air will increase by almost 50 percent.[23]

★ ★ ★

I ASKED TSERING TSOMO AT THE TIBETAN CENTRE FOR HUMAN RIGHTS AND Democracy about the future of Tibet in relation to mining. She talked about the Western Development Strategy (Open-Up-the-West campaign), which runs from 2000 to 2050: "I really cannot imagine after 50 years how the Tibetan Plateau will turn out to be. I mean, we really don't know whether a single nomad would be able to survive as a nomad after 50 years. The scenario now looks really scary because they are talking about doing these really exploitative, exclusionary development practices for the next 50 years."

So what can be done to stop this from happening? "We need a united approach from the international community to counter China when China is doing wrong," says Tsomo. "We should have the courage and the moral strength to say that yes, this is wrong, and this is what we stand for, these are our principles. We need to have that kind of approach. And more than that,

I also believe that there should be an international trade system where no country should be allowed to use conflict minerals or resources to engage in international trade practices."

If Tibetans vehemently protest against mining operations—sometimes at the cost of their own lives—then these minerals are conflict minerals: conflict gold, conflict copper, conflict lithium. But this concept may be very difficult for the international community to enforce, as Chinese officials are not likely to come clean about the exact source of the minerals used in their products.

Tsering Tsomo points out that Tibetans are not the only ones affected by mining pollution: "We have to take into consideration not only the human rights of the Tibetan people, but also the human rights of billions of people in the downstream Asian countries. They are also affected by the pollution of Tibetan water. They depend on Tibetan water for their livelihood. And if these water systems are polluted, what kind of human rights are we talking about? The Asian downstream countries have the right to ask China—to actually confront China—on taking responsibilities, asking them not to dump chemical waste into the water system. Because this water is not owned only by the Chinese government. Water has no border."

PART THREE

THE POLITICS OF WATER

China is engaged in the greatest water grab in history. Not only is it dam-ming the rivers on the plateau, it is financing and building mega-dams in Pakistan, Laos, Burma and elsewhere and making agreements to take the power. China-India disputes have shifted from land to water. Water is the new divide and is going centre stage in politics. Only China has the capacity to build these mega-dams and the power to crush resistance. This is effec-tively war without a shot being fired.

—Indian geopolitical analyst Brahma Chellaney⋆

⋆ Quoted in John Vidal's article, "China and India 'Water Grab' Dams Put Ecology of Himalayas in Danger," *The Observer*, August 10, 2013.

The Megadeltas of Asia

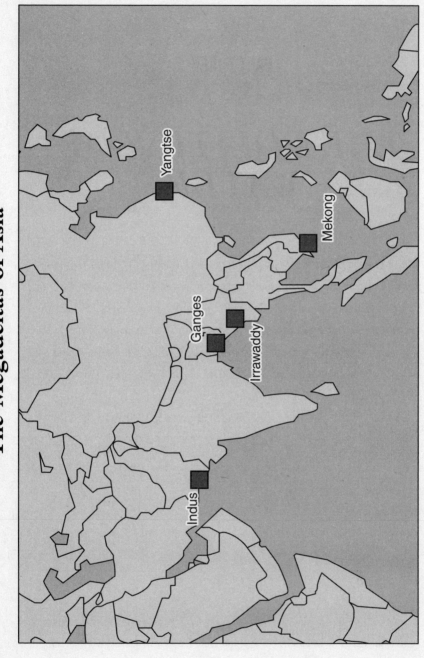

Yangtse

Mekong

Ganges

Irrawaddy

Indus

At the tail end of the rivers originating on the Tibetan Plateau are the largest deltas in the world, with intensive rice growing.

CHAPTER EIGHT

Downstream Blues

Southeast Asia: What Is at Stake for Food Security?

At the tail end of the mighty rivers flowing from Tibet lie the largest deltas in the world. Five megadeltas stand out: the Yangtse (an intensive rice growing and inland fishing region close to Shanghai), the Mekong (a major rice producer and aquaculture center for Vietnam), the Irrawaddy (a major rice producer for Burma), the Ganges-Brahmaputra (the agricultural heartlands of India and Bangladesh), and the Indus (a major agricultural zone for Pakistan). These megadeltas act as rice bowls for nearby megacities. One way or another, nearly 2 billion people rely on Tibet's rivers for their water—for drinking, fisheries, agriculture, and industry. For thousands of years, that water has flowed freely from Tibet to the nations downstream without traces of pollution. But under Chinese occupation of Tibet, the geopolitical situation has been turned on its ear. China is a water hog, with an eye on water diversion that could cause a significant drop in river flow. China has its hands on the tap for the whole of Asia: it can turn the water on or off via dams.

Water and food security are major concerns for downstream nations. By far the greatest water usage in Asia is for irrigation for crops, including rice, cotton, and rubber. Most of the world's rice is grown and consumed in Asia. India and China produce and consume up to half of the world's rice supplies. The world's highest per capita consumption of rice is in Burma, Bangladesh, Cambodia, Laos, Thailand, Vietnam, and Indonesia. Rice is very water-intensive: it takes around 250 to 600 gallons of water to grow a pound of rice. Asia is locked into rice as a staple food, although Pakistan and parts of India depend on wheat. As demand for rice balloons, demand for water will soar too. The only way to reduce this water demand would be to develop more efficient methods of cultivating rice, or substitute other crops. It takes about ten times more water to raise a pound of beef than to grow a pound of rice. As a wealthy middle class has grown in China and the diet has become more meat-centric, this has placed more water stress on the region.

★ ★ ★

RIVERS CARRY A LOT MORE THAN WATER—THEY ALSO BRING FISH AND NUTRIENT-rich sediment, or silt. Both are blocked by large dams. Dam builders curse silt because it can break turbines and should be filtered out. But the mega-deltas of Asia need all the deposits of silt they can get to prevent sinking and to counter rising sea levels. According to a 2014 report from the IPCC, "Most large deltas in Asia are sinking (as a result of groundwater withdrawal, floodplain engineering, and trapping of sediments by dams) much faster than global sea-level is rising."[1]

For farmers, silt is a life-giver: it is essential for agriculture. Fast-moving water in rivers picks up organic matter like vegetation, topsoil, animal waste, dead fish, and snail shells and mashes it all together. Silt, the resulting "cocktail," contains all the precious nutrients needed for growing plants: nitrogen, phosphorus, potassium, magnesium, and calcium. If that sediment is withheld, farmers must use artificial fertilizer, adding considerably to their production costs. Chinese farmers make heavy use of artificial fertilizers such as nitrogen, which increases crop yields but comes at an environmental cost. (It is estimated that 3 to 5 percent of nitrogen fertilizer is converted directly into nitrous oxide, a greenhouse gas thought to be 300 times more potent than CO_2.) Indirectly, silt provides food for fish. Hidden in silt are items like worms and insect larvae, which fish feed on.

Fisheries provide a major source of protein in Southeast Asia. Wild fish migration patterns have been severely disrupted by dam building. The fish catch has dropped drastically in the last two decades in Cambodia as a direct result of dam building upstream in China. Fish farming provides an alternative source of protein, with the raising of fish in cages—but those fish have to be fed, and there are aquacultural pollution problems to deal with. Another potential downstream hazard for food production is pollution of transboundary rivers from Tibet due to mining or industry. This could poison fish stocks and affect the cultivation of rice. Because of the great length of the rivers, pollution from Tibet will likely dissipate by the time it reaches neighboring nations, but that could change as more large-scale mining ventures start up in Tibet. If heavy metals from mining should leach into the rivers, this can work its way into the food chain.

★ ★ ★

THIS CHAPTER LOOKS AT THE TRANSBOUNDARY RIVERS THAT FLOW FROM THE eastern side of the Tibetan Plateau into Asian nations downstream, with special focus on ecosystem impact—and water and food security—in Cambodia and Burma. But two major rivers flowing east from Tibet have no transboundary issues: the Yellow and the Yangtse, both running to coastal China. Well, not quite running all the way: both rivers may fail to meet the sea. The Yellow and the Yangtse are less glacier-dependent for their flow than other rivers sourced on the Tibetan plateau, and they are more dependent on seasonal monsoon rains, which are affected by climate change factors. Both the Yellow and the Yangtse are prime cases of what can happen to the food chain when pollution and damming get completely out of hand.

The Yellow River flows 3,400 miles from Tibetan Plateau grasslands to the Bohai Sea. En route, it supplies water to 140 million people, passing through densely populated regions and heavy industrial zones. The Yellow River gets its moniker from the huge amounts of muddy silt it carries. But silt and mud are not all that is being carried along by the Yellow River these days. Severe pollution has made a third of the Yellow River unusable due to factory discharges and sewage from fast-expanding cities. In 2007, a survey by the Yellow River Conservancy Committee found that more than 33 percent of the river system registered worse than Level Five.[2] According to criteria used by the UN Environment Program, Level Five is unfit for drinking, aquaculture, industrial use, and agriculture. The report says waste and sewage discharged into the Yellow River totaled over 4 billion tons, mainly from industry and manufacturing. On top of that, the Yellow River is strangled by megadams in its upper reaches.

In 1972, for the first time in China's recorded history, the Yellow River dried up in patches and failed to reach the sea. Since then, the river has failed to reach the sea so often that some scientists have suggested it should be considered an inland body of water. "The once mighty [Yellow River] has by now become a small, filthy stream that cannot even flush much of its sediment into the sea," says Ma Jun, China's leading water activist.[3]

In 2006, China's environmental protection minister was quoted as saying about half of China's 21,000 chemical factories were in the vicinity of the Yellow and the Yangtse.[4] Obviously chemical factories and freshwater rivers are not a good combination. Protests have erupted around China from farmers complaining that uncontrolled factory discharges are poisoning the water and ruining crops. In October 2006, the Yellow River turned bright red—at least in the water around the western city of Lanzhou. State news agency Xinhua blamed the red and smelly slick on a sewage discharge.[5] In 2010, oil leaked from the Lanzhou-to-Changsha pipeline, contaminating part of the Yellow River near Sanmenxia Dam.

In December 2010, the *South China Morning Post* quoted a Chinese government official as saying that 8 million acres of land in China is too polluted to grow crops.[6] That's an area the size of Belgium. Samples of cadmium-contaminated rice were traced back to Henan Province, near the Yellow River, and Hunan Province, near the Yangtse. The toxic rice results from growing crops in paddies surrounded by factories that discharge waste. Contamination of China's soil and water due to industrial pollution may mean a shift to more reliance on imported food in the future. Large-scale, Chinese-run farms have surfaced (or are in the works) in several countries, including Kenya, Zimbabwe, Brazil, Russia, Argentina, and Australia. In this form of food outsourcing, China prefers to use its own farm workers; the crops grown are destined to be shipped directly to China.

★　★　★

THE YANGTSE RIVER RISES IN THE TANGGULA MOUNTAIN RANGE IN AMDO AT AROUND 16,400 feet and flows for 3,900 miles to China's east coast near Shanghai. Except that these days, the river mostly fails to reach the sea. Where to start on the Yangtse? There are so many large dams under construction or on the drawing board that you have to wonder how anything—or anybody—will survive along this river. The Yangtse is the longest river in Asia: the Yangtse watershed is home to around 400 million people, or a third of China's population. Around 200 million people live close to the banks of the river itself. An estimated 60 percent of the river is polluted from billions of tons of untreated effluent. In February and March 2013, thousands of dead pigs were found floating down the Huangpu River, a Yangtse tributary that runs through Shanghai. In September 2013, a 25-mile stretch of the Fuhe River, a Yangtse tributary in central China, was completely covered in dead fish. The death of the fish was directly attributed to ammonia discharge from a chemical factory.[7]

If that's how China treats its own rivers downstream, then transboundary rivers could be in deep trouble. And that includes the river that must be shared among five nations downstream: the Mekong.

★ ★ ★

THE MEKONG RIVER STARTS OUT AS A TRICKLE IN SNOWBOUND COUNTRY AROUND 17,000 feet in Qinghai. The river gathers momentum, becoming a roaring torrent as it swirls through deep gorges, dropping an astonishing 14,700 feet in elevation through Tibet and China over a distance of 1,100 miles before turning tamer in Laos. The entire length of the river is estimated at 2,700 miles. The river is known under many names as it courses through different nations: Dza Chu (Tibet), Lancang Jiang (China), Mekaung Myit (Burma), Menam Khong (Thailand), Tonle Thom (Cambodia), and Song Me Kong (Vietnam). There are more name variations for upper, middle, or lower reaches within China. In Vietnam, at the tail end of the river, the sprawling Mekong Delta is called Song Cuu Long (Nine Dragons River). Downstream from China, there are around 60 million people in the Mekong Basin waiting for its waters—mostly subsistence farmers and fishermen.

Damming the Mekong is highly controversial because the river runs through six nations. Of all the world's major rivers, the Mekong is the last to see dam activity or other development. French Indochina deemed the Mekong useless for navigation due to insurmountable rapids in lower Laos, and five decades of warfare and insurgency from the 1940s to the 1980s kept engineers away from the river. The first dam to be constructed was Manwan Dam, completed in Yunnan in 1994. Since then, four more megadams have been built on the lower Mekong in China: Jinghong, Dachaoshan, Xiaowan, and Nuozhadu.

Although the Mekong is sourced in Qinghai on the Tibetan Plateau, the current impact on the nations downstream is from the completed megadams in lowland areas of Yunnan, close to the border with Laos. On the drawing board, however, are plans to build megadams on the upper Mekong, on the Tibetan Plateau: some dams are under construction in the Chamdo area of northeastern Tibet. And in the distant future, there are plans on the drawing board to divert Tibet's Mekong waters to the northeast.

The Mekong River is the world's largest inland fishery, with over 2.5 million tons of fish products per year. But dams are severely impacting the natural ecosystem in the river. Many fish are unable to travel to feed or spawn because the dams block the river. Fish production in the Mekong is decreasing every year as more dams are being built in China. Not listening to vigorous protest from the downstream nations, Chinese engineers are forging ahead with construction of three more megadams to complete a cascade of eight dams on the lower Mekong, with more to follow further upstream in Tibet in the future.

James Clad, a senior research fellow at the Institute for National Strategic Studies at the National Defense University in Washington, says China's presence and impact, potential and real, on the Mekong is "so predominant, so overwhelming, that it does affect, literally, the ability of these countries to continue earning a living, irrigating their fields in the way that they've been accustomed to for millennia." He called Chinese dam construction on the Mekong "probably the most dramatic use of water resources to reorder a geopolitical area that I've ever seen."[8]

In an attempt to negotiate transboundary issues along the Mekong, the Mekong River Commission (MRC) was set up in 1995 with a mandate to protect the river. But China and Burma resolutely refused to join; they sit on the sidelines as "dialogue partners" and are thus not bound by any agreements reached. The MRC has consumed millions of dollars from various grants and government bodies, but this has produced little or no action for preserving the Mekong. In November 2007, a petition was delivered to the MRC demanding that the organization fulfill its mission to protect the river, in light of compelling scientific evidence that warns of the disastrous consequences of damming the lower Mekong. The petition was endorsed by 200 organizations and individuals from 30 countries, with unprecedented support from civil society groups from Mekong countries. The MRC has no teeth: it looks like the organization will not be able to stall the dam-building ambitions of Laos.

★　★　★

AROUND 44 PERCENT OF THE LENGTH OF THE MEKONG RUNS WITHIN TIBET AND China. After leaving China, the longest stretch of the Mekong flows through Laos along shared river borders with Burma and Thailand. Intent on becoming the battery of Asia by exporting hydropower, Laos has proposed nine major dams on the Mekong, claiming that if the river is already dammed upstream, then they should go ahead and dam it downstream. In other words, if the river is already dead upstream, might as well drive some nails into the coffin downstream. In addition, there are plans to dam tributaries of the Mekong—such as the Nam Ou, where Sinohydro has blueprints for a seven-dam cascade. Laos does not actually need these dams: the plan is to export hydropower to neighboring Thailand, Vietnam, and China. These dams will not benefit the local Laotian population: they will destroy farmland, displace thousands, and ruin fisheries. Laos is being exploited by its neighbors selling its valuable resources in the form of hydropower, mining (copper, gold), timber, and rubber.

The main player in potential dam building on the Mekong in Laos is Thailand. In 2014, construction started on Xayaburi Dam, on the Mekong south of Luang Prabang, with a completion date set for 2019. The massive 1,285 MW dam is a joint Thai-Laotian venture, with 95 percent of the electricity destined for export to Thailand. Xayaburi Dam was the first significant test for the 1995 MRC treaty, which required the agreement of MRC members before building any dam on the Mekong mainstream. But such agreement was never sought for Xayaburi Dam. Thailand refused to study the dam's transboundary impact before beginning construction; the environmental impact assessment only examines an area six miles downstream. Various groups called for a ten-year delay on Xayaburi to study transboundary impact, but the requests were ignored. This sets a dangerous precedent for further dam building in Laos.

★   ★   ★

IF THE PROPOSED DAMS IN CHINA AND LAOS ARE ALL BUILT, THE MEKONG WILL NO longer be a river—it will be a cascade of still-water lakes. Watching ongoing dam construction in China and proposed dam building in Laos with considerable consternation is Vietnam. That's because Vietnam's Mekong Delta is vital for the nation's food security. The delta, home to 18 million people, is by far Vietnam's most productive region for agriculture and aquaculture. It embraces an area of 15,000 square miles, with water coverage varying by season. The delta comprises a quarter of Vietnam's total area under agriculture and provides close to half of Vietnam's national output of cereals, mainly in the form of rice cultivation. The Mekong River is a lifeline. China's megadams in Yunnan trap large amounts of nutrient-rich silt, which means the fertility of the Mekong Delta, vital for rice cultivation, will suffer, leading to a decline in productivity. The Mekong Delta suffers from saltwater intrusion, which damages crops. This is likely due to sea-level rise caused by climate-change factors, but a contributing cause is that China's dam construction on the Mekong may reduce the flow of freshwater to the region. Saltwater from the South China Sea now reaches some 35 miles into the delta at times. Similar problems of saltwater intrusion are experienced in the Ganges-Brahmaputra Delta and the Indus Delta. Research is under way to create a strain of rice that is salt resistant, but that could take time—and ultimately it does not solve the underlying problems.

On the map, it looks as if Vietnam's Mekong Delta is the tail end of the Mekong River, but actually there is another distinct tail end where the river backs up into Cambodia, at Lake Tonle Sap.

★   ★   ★

PREAK TOAL, LAKE TONLE SAP, CAMBODIA, FEBRUARY 2005: WE HAVE not set foot on dry land for a week. In the flooded forest, we sometimes scramble from our kayaks to an observation platform built high in the trees to check on bird life. At night, we sleep in the treetops in special hammocks with mosquito netting enclosing the top. You have to make sure your bladder is empty before climbing into your hammock, because a trip to the outhouse is not possible at night.

We're out paddling early in the morning because that's when the birds are most active. Five of us, in three kayaks, have launched an expedition into this remote region to observe the bird colonies at Preak Toal. The kayaks belong to Jock, an adventure traveler and photographer. Guiding us are two rangers. Vanna, who speaks some English, is a former soldier now involved in a very different kind of combat—a battle to save rare species. A ranger's job involves counting birds, hatchlings, and eggs. On this trip, Vanna is needed to get us past fish gates, which are jealously guarded. To keep poachers at bay, Vanna carries an AK-47 assault rifle to show that the rangers mean business. The poachers may also be armed and often work at night to escape detection. At a stop along the route, the AK-47 has been left casually stowed in the backseat of a double kayak—and I'm thinking that if the AK-47 were to accidentally go off, that would sink this whole venture.

In the morning, I have a front-row seat for the splendors of Preak Toal, viewed from the cockpit of a kayak. Kayaking around a bend in the river, I spot a dark cluster in the air and track up with binoculars. I have chanced upon one of the great wonders of the avian world: a thermal with at least

70 large, endangered birds wheeling around. One species, the painted stork, is an elegant, streamlined flyer with a long bill. Another, the spot-billed pelican, is a slower, heavier bird that reminds me of a flying boat. Higher up, I sight a species with a majestic six-foot wingspan, a lesser adjutant, circling languidly. Over millennia, birds like these have honed the ability to sense thermals—pockets of warm air swirling up from the earth's surface—that enable them to gain altitude, then glide effortlessly wherever they want. And for centuries, humankind has envied birds for their freedom in the air and sought to solve the mysteries of flight and other avian secrets.

One of those secrets was unveiled right here, at Cambodia's Preak Toal, in 1994. That was the year ornithologists first discovered large colonies of nesting waterbirds in this remote part of the country at the northwest edge of Lake Tonle Sap. Unfortunately, poachers had discovered the site much earlier. During the 1990s, they removed bird eggs by the thousands, as well as chicks to be fattened up for the cooking pot. According to French ornithologist Frederic Goes, Cambodia's leading bird expert, one year a single poacher was caught with more than 1,000 eggs in his boat. Reeling from these losses, species including the greater adjutant and milky stork tottered on the brink of extinction.

Preak Toal, which encompasses 52,737 acres of wetlands and flooded forest, is recognized as Asia's premier habitat for large waterbirds. In 1997, the United Nations declared Lake Tonle Sap and its shores (including Preak Toal) a UNESCO Biosphere Reserve. Over 100 species of birds have been spotted here, 15 of them endangered. Among the species that nest here are Asia's only known colonies of the glossy ibis and milky stork, as well as the continent's largest colonies of the greater adjutant, Asian openbill, painted stork, black-headed ibis, Oriental darter, and spot-billed pelican. Numbers of each species range from 1,500 pairs for the pelican down to just half a dozen pairs for the milky stork, the rarest of Asia's big waterbirds.

Kayaking in this region, we sight flocks of Indian shags, Oriental darters drying their wings, greyheaded fish eagles swooping for a catch, and storkbilled kingfishers flashing by in a swirl of color. The diversity of avian life is amazing. It's not difficult to work out what attracts the birds: they're here for the lake's abundance and diversity of fish. More than 200 species of fish have been discovered in Lake Tonle Sap. Each kind of bird has its own specialized technique for landing such plentiful prey. There are waders (herons and egrets), strikers (kingfishers), divers (darters), and surface skimmers (terns).

In February, the birds get a lot of competition from humans. February is the start of the official fishing season. An extraordinary cottage industry gets underway in this part of the biosphere reserve, designated a "multiple-use zone." The waters and shorelines of the vast lake are partitioned off with long bamboo fences and fish gates into a maze of commercial fishing lots patrolled by armed guards. Lot owners pay hefty sums for concession rights, which are leased for two-year periods to the highest bidder. To maximize profits, concession owners sublease their fishing rights.

And where do all the fish come from? They are here due to the bizarre annual flood pulse of Lake Tonle Sap. In the monsoon season, the Mekong swells with up to 50 times more water than in the dry season. Lake Tonle Sap acts like a backup valve for the high flow of the Mekong. At this time, the Tonle Sap River actually undergoes a reversal of current, with water flowing into the lake and flooding rainforest for up to 25 miles around. And with the monsoon waters come billions of fish fry, tiny juvenile fish that fatten up over the course of four or five months. When floodwaters recede and the lake shrinks, it turns into one of the richest fishing grounds in the world, yielding as much as 15 tons of fish per square mile of water surface. Fish are caught with nets and bamboo traps; some are even caught in the branches of trees or in the mud. It is estimated that over 60 percent of Cambodia's annual catch comes from Lake Tonle Sap or the Tonle Sap River, which connects the lake to the Mekong. This largely comprises migratory fish species. When the floodwaters recede, the fattened fish depart via Tonle Sap River, heading toward the Mekong Delta or northward to Laos and China. They make easy pickings for fishing nets.

Lake Tonle Sap is a special ecosystem that has adapted to an annual flood pulse. It is known as the "beating heart" of Cambodia. But all is not well with the pulse. It is irregular now, skipping beats and sometimes very weak. Vanna, our guide, says that the 2003–2004 fishing season was the worst year on record. The Mekong's flow was at record low levels, and the flooding season at Tonle Sap lasted only three months instead of five. As a result, fish had less time to mature. The fish haul was around half the usual catch at Tonle Sap.

The timing coincided with the filling of the reservoir for the just-completed Dachaoshan Dam on the lower Mekong. The dams on the Mekong in China could well be holding back floodwaters that would otherwise surge down into Cambodia. And that weakens Tonle Sap's flood pulse, upon which the entire ecosystem depends. Chinese authorities routinely deny that its Mekong megadams in Yunnan have any effect on the nations downstream, frequently citing climate change as the cause of low river levels.

Regardless of the river-flow factors, there are two reasons why China's megadams are having a huge impact on fisheries in Cambodia. Lake Tonle Sap acts as an important nursery for many wild, migrating fish species. Dams block fish migration as there is no way for fish to get around a dam wall that is over 300 feet high. And megadams block the flow of silt coming down the Mekong. That silt previously ended up in the flooded forest around Lake Tonle Sap, fertilizing the vegetation. Since the fish feed on floating vegetation, silt plays a vital role. According to Finnish researcher Matti Kammu, China's first two megadams captured half the flow of silt coursing down the Mekong. He says that if a cascade of eight megadams is completed in Yunnan, it would hold back more than 90 percent of the sediment load.[9]

A report issued in May 2009 by the United Nations Environment Programme warned that these dams are "the single greatest threat" to the future of the river and its fecundity. The five dams now operational in Yunnan mean that Mekong waters will rise and fall at the whim of engineers, not from natural causes. Half the flow of the Mekong may be stalled in Yunnan if Chinese engineers decide to hold back water for release in the dry season, or if they decide to impound water for flood control. That could weaken or even eliminate the river's annual flood pulse, one of the natural wonders of the world, and wreck the ecosystems that depend on it. Aviva Imhof, campaigns director at the International Rivers network, says the dams will cause incalculable damage downstream. "China is acting at the height of irresponsibility," says Imhof. "Its dams will wreak havoc with the Mekong ecosystem as far downstream as the Tonle Sap. They could sound the death knell for fisheries which provide food for over 60 million people."[10]

China's megadam building in Yunnan amounts to a slow strangulation of the Mekong. It may take 5 to 15 years for the Chinese-built dams to have real impact, but when that happens, it will be disastrous for Cambodia's fisheries. And that will be catastrophic for the nation. According to Mekong expert Milton Osborne, "nearly 80 percent, or some would say over 80 percent, of the animal protein intake of the Cambodian population comes from fish taken out of the Mekong and its associated river systems, including the Cambodian great lake."[11] Cambodians are more dependent on wild protein from fish than practically any other country on earth. The river fisheries of Cambodia are essential to its food security. Although Cambodia is fostering development of aquaculture, with the raising of fish in cages, this cannot match the wild fish catch.

★　★　★

AFTER A SOJOURN IN THE FLOODED FOREST, WE KAYAK BACK TO PREAK TOAL VILLAGE. Some wooden structures like a school and a monastery have been built on high stilts to allow for flooding, but most residents live in floating homes that rise and fall with the waters. The floating homes are well maintained, with vegetable and flower gardens, electric generators, and TV antennas sprouting from rooftops. Some floating homes have large cages beneath them where captive fish are raised. The pungent smell of fish paste pervades the air. On the porches of the floating houses, large quantities of sardine-like *trey riel* are being processed into a fermented fish paste called *prahok*, which is an excellent source of protein and calcium. It's Sunday, and a special boat is running around the village to pick up children from families of the fishing community. They go to a classroom for a brief orientation and then depart on a field trip to see the birds along a tributary at Preak Toal. This is part of an innovative educational community program at the floating village. These kids could be future guides and rangers and managers. If the waterbirds nesting at Preak Toal are to have any chance of survival, the future rests in their hands.

Vanna takes us over to an unusual floating pen. Through the floorboards, we see dozens of crocodiles, which are raised in captivity for lucrative sales to Thai, Vietnamese, and Chinese traders. Hunters at Tonle Sap go after reptiles like pythons, cobras, turtles, and lizards. But due to the work of rangers, locals have been warned off hunting for the eggs and chicks of large waterbirds and are educated about protecting these endangered species instead.

Due to a dwindling fish catch, fishermen at Tonle Sap are turning their attention to harvesting water snakes from the flooded forest. The annual catch is thought to be several million water snakes (from eight species), attesting to the extraordinary fecundity of Tonle Sap's ecosystem. But harvesting that number of water snakes on an annual basis is most likely not sustainable. The water snakes are mainly fed to captive crocodiles, while others are sold for food or for their skins.[12]

★ ★ ★

GREAT CIVILIZATIONS RISE AND FALL ON GREAT RIVERS, BUT THE CITY OF ANGKOR ROSE instead on a lake. Just north of Lake Tonle Sap lie the ancient ruins of Angkor. The mighty Khmer Empire, which once ruled large swaths of present-day Southeast Asia, had its center at Angkor, which depended on the annual flooding of Lake Tonle Sap for an abundant supply of fish and for rice harvests several times a year. Bas-reliefs at the Bayon in Angkor Thom, dating from 800 years ago, show fish life so abundant that it impeded the progress of canoes across the lake. Thriving on the flood pulse of Lake Tonle Sap, Angkor grew into the greatest metropolis in Asia. At its zenith in the twelfth century, it may have supported 750,000 people. Under attack from neighboring Vietnam and Thailand, the Khmer Empire collapsed in the fourteenth century, and Angkor was abandoned. And now, in the twenty-first century, Cambodia faces another disaster: the specter of collapsing fisheries at Lake Tonle Sap.

Given this scenario, it seems incredible that Cambodia would even consider the building of dams on the Mekong—or on its tributaries—within its own territory. In 2012, government approval was given for construction of the 400 MW Lower Sesan 2 Dam, on the Sesan River, a tributary about 15 miles from the Mekong in northeastern Cambodia. This is a 90 percent joint venture between China's Hydrolancang International Energy and Cambodia's Royal Group, with the remaining 10 percent owned by a subsidiary of Vietnam Electricity Group. Hydrolancang is a subsidiary of Huaneng Group, which has built megadams in Yunnan.

Lurking in the wings is Chinese megadam builder Sinohydro, which completed Kamchay Dam in Cambodia's southwest. Sinohydro and other Chinese consortiums are keen on building megadams on Cambodia's rivers, including the Mekong. These dam proposals have been strongly protested by villagers in the affected regions, but the deals are signed with Cambodia's prime minister Hun Sen, who has held the reins of power since 1985—and who has never hesitated to unleash security forces to stamp out any hint of opposition to his plans. Hun Sen's power base is propped up by China, which treats Cambodia like a fiefdom. China is the biggest investor in Cambodia and the leading aid donor. There is rapidly expanding Chinese interest in exploiting Cambodia's mining, forestry, and oil sectors, with proposed Chinese-built railways and highways to allow access. Illegal exploitation goes on under the radar, such as the smuggling out of rare rosewood to China for use in furniture making.

★ ★ ★

IN BURMA (MYANMAR), CHINA IS A MAJOR PLAYER IN RESOURCE EXPLOITATION, from mining and logging to hydropower. This is a case of one repressive regime dealing with another, and the Burmese people are the ultimate losers. They see very little benefit from these projects. The profits line the pockets of the repressive Burmese military junta, which has wielded absolute power since 1962. As a pariah state, Burma was long under embargo by the West, and China remained the nation's only real ally and economic backer. In 2011, Burma finally set out to end its isolation and re-establish relations with the outside world. This means Burma is no longer totally reliant on China as its economic backer, which changes the picture by giving Burma more choices, though Chinese influence remains strong. The situation in Burma is complicated by military repression of ethnic groups who are strongly opposed to the exploitation of their resources. Burma has few environmental protection laws in place.

The Salween is among the last wild rivers of Asia—with imminent threat of dam building getting under way in Yunnan and in Burma. Within China, plans for a cascade of megadams are proceeding after being delayed for a decade by protest over environmental concerns. Once building of this cascade gets under way, the dams will severely impact farmers and fishermen who depend on the river ecosystems for their livelihood in Burma. The long arm of Chinese dam builders reaches across the border into Burma, and here they have run into some trouble.

According to the NGO International Rivers, "the proposed dams in Burma are located in active civil war zones, which is partly why they have proven problematic to develop. Since project preparations began, there has been increased militarization at the dam sites, which has been linked to the escalating abuse of local populations. According to Human Rights Watch,

Shan Women's Action Network and other relief groups, members of ethnic minority groups like the Kachin, Shan and Karen are not only being systematically and forcibly moved from their homes, but in some cases robbed, tortured, raped or executed."[13]

Six megadams on the Salween River in Burma are under planning and development with investment from five Chinese corporations, the Electricity Generation Authority of Thailand (EGAT), and three Burmese corporations. These dams are shrouded in secrecy, but a few details have emerged. Kunlong Dam is a 1,400 MW project; its electricity output will be exported to China, just across the border. Hatgyi Dam is a venture involving China's Sinohydro and Thailand's EGAT, with 75 percent of the power slated for export to Thailand. Hatgyi's environmental impact assessment was broadly criticized by experts and NGOs for downplaying the environmental and human impacts, and for making dubious claims about the extent of opposition to the project by local ethnic Karen people. Tasang Dam, located in southern Shan State, is slated to be become the largest in Southeast Asia, with a capacity of 7,000 MW. The project is under construction by China's Three Gorges Project Corporation in a joint venture with EGAT, with 85 percent of the output expected to go to Thailand. Construction of the dam has entailed rampant environmental damage and widespread human rights abuses, with Burmese being press-ganged into forced labor and others raped or killed by Burmese military. Over 60,000 villagers have been displaced from the dam site and projected reservoir zone, with tens of thousands more expected to be forcibly moved. In June 2011, fighting around the dam site spread to other Chinese-backed dam sites, with refugees fleeing these areas.

★　★　★

BURMA'S MOST IMPORTANT WATERWAY IS THE IRRAWADDY RIVER, WHICH IS actually formed from two tributaries called the N'Mai and Mali rivers that converge near Myitkyina. Other feeders, such as the Dulong Jiang, come in from Tibet via Yunnan, and downstream more tributaries engorge the river as it flows across the nation, emerging at the Irrawaddy Delta and the Andaman Sea. According to the NGO Burma Rivers Network, "Burma's military government signed an agreement with [state-owned] China Power Investment Corporation in May 2007 for the implementation of seven large dams along the Irrawaddy, Mali, and N'Mai Rivers in Kachin State. The largest of the seven, the Myitsone Dam, is located at the confluence of the Mali and N'Mai Rivers at the creation of the Irrawaddy. The dam would destroy the confluence [most likely through flooding] of one of the most significant cultural heritage sites for the Kachin people and an important landmark for all of Burma."[14]

These dams fall within Kachin State, where ethnic Kachin people have waged decades of warfare with the Burmese military over resource extraction on their lands, which are rich in jade, gold, and tropical hardwood. A ceasefire lasted 17 years—until 2011, when Myitsone Dam got under way. The blueprint for Myitsone Dam is for a structure 500 feet in wall height, with a colossal capacity of 3,200 MW. And where is this huge amount of hydroelectricity slated to go? Apparently, 90 percent of the hydroelectric output is earmarked for export to China through some system of power transfer, probably ultra-high voltage lines. This amounts to neocolonialism. The reservoir of the dam will flood an area larger than Singapore—in one of the world's hotspots of biodiversity. Animals impacted include the highly endangered Irrawaddy dolphin. An estimated 10,000 people will be displaced, losing their livelihoods and natural resource base. Construction for Myitsone Dam started in December 2009. In April 2010, the dam builders were temporarily shut down when the offices and equipment for Asia World and the Ministry of Electric Power were hit by a series of bomb blasts. In June 2011, the Burmese army attacked a Kachin Independence Army outpost near the dam site, ending the 17-year ceasefire. Since then, more than 75,000 Kachins have been displaced by fighting between the two groups. In September 2011, in a rare victory for anti-dam campaigners, Burmese president Thein Sein announced the suspension of the Myitsone Dam project. However, he did not cancel the project. He suspended it for the duration of his term in office, which runs to 2015.

In April 2012, I hopped on a flight from Rangoon to Myitkyina. I hired a Kachin guide with a motorcycle and we headed for the site of Myitsone Dam. Here's what I learned. Access to the dam site is completely sealed off, but we managed to cruise past it on a hired boat. Locals confirmed that Chinese workers are still at the site and are active at night, under cover of darkness, though it is not clear what they are doing. Close to Myitsone, large-scale gold mining and logging continues at breakneck pace. The Kachin guide took me to a Chinese-built village where people had been forcibly resettled in rows of neat wooden houses. But Kachin people in five villages that were bulldozed in 2010 to make way for the Myitsone project have not been allowed to go back to the area. The more I look at these factors, the more it seems Chinese engineers are just biding their time, waiting for the project to resume. Back in Myitkyina, I found I could not get out of the town. Fighting had broken out between Kachin and Burmese troops, and road, river, and rail travel were not considered safe. Eventually, I flew south to the town of Bhamo.

President Thein Sein made no announcement about the other six Chinese-engineered megadams slated to be built on Irrawaddy tributaries, which will have a similar impact on the Irrawaddy as Myitsone Dam. Power from these dams would most likely be exported to China, India, or Thailand. All in all, the suspension of the dam's construction was a hollow victory for Burma's anti-dam crusaders. Ethnic Kachin groups declared their intention to attack Chinese dam-building sites in the north.

★ ★ ★

CHINESE COMPANIES ARE HELPING THEMSELVES TO BURMA'S NATURAL RESOURCES IN lucrative deals with Burma's military junta. Running from the Burmese coastal port of Kaukpyu all the way to Kunming in Yunnan are two parallel pipelines: one for sending offshore natural gas to China, and the other for transporting oil that comes from the Middle East and Africa. Tropical hardwoods like teak are being exploited by operations from China, India, and Thailand. Around 75 percent of the world's teak market comes from the forests of Burma. China has some legal teak imports from Burma, but there is a much bigger trade in illegal teak importing. As China shares a land border with Burma, teak can be smuggled out at night. Burma recently banned all exports of virgin teak.

Chinese mining companies appear to use the same tactics in Burma as they do in Tibet: land grabbing, excluding locals from planning, no concern for pollution, and the suppression of any protest with brutal force through military supplied by the Burmese junta. Burma's largest copper mine at Leptadaung, 280 miles north of Rangoon, is highly controversial. The mine is a billion-dollar joint venture between Wanbao, a subsidiary of a Chinese weapons maker, and a holding company backed by Burma's military. Locals say the project entails confiscation of thousands of acres of farmland and would create significant pollution. Buddhist monks say the development would damage or destroy sacred sites. In November 2012, there was a brutal crackdown on demonstrators by police who used military-grade smoke grenades containing white phosphorus, leaving a hundred protesters injured, some with severe burns.

In a distinctly neocolonial situation, China is doing what history's worst colonizers have done—rampantly exploiting its neighbors with scant regard for the environment, or for the welfare of the people.

CHAPTER NINE

Himalayan Water Wars

Why Can't They Just Leave the Rivers Alone?

Shifting the focus from Southeast Asia to the Himalayan region brings up more intense geopolitical intrigue as China squares off with rival India. Himalayan rivers—largely untouched until the 2000s—have become the object of a huge water grab as China, India, Nepal, Pakistan, and Bhutan seek electricity to power their economies. The Himalayan region is sitting on massive hydro potential, and a dam-building frenzy is getting under way. Here, two major dam builders are going at it: China and India. China is intent on transferring the power generated by Tibetan dams to mining and industrial sites. India wants to transfer hydropower from Sikkim and Arunachal Pradesh to other states. And both nations have extensive water-diversion plans in the works.

The figures are staggering. China has plans for more than 100 large dams in Himalayan regions, and it has a stake in dam building and financing in both Nepal and Pakistan. India envisages building a mind-boggling 290 large dams and is involved in construction of dams in neighboring Bhutan. That totals around 400 large dams for the Great Himalayan Watershed region.[1] If they are all undertaken, this would become the most heavily dammed region in the world. The Himalayan region is one of the youngest and most unstable mountain regions in the world. Neither Chinese nor Indian engineers seem to have conducted proper assessments on the impact of gouging out millions of tons of rock and earth to build megadams and tunnels and store millions of gallons of water in reservoirs. This activity could trigger major landslides and possibly earthquakes—which in turn could crack concrete dams and breach them.

In this race to dam the Himalayas, the vital river ecosystems will become casualties—and millions of people living along the riverbanks will be the losers. The environmental impact of all this dam building will be devastating because water and food security problems in the Indian subcontinent are much magnified due to population factors. The Mekong River countries (embracing Burma, Thailand, Laos, Cambodia, and Vietnam) have a combined total population of around 240 million people (as of 2014). In comparison, Bangladesh alone has a population of around 165 million (as of 2014), most of whom are dependent on rivers sourced in Tibet. The same goes for Pakistan, with a population of 180 million (as of 2014). And over 400 million people in northern India depend on Tibet's waters (out of a total of 1.3 billion people in India). That's an awful lot of people waiting for the water from Tibet—over 750 million of them.

The Indian subcontinent populations are increasing at a fast pace, with enormous pressure to boost food production. With severe groundwater problems in India, Bangladesh, and Pakistan, there will inevitably be rising tensions over shared water resources, among farmers and between farmers and urban dwellers. The greatest challenge will be to prevent transboundary water conflicts from erupting between China, India, Pakistan, and Bangladesh.

The geopolitical picture for the Great Himalayan Watershed region is highly complex. In this chapter, some of those complexities are explored on three transboundary river basins—the Brahmaputra, Ganges, and Indus.

These rivers rise from roughly the same area—close to Mount Kailash—and flow toward megadeltas that meet the sea.

★ ★ ★

IN THE LATE NINETEENTH AND EARLY TWENTIETH CENTURY, MOUNT KAILASH IN FAR western Tibet assumed mythical dimensions among Western geographers and explorers. For a long time, a high mountain in Tibet was reputed to be the source of all the great rivers of India. But Tibet was inaccessible at the time, so geographers were unsure if this was myth or fact. Finding the source of India's great rivers was a prime geographer's puzzle, on par with finding the source of the Nile.

To get accurate mapping data for Tibet, in the 1860s the British-run Survey of India started training Indian undercover agents. Having observed that Indian pilgrims were permitted to visit sacred places in Tibet and that Indian traders were allowed to venture across the border, the British hit on the idea of disguising Indian agents as pilgrims to gather intelligence. They used the strangest map-making equipment ever conceived. An agent paced out distances on foot, painstakingly measured with pilgrim prayer beads. A Tibetan rosary normally holds 108 beads. For every 100 paces, a bead could be dropped: the distance of a mile might equate to exactly 2000 paces. Tiny beads of silver recorded the miles, rather like an abacus. The native explorer's neck amulet cleverly concealed a miniature compass for recording bearings. A hollow walking stick hid a miniature boiling-point thermometer, used to determine elevation. Tibetan pilgrims commonly twirl a handheld prayer wheel inscribed with sacred mantras: hidden inside the explorer model was a blank scroll on which measurements and map data could secretly be recorded. This secret logbook could easily be retrieved by removing the top of the prayer-wheel cylinder—discreetly, of course.

The riddle of the Yarlung Tsangpo foxed British geographers for over a century. Was it the same river as the Brahmaputra? Or did it flow into the Irrawaddy River or elsewhere? In the summer of 1880, an Indian agent called Kintup was dispatched to the Tsangpo Gorges region. His mission was to follow the Tsangpo all the way into India. If that proved impossible, he was to cut and mark 500 small logs, attach some tubes to identify them, and then launch them into the Tsangpo over a period of a week. After overcoming many travails, in November 1883 Kintup tossed the marked logs into the Tsangpo in far eastern Tibet, but due to failure in communications, nobody was there to witness the logs floating into India.

Eventually, it was established that the Yarlung Tsangpo made a dramatic turn in eastern Tibet and became the Brahmaputra. And it was discovered that the headwaters of four of India's mightiest rivers lay within 70 miles of Mount Kailash—the Yarlung Tsangpo, Karnali, Sutlej, and Indus rivers. Remarkably, these rivers meet the sea as far as 1,900 miles apart, ranging from the Ganges-Brahmaputra Delta in the east to the Indus Delta in the west.

The Tibetans knew about the rivers all along but did not want to reveal the mysteries to outsiders. In Tibetan, the four rivers are known by more prosaic names, identified with four cardinal directions and four legendary animals. Thus the Yarlung Tsangpo becomes the "River from the Horse-Mouth" (Tamchok Khambab, to the east); the Karnali, the "River from the Peacock-Mouth" (Mabchu Khambab, to the south); the Sutlej, the "River from the Elephant-Mouth" (Langchan Khambab, in the west); and the Indus, the "River Issuing from the Lion's Mouth" (Sengghe Khambab, in the north).

Back in the nineteenth and early twentieth century, these rivers flowed freely, as they had for millennia, barely touched by Tibetans, supplying the entire Indian subcontinent with all its water needs, mainly for agriculture. The setup was simple: Tibet had abundant water, India got all the water it needed. The Indus and Sutlej flowed directly from Tibet into India. The Karnali coursed through Nepal before entering India as a major feeder of the Ganges. Nepal presented no water-flow problems as it was undeveloped.

And the Yarlung Tsangpo meandered all the way across Tibet before heading south for India.

This idyllic water arrangement between Tibet and India underwent a drastic transformation after World War II. In 1947, India gained independence from the British but was partitioned into the Union of India and the Dominion of Pakistan (comprising present-day Pakistan and Bangladesh). In 1950, China invaded central Tibet, putting new masters in control of the rivers. In 1971, Bangladesh declared independence from Pakistan.

By this time the geopolitical picture completely changed, with a river situation that would eventually turn into a nightmare for the nations downstream. The Tsangpo-Brahmaputra courses through Chinese-controlled Tibet and through India before reaching Bangladesh. The Indus and Sutlej now flow from Tibet through India before reaching Pakistan, where the two rivers join. Since both China and India are big dam builders and water diverters, that puts Pakistan and Bangladesh at the wrong end of these rivers when it comes to getting their fair share of desperately needed water. Both nations have negotiated water-sharing treaties with India, but fighting over water resources continues. Despite repeated attempts, India has not been able to negotiate any water-sharing treaties with China.

★ ★ ★

THE YARLUNG TSANGPO (BRAHMAPUTRA) RIVER TOPS THE WORRY LIST FOR BOTH India and Bangladesh because China has begun to dam it. And when China sets out to dam a river, they do not go about it in a small way. India and Bangladesh also fear diversion of the waters of the Tsangpo by Chinese engineers. "So much water in the Yarlung Tsangpo runs out of China, it's a huge waste," says retired general Guo Kai in an interview.[2] Guo Kai is a self-educated hydrologist who collaborated with a colleague, Li Ling, to write a book, *Tibet's Waters Will Save China*, published in China in 2003. The book advocates large-scale water diversion from the Yarlung Tsangpo to parched areas of northern China. Guo makes the astounding claim that

India and Bangladesh get so much rainfall that they suffer from flooding, so if China diverted water from the Tsangpo, all three nations would benefit.

Thus far, no official plans have been announced for diverting the Tsangpo, but then China rarely announces plans anyway. Chinese authorities have been secretive about plans to dam the Yarlung Tsangpo, one of Asia's last major wild rivers. In the early 2000s it was announced that a five-dam cascade would be initiated to the east of Lhasa, in Shannan Prefecture. Zhangmu Dam, on the midreaches of the Tsangpo, is slated for completion in 2015. Located in a gorge 86 miles southeast of Lhasa, at an altitude of 10,700 feet, Zhangmu Dam is expected to generate 540 MW of electricity. Its height is 380 feet and length 1,280 feet. Construction is also under way on 360 MW Gyatsa (Jiacha) Dam and on 510 MW Jiexu Dam.

Why so many dams in this region? They are needed to power nearby mining operations. A copper-gold-silver seam runs across Tibet, paralleling the Tsangpo. Double trouble: pollution of heavy metals from mining operations could easily find its way back into the Tsangpo, with dire consequences downstream.

China blithely assures India and Bangladesh that these are run-of-the-river dams that will have little or no impact downstream. But this dam cascade appears to be just the start of things; up and coming are three more large dams, now in advanced planning stages. Close to Zhangmu is Dagu Dam at 640 MW capacity. Also on the drawing board for the Tsangpo is Bayu Dam at 710 MW. And above the Great Bend, on a tributary known as the Yiwong River, is Zhongyu Dam, which eclipses all these dams at 800 MW capacity. Within Tibet, at least 20 large dams are planned for the Tsangpo River and its tributaries, including the colossal 38 GW Motuo Dam at the Great Bend (described in chapter 3). If Motuo Dam gets under way, the Tsangpo-Brahmaputra River will never be the same again.

India and Bangladesh are highly vulnerable to changes in river flow on the Tsangpo-Brahmaputra, which is the largest river by volume in both nations. In fact, it ranks among the world's top five rivers for greatest average discharge and for greatest sediment load. Swelled by tributaries in

Tibet, Arunachal Pradesh and Sikkim (India), and Bhutan—and eventually joining forces with the Ganges—the Brahmaputra bears huge quantities of nutrient-rich silt. This silt is essential for agriculture—and necessary to bolster the Ganges-Brahmaputra Delta against rising sea levels. Dulal Goswami, an environmental scientist at Guwahati University in Assam, calculates that the Brahmaputra carries around 400 million tons of sediment each year.[3]

It is debatable how much flow for the river in India actually comes from Tibet. Some sources claim only 20 percent of the flow comes from Tibet, while others say it is 40 percent, with tributaries swelling the river on the Indian side providing the main flow. Being upstream, China definitely has the upper hand. It can use water control as a strategic tactic to gain leverage over rival India. There have been intermittent skirmishes between Chinese and Indian troops over territorial claims at the borders of Tibet, but now the battleground appears to have shifted to water politics. And China has its eyes on Arunachal Pradesh.

★ ★ ★

AFTER THE YARLUNG TSANGPO LEAVES TIBET AND ENTERS INDIA, IT FLOWS THROUGH the states of Arunachal Pradesh and Assam, which are blessed with rich biodiversity, supporting a wide range of unusual flora and fauna. These areas are largely tribal, with a great diversity of ethnic groups. Chinese maps routinely claim the Arunachal Pradesh region of northeast India as "south Tibet." And on one particular map—the HydroChina map from Beijing—you can see why. This dam-inventory map indicates the construction of Chinese megadams right in Arunachal. Due to precipitous drops in elevation, the Arunachal region has tremendous potential for hydropower—and it is the focus of India's ambitious megadam construction program.

India is among the world's most prolific dam builders, with an estimated 4,300 large dams. That's significantly short of China's estimated 26,000 large dams, but still significant in comparison with other nations.

As the world's largest democracy, India's megadam-building program has attracted a lot of activist heat. Among the prominent anti-dam campaigners is novelist Arundhati Roy, who argues, "Big Dams are undemocratic. They're a Government's way of accumulating authority (deciding who will get how much water and who will grow what where). They're a brazen means of taking water, land and irrigation away from the poor and gifting it to the rich. Their reservoirs displace huge populations of people leaving them homeless and destitute. Ecologically, they're in the doghouse. They cause floods, water-logging, salinity, they spread disease."[4]

Arundhati Roy claims, "For over half a century we've believed that Big Dams would deliver the people of India from hunger and poverty. The opposite has happened. Big Dams have pushed the country to the brink of a political and ecological emergency. They have uprooted 40 million people, most of them Tribal and Dalit, from their forests and rivers, from lands and homes where they and their ancestors have lived for thousands of years. They have lost everything."[5]

Roy says one-fifth of the population of India—200 million—doesn't have safe drinking water, and two-thirds lack basic sanitation.[6] Half of India still lives below the poverty line (defined as earning less than two dollars a day), and about a third—more than the entire population of the United States—lives on less than a dollar a day.[7] Despite India's extensive dam building, a third of the rural population lacks electricity. For the rural areas that do have access, supply is intermittent and unreliable, with frequent blackouts and load shedding.

Oblivious to its critics, India plans to double its hydro capacity by 2022. The greatest hydro potential is locked in the regions bordering Tibet, in the states of Sikkim and Arunachal Pradesh. Many rivers rise on the Indian side of the Himalayas; others originate in Tibet and are transboundary. India's bizarre response to the threat of China's dam building on the Yarlung Tsangpo is to build dams downstream on Brahmaputra tributaries to "claim" the rivers there. New Delhi argues that if it has to go to the International Court of Justice to counter Chinese dam building and diversion on the Yarlung Tsangpo, then it must show beneficial use of the river in India by building its own dams. Under international law, a country's right over natural resources it shares with other nations becomes stronger if it is already putting these resources to use.

But other motives seem to be at work—corruption, greed, large amounts of money being pocketed. And building 160 large dams is certainly overkill if you want to establish dam presence. In what is thought to be India's largest-ever hydropower venture, proposals call for the building of scores of megadams across Arunachal Pradesh, one of the world's most seismically active regions. Three megadams, each over 2,700 MW capacity, have been proposed on the Siang River, connecting the Tsangpo to the Brahmaputra. Dam plans are being pushed through without proper environmental impact assessments, and without consultation with locals. Total power generation of these 160 proposed dams is estimated to be over 60,000 MW, but the adjoining state of Assam would receive only 50 MW as a royalty. The rest would be transferred out of the region. Megawatts or protein? The staple food of Assam is fish—the key source of protein for over 80 percent of the population. And that is why these dam proposals have generated fierce protest: the All Assam Students Union (AASU) has led a coalition of 40 NGOs and ethnic groups to prevent dam construction.

Unlike China, where anti-dam protest is violently suppressed by military and paramilitary forces, protest in India has managed to cancel some megadam projects or delay them with well-organized campaigns and even hunger strikes. Opposition by the AASU coalition shut down construction of the 2,000 MW Subansiri Dam on a Brahmaputra tributary near the Arunachal-Assam border. Since 2010, protesters have prevented delivery of the turbines for the hydropower project, manufactured by French company Alstom in India. Samujjal Bhattacharya, adviser to the AASU, says, "The people of the north-east will become a pawn in the race between Beijing and New Delhi." Calling each of the megadams a "hydro-bomb," he says, "We are not against development. But if development comes at the cost of the life, security and civilization of the people of Assam, no way would it be allowed."[8]

* * *

LOOKING ON WITH CONSIDERABLE ALARM AT BOTH CHINESE AND INDIAN DAM building in progress on the Brahmaputra and its tributaries is the impoverished nation of Bangladesh. Bangladesh is heavily reliant on the waters of the Brahmaputra (called the Jamuna once it enters the country, but to avoid confusion, the river is still referred to as the Brahmaputra here).

Over 90 percent of Bangladesh's river flows come from waters that originate outside its boundaries. Around 80 percent of Bangladesh's farmers are dependent on water that flows in from India—mainly via the Ganges and Brahmaputra rivers—for irrigation, nutrient-rich silt, and for fisheries. Up to 75 percent of the Bangladeshi diet comes from fish. Rice is a major staple. Put all those statistics together and you can understand why tampering with water flows on the Brahmaputra both in Tibet and in India will significantly impact Bangladesh. Rapid changes in river water levels could lead to disaster, and that could lead to millions of refugees. India has a way of dealing with this: it is building a security barrier to keep Bangladeshis out.

* * *

NORTHWESTERN BANGLADESH, NOVEMBER 2009: AS WE ARE DRIVING ALONG IN the jeep, I spot the fence. This is the barrier that Bangladeshis routinely claim does not exist. It is a six-foot-high double row of wire fencing, topped with barbed wire—the same kind you would expect to find at the perimeter of a prison. India has gone to the immense trouble of building this fence to box in desperate Bangladeshis. We quickly jump from the jeep and manage to snap a few photos before armed security personnel descend, demanding to know what we're doing. We're photographing a nonexistent fence, of course.

How long is the fence? That's not clear because it is still being built. I later found this reference in a *National Geographic* story about Bangladesh: "To block immigration from Bangladesh, India is erecting a six-foot barrier of barbed wire and concrete along the 2,500-mile border."[9] The fence is being erected all the way around Bangladesh, except where major rivers like the Ganges and the Brahmaputra enter Bangladesh from India. Indian security guards have shot and killed Bangladeshis attempting to cross illegally into India. India claims the fence is being built to keep out smugglers, but the real target is refugees.

Bangladesh is mostly flat, and not much is above sea level, especially in the Ganges-Brahmaputra Delta. Embracing an area of 40,540 square miles, the Ganges-Brahmaputra Delta is the world's largest. About two-thirds of the delta lies in Bangladesh, and a third in the adjoining Indian state of West Bengal. The delta includes two megacities: Kolkata (population 16 million) to the east, and Dhaka (population 15 million) to the west. The delta is one of the most densely populated regions on the planet—home to over 100 million people. And more than 300 million people depend on the crops produced here, which in turn rely on nutrient-rich silt coursing in on the rivers from Tibet. That silt, or sediment, performs other very important functions. Inland sediment is swept down by the river over long periods of time and deposited at the mouth of the delta: this process is necessary to maintain the delta and counter strong eroding forces from the ocean. As sediment is withheld by dam-building activity, the Ganges-Brahmaputra Delta is slowly sinking, making it vulnerable to rising sea level. Saltwater intrusion means damage to crops and contamination of groundwater. A sinking delta is highly vulnerable to climate change factors, with recent years seeing an increase in monsoonal flooding and the incidence of extreme climate events like Cyclone Alia, which ripped through the Ganges-Brahmaputra Delta in May 2009, leaving hundreds dead and thousands homeless. In the close future, large areas of Bangladesh could be flooded, mainly due to rising sea level.

Bangladeshi climate scientist Atiq Rahman calls the situation "climate genocide," referring to the potential disastrous flooding of Bangladesh, where large areas of the nation could simply disappear under water. Quoted in a 2008 interview, he says, "From now on, we need to have a system where, for every 10,000 tonnes of carbon you emit, you have to take a Bangladeshi family to live with you. It is your responsibility."[10] Rahman's appeal is directed to Western nations, but in fact the world's top three carbon dioxide emitters, based on 2013 figures, are China, the United States, and India. Under this system, China would have to take in an awful lot of Bangladeshi families, since China burns around half the world's coal. India, another great carbon emitter, wants nothing to do with Bangladeshi refugees, as evidenced by the building of its 2,500-mile barrier.

★   ★   ★

I HAVE COME TO BANGLADESH TO GET A GLIMPSE OF THE FUTURE—TO SEE REFUgees, in fact. In northwestern Bangladesh, they are known as squatters. If future projections hold, Bangladesh will see tens of millions of refugees over the next few decades, for several reasons. It is the most densely populated nation on earth—and its population continues to rise. And yet the land area under cultivation could shrink dramatically due to wide-scale flooding and other factors. Low-lying Bangladesh is under siege from all directions. In the north, glacial meltdown in the Himalayas and monsoon rains cause flooding. In the south, there is saltwater intrusion due to rising sea levels. Increased salinity damages groundwater and crops. Cyclones and tidal surges batter the coast. Bangladesh is considered ground zero for climate change. The nation has tens of millions who scratch out a meager living. Almost half the population of Bangladesh lives below the poverty level—earning less than two dollars a day.

Compounding these problems is the issue of Bangladesh's groundwater. With the intent of improving water supply, millions of tube wells were sunk across Bangladesh by well-meaning agencies like UNICEF and the World Bank, but they tapped into water laced with arsenic, which derives from arsenic-rich bedrock. The result is that tens of thousands of Bangladeshis have been poisoned. Arsenic poisoning is cumulative over the years and leads to premature death. The tube wells have yet to be cleaned up.

Bangladesh is a flat, low-lying nation crisscrossed by more than 300 rivers. Hundreds of islands, called *chars*, are sprinkled in the middle of the rivers, creating a curious topography. The islands—part sediment, part compacted mud, and part sand—are formed from rich sediment coursing down from Tibet and India. *Char* means "river island," but these are glorified sandbars.

Living on shifting sands, squatters lay claim to these tiny islands of sediment to grow crops before they are flooded. In theory, the islands belong to the government, which turns a blind eye and provides no support for squatters living on them. There are estimated to be up to 5 million char dwellers in Bangladesh along the Brahmaputra and its tributaries. There are large numbers of char dwellers on the same river and tributaries in Assam in India. Many islands are destroyed and reformed by flooding each year. The only way to reach the chars is by boat; kayaks enable easy access to these remote islands of sediment.

We've brought two tandem kayaks, which are very stable in the water, especially when weighed down with food and camping supplies. Kayak logistics are in the hands of Jock, who has paddled many rivers in Asia and the Himalayas. We have added two local guides—Gini and Jamal—who can communicate with villagers en route.

We get off to a rough start on this trip. Our kayaks are held to ransom on arrival in Dhaka, which results in a week dedicated to traveling back and forth to the airport, grappling with Bangladesh's legendary graft and corruption merchants. Customs is looking for some kind of special paperwork—in the form of US greenbacks. Things get tangled up in reams of Byzantine bureaucracy. Just when it looks like the kayaks will be released, some obscure document goes "missing" and requires trundling back through ten offices, groveling for the right chops and stamps.

★ ★ ★

BREAKFAST IN BANGLADESH: IN THE MIDDLE OF NOWHERE, AT A SANDY RIVERBANK UP by the Indian border, our campsite attracts a crowd of around 60, pouring in to see the foreigners and their strange red boats. It's a startling introduction to Bangladesh's top problem: *people.* There are far too many of them in this small nation: too many mouths to feed, not enough resources. Not enough water to irrigate the fields of rice, the staple food of the nation. There is talk of introducing population limit measures such as a one-child-per-family stipulation. The head count is over 160 million Bangladeshis, and growing fast.

Crowds of the curious and the excited press in for a closer look at us. Unfortunately, cell-phone reception in this remote part of the north is excellent, and the word has gotten around. The women—all grouped together, young and old—criticize our amateur cooking of eggs and rice. Cheeky boys delight in mimicking our every movement and vocalization. And the men gather to study the marvelous kayaks in great detail.

Due to sandbars and very low water levels, we end up wading down-river a fair bit with the kayaks in tow. Finding the deeper part of the Teesta River and getting lost in the sandbars are our chief preoccupations. The Teesta is sourced in the glacier-fed regions of the Indian Himalayas, but it has been so tapped for irrigation and other uses that it is practically dry in places. That makes it very difficult for fishermen and farmers to make a living. And despite this, there are plans by Indian engineers to build a dozen large dams on the Teesta. So this is what a dying river looks like: you cannot even paddle a kayak along it without hitting a sandbar.

Kayaks are the ultimate icebreakers: people along the river marvel at them. They debate the functions of the kayak parts, deciding that the rear hatch must be the toilet, because Bangladeshi fishing boats have an over-hanging structure at the back that serves this purpose. They are amazed by the blowing of air into the sides of the kayaks to streamline them in the water. They love the lightweight carbon-fiber paddles and are fascinated by our double-paddle technique, since all the local vessels use single oars. And we are equally fascinated by the boats that ply the river: small fishing craft, the odd vessel with a makeshift sail, and the wooden, cross-river ferry boats occasionally loaded with oxen as well as people. Bangladeshis assume that we are surveyors of some sort, as those are the only foreigners they have seen in these parts. So when we stop to take photos or film, they are sure we are surveying for some project.

Bangladeshis touch the open palm to the heart after shaking hands. It is a wonderful custom—denoting the seal of sincerity. We shake many hands along the way, sparking many hand-to-heart gestures. And have many heart-to-heart talks. Once people get over their initial shyness—and their distrust of outsiders—they open up and tell their stories. Erosion constantly eats away at the islands; many families have moved countless times as the sands shift or disappear beneath their feet. This could happen in a month, or it could happen overnight—nobody knows. Sometimes the sandy banks of the river completely collapse, a kind of "sandquake" that demolishes makeshift housing. The chars are scenes of desperate poverty: mud walls, thatched roofs, earth floors. No electricity. The river supplies the running water.

★   ★   ★

AFTER A WEEK OF PADDLING THE TEESTA RIVER, WE ROUND A CORNER INTO A MUCH broader flow of water—the Brahmaputra River. It is odd to think that the river started its journey at Mount Kailash, so far away in Tibet. We paddle on toward Gaibanda, where we make a longer stop at a floating hospital, an extraordinary venture run by the NGO Friendship. In a country that may be subject to large-scale flooding due to the impact of climate change, the floating hospital provides a unique solution for medical outreach. Here, it serves the people of the chars, most of whom have never seen a doctor, let alone a hospital. The floating hospital is the idea of adventurer Yves Marre, who brought in a disused oil barge from France and had it refitted as a hospital. He arranges for weeklong camps to be held, with volunteer teams of specialist doctors flying in from Europe. This week, the emphasis is on eye surgery. The Friendship mandate has expanded into education, vocational training, and micro-investing initiatives among the disadvantaged people of northern Bangladesh.

At Gaibanda we pack up the kayaks and head back for the capital, Dhaka. Later, we catch up with Yves Marre on the outskirts of Dhaka, at a shipyard where he is testing out several new boats. One is a prototype for a stronger fishing vessel that can withstand storms; it is made from layers of jute (a traditional fiber) and high-tech fiberglass. Marre envisages floating solutions to Bangladesh's other pressing problems. "We have started with the floating hospital, but we have many other projects: floating ambulances, floating homes, floating schools, and floating gardens. Everything in Bangladesh will have to float sooner or later," he tells me.[11] He has been working with top French naval designers to produce fast, motorized catamarans that can serve as emergency vessels to handle disaster management and flood relief. Marre outlines plans for a vessel that would enable rapid deployment of small containers loaded with medical and disaster relief supplies in a situation such as a cyclone or storm surge.

Bangladesh is looking to floating solutions to counter imminent flooding. Farmers are switching from keeping chickens to herding ducks, because ducks float. Aquaculture, with farming of fish in ponds or cages, is under development. However, aquaculture comes with its own raft of environmental issues that can affect the delta—from stripping mangroves for shrimp farming to groundwater depletion for fish farming. An intriguing pilot project is the development of freshwater floating gardens, under investigation in southern cities. In prototype models, a raft of bamboo slats is seated on car tires for flotation. Mulch is then added as a floating seed bed to grow cucumber, tomatoes, pumpkin, and cabbage. In liaison with scientists in Japan, researchers are working to create new strains of rice, such as flood-tolerant rice (which can withstand total immersion for two weeks) and saline-resistant strains. Saline-resistant strains are needed because the Ganges-Brahmaputra Delta is experiencing saltwater intrusion, which kills crops and damages groundwater supplies. And the reason for saltwater intrusion may well be that a reduced volume of water and sediment is coming into the delta from both the Brahmaputra and the Ganges rivers.

But can floating gardens, floating schools, and floating homes handle a large-scale refugee crisis in Bangladesh? That seems unlikely given the sheer numbers of people involved. This seems more like a Noah's Ark solution—one that can save a select few, not the masses of humanity.

★ ★ ★

In 2010, Pakistan experienced a large-scale refugee crisis. Over 20 million people were affected when major flooding hit Pakistan. Engorged by unusually heavy monsoon rains, the Indus River, which runs the length of the country, flooded its banks. In the worst flooding in 80 years, more than 1,750 were killed, and 1.8 million homes were destroyed. What is striking about the flooding in Pakistan is that the government proved totally incapable of dealing with a disaster of this scale. The head of the Disaster Relief Authority could only find $6 million to spend on flood relief.[12] The United Nations World Food Programme had to step in to feed millions of Pakistanis affected by the flooding. Flood relief was marred by tribal clashes and by widespread corruption. The cause of the excessive flooding is unclear, but it seems to fit into the pattern of extreme weather that has lashed Asia over the past decades, from deadly cyclones in Burma to vicious tidal surges in Bangladesh.

The fate of Pakistan is bound to the Indus River system. Pakistan is extremely arid, with fertile valleys dependent on two major rivers from Tibet throwing out a lifeline. Sourced close to Mount Kailash, the Indus and Sutlej rivers run across northwestern India before entering Pakistan, where they join for the run to the Indus Delta and merge into the Arabian Sea near the port city of Karachi. The Indus River covers a distance of around 1,800 miles from source to sea. Apart from flooding in 2010, the Indus River has mostly run dry for its last few hundred miles to the sea. The Indus Delta, once an area rich in mangrove swamps and fish, is stagnating and slowly sinking, with half the mangroves gone—along with all the fish. James Syvitski, chairman of the International Geosphere Biosphere Programme, was involved in a study of 33 at-risk deltas worldwide. He claims that dams are predominantly responsible for sinking deltas in Pakistan, India, and Bangladesh. The Indus Delta, he says, has seen an 80 percent reduction in sediment since the early twentieth century, due to extensive damming and canal building along the Indus River.[13] Because freshwater and sediment do not reach the delta in the same volume as before, the sea can advance, bringing with it salt that is deadly to farmland. This has resulted in mass migration out of the Indus Delta.

The Indus River is extremely sensitive to climate-change factors. An estimated 70 to 80 percent of its flow derives from glaciers, the highest proportion of any river in Asia. The Ganges, by comparison, derives around 30 to 40 percent of its flow from glaciers. For this reason, the Indus is expected to see high flow in the first half of the century as glaciers melt down, then receding flow later in the century, then no flow at all. The Indus River waters more than 80 percent of the crops of Pakistan—including rice, wheat, and cotton—through an extensive network of canals, barrages, and dams. Initiated by British colonial engineers, this is the largest irrigated area on the planet.

Due to the importance of the Indus for Pakistan's survival, a water-sharing agreement was negotiated with India in 1960. Pakistan received rights to the Indus River (sourced in Tibet) plus two more tributaries, while India gained rights to the Sutlej River (also sourced in Tibet) and two tributaries. India was quick to lay claim to the power potential of the Sutlej through construction of 1,325 MW Bhakra Dam, completed in 1963.

To understand how geopolitical problems can flare up in relation to rivers and dams, look no further than the northern corner of Pakistan, where its borders meet those of India and China. Since 1947, intermittent wars have been fought over the region of Kashmir, stemming from unresolved border disputes between rivals India and Pakistan. The Indian state of Jammu and Kashmir sits on one side, and on the other lies Pakistan-controlled Kashmir, also known as the Northern Areas. India does not recognize Pakistan's territorial claim and refers to the region as "Pakistan-occupied Kashmir." Across the border from Jammu and Kashmir to the northeast, India claims the 14,400-square-mile desert region of Aksai Chin, which sits in Tibet and has been occupied by China since the 1960s.

Pakistan aims to cement its claim to the disputed territory of the Northern Areas by building megadams in the region in collaboration with large Chinese consortiums. The first of these, the 969 MW Neelum-Jhelum Dam, is under construction by China's Gezhouba Group. It is on the Neelum River, a waterway shared by India, which has its own dam project in the works. However, experts believe that the river can supply energy and irrigation to one side of the border, but not both. Wrangling over the competing dams is ongoing.

On the drawing board for the Northern Areas are more megadams to be built by Chinese consortiums. China has pledged $15 billion to develop this disputed region of Pakistan. Chinese dam building comes with a complete package of financing, Chinese engineers, and scores of Chinese migrant workers. Also part of the package: a large contingent of Chinese military and paramilitary forces to ensure that dam workers are not attacked by militant forces operating in this volatile region. The presence of Chinese troops does not sit well with India, just across the border in Kashmir.

China is extending its influence in Pakistan through the energy sector, building nuclear power plants and coal-fired plants. On the coast of Pakistan, the deep-water port of Gwadar—built and operated by a Chinese company—gives China access to shipping on the Arabian Sea. Gwadar worries India because it could be used by Chinese naval vessels on patrol, extending China's reach in this maritime region.

★ ★ ★

ALSO WORRISOME TO INDIA IS CHINA'S EXPANDING INFLUENCE OVER THE NATION of Nepal. As well as building megadams in Pakistan, Chinese consortiums have an eye on dam construction in Nepal, but here they run into competition from Indian and foreign dam-building consortiums. Because of big drops in elevation in the Himalayan range that forms its northern border, Nepal has huge hydropower potential: it could generate up to 42,000 MW of electricity. Nepal's existing dams are small in scale. Decades of civil war, insurgency, and unrest in Nepal have stymied attempts by foreign dam builders to exploit its vast hydro wealth.

Nepal is a small, landlocked Himalayan nation with a population of 28 million. Sandwiched between the giants of India and China, it has a unique geostrategic position. Once heavily reliant on trade with India, Nepal is now turning to deals with China via road connections through Tibet. China is slowly building a railway westward from Lhasa toward the Nepalese border. In 2005, when India suspended its supply of weapons to the Nepalese army, the Nepalese turned to China for help. The Chinese promptly pledged a million dollars in military aid and dispatched truckloads of weapons overland from Tibet into Nepal. Since then, China has provided extensive military and economic aid to Nepal. As a result of these initiatives, Nepal has bent over backward to fall in line with Chinese ideology. The press is blatantly pro-Chinese. Nepalese police and authorities go to ridiculous lengths to silence the 20,000 exiled Tibetans living in Nepal. Tibetans are not allowed to stage any anti-China protests in Nepal, and may be thrown into jail if they hold demonstrations.

Extensive Chinese assistance with infrastructure and military aid has opened the door to heavy investment by Chinese companies. Chinese dam builders Sinohydro and Three Gorges Project Corporation have shown interest in dam projects in Nepal. Where these corporations tread, Great Walls of Concrete are sure to follow. The Three Gorges Project Corporation has an eye on potential construction of West Seti Dam, on a Karnali River tributary in far western Nepal. West Seti Dam has a projected wall height of 600 feet and output of 750 MW, with most of the power earmarked for export to India. Also under consideration for dam-building potential is the powerful Arun River, which rises in Tibet near Mount Everest. On the Tibetan side, Chinese dam builders have plans for construction of a cascade of dams on the Arun. On the Nepalese side, there are plans for a 600 MW megadam, to be built by an Indian consortium. Other Indian-built mega-dams are in the works for the upper Karnali and upper Marsyangdi rivers. That would spell the end of these rivers for whitewater rafting runs: both rivers are already under siege from smaller dams in operation.

★   ★   ★

COURSING THROUGH NEPAL ARE THREE TRANSBOUNDARY RIVERS THAT FEED INTO India's most sacred river, the Ganges. The Karnali (sourced near Mount Kailash), the Bhote Kosi (sourced near Mount Shishapangma), and the Arun (sourced near Mount Everest) plummet from the Tibetan highlands through deep valleys into Nepal, then onward into India.

The Ganges is not sourced in Tibet; it rises in the Indian Himalayas. As a transboundary river, the Ganges is highlighted here because India is diverting part of its waters close to its border with Bangladesh. At the heart of the matter is water and food security. Like China, India is desperate for water and is grabbing water resources through damming and diversion. India suffers from acute water scarcity, a paradox in a land that is deluged by lengthy monsoon seasons. India's surface water is mostly polluted, and half of its rural water supply could be contaminated with toxic bacteria.[14] In addition, scores of wells sunk by UNICEF and other aid agencies in the 1980s have contributed to fluoride poisoning (due to excessive fluoride dissolving from granite rocks) because the source of the well water was not tested properly.

India is the world's largest groundwater user. Groundwater has been heavily depleted for agricultural use; water tables are falling fast over most of the nation, particularly in central and southern India, where aquifers take thousands of years to be filled. If aquifers are depleted, this could precipitate a major food crisis. Groundwater supplies in major cities like Delhi, Mumbai, and Hyderabad are dangerously low.[15]

China plans to divert water from water-rich Tibet and the southwest to the dry north. India plans to divert water from its water-rich north to its dry south. A big bone of contention between India and Bangladesh is diversion of water along the Ganges for irrigation. At the Farakka Barrage, only 11 miles from the Bangladeshi border, water is partly diverted from the Ganges to feed the parched Hooghly River, which serves the megacity of Kolkata (formerly spelled Calcutta). In 1996, a complex treaty on sharing the Ganges waters at Farakka was concluded between Bangladesh and India, but Bangladesh remains bitter about the deal. Bangladesh claims diversion at the Farakka Barrage dries out not only northwest of the country, but also contributes to drying of the Sundarbans region of the Ganges-Brahmaputra Delta.

★   ★   ★

VARANASI, UTTAR PRADESH, JANUARY 2012: IT'S STANDING ROOM ONLY ON THE *ghats,* the tiered steps leading to the best spots on the Ganges to bathe. Varanasi is one of the oldest pilgrimage sites on the planet, and still going strong. My mid-January visit coincides with the auspicious holy day of Makar Sankranti. Thousands of Indian devotees have poured in from surrounding villages to conduct rituals at the banks of the Ganges; a solid wall of worshippers lines the most popular ghats. Brahmins offer blessings. Yogis smeared in ashes follow their arcane practices. In Indian mythology, Mount Kailash is claimed as the source of the Ganges. According to legend, the goddess Ganga was locked in the matted hair of Lord Shiva, resident at the summit of Kailash. Shiva eventually released her, and she created the flow of the Ganges. The ritual of ablutions in the holy Ganges is one of the most ancient on earth. Devotees make offerings to the goddess Ganga by floating flowers and candles onto the river. And they fill up containers with precious holy water.

It is believed that the goddess Ganga will wash away all sins, which is ironic considering the pollution levels in the river. Here lies a great paradox: the river most sacred to the Hindus across India has not been treated with due respect for its water quality. The banks of the Ganges River are heavily populated and stacked with industrial enterprises. Floating along is a toxic soup of heavy metals resulting from uncontrolled dumping of industrial effluent from the tanneries, factories, and brick kilns that line the Ganges. The river has a fecal coliform count that is off the charts. Taking this into account, do worshippers who visit the Ganges and collect holy water actually drink that water? How can they be so oblivious to the water-pollution problems? It boggles the mind. This is not confined to the Ganges. It's the same horrific problem on rivers in other parts of India and China, and elsewhere in Asia—with very poor controls on sewage, industrial discharge and mining runoff, among other pollutants.

★ ★ ★

KOLKATA, JANUARY 2012: I AM UP AT THE CRACK OF DAWN. IT'S SURPRISINGLY chilly. Under makeshift cardboard shelters on the streets, entire families are huddled together, wrapped in blankets. They are among the tens of thousands living on the streets of Kolkata. Early morning in Kolkata has a surreal edge: on the foggy streets, all is quiet, with no sign of chaotic traffic. Stray dogs rummage in garbage piles. A rickshaw wallah, muffled in a scarf, is warming his hands with hot tea.

My destination is a municipal water-tanker filling station. This facility distributes water to those who have no access. I manage to hitch a ride with one of the water tankers and sit in the front cabin. We drive out to Topsia, a poor area. People are waiting. Lots of people, with plastic containers, buckets, empty vessels. I stand on top of the tanker next to a man with a large hose to take some photos. The hose passes between jostling residents; people get impatient for their turn. An argument breaks out over who gets the hose next, followed by shouting and escalating confrontations. Within 15 minutes, the water tanker is empty and the driver coils up the hose. The residents of the area head home, lugging their precious cargoes of water. We head back to refill the tanker and drive to another area to distribute water.

The water tanker gets me thinking about the future. Kolkata is a city of 16 million—what will it be like by the year 2030? Will there be enough water tankers to go around? What about India? And what will Asia be like by 2030? It occurs to me that future scenarios could have a lot in common with the water tankers of Kolkata: people fighting over water, people getting up in the morning and battling with their neighbors over water. This is a scary future, with urbanized, overpopulated regions, and people desperate for food. Pakistan and Bangladesh fighting with India over diverted water. India fighting with China over water diversion and damming on a grand scale.

★ ★ ★

DUE TO RAPID POPULATION GROWTH IN ASIA, CROP YIELDS NEED TO INCREASE dramatically by 2030, but instead there could be a shortfall due to climate change and depletion of groundwater. Demand for food and energy could soar by 30 or 40 percent. Asia has the most water-intensive agriculture in the world. Demand for water could soar by 50 percent or more.

Throughout Asia, more and more rural people are moving to cities, placing greater demand on water resources. By 2030, it is estimated that over 60 percent of China's population will be urban dwellers, while in India, urban dwellers could compose 40 percent of the population.[16]

The United Nations Environment Programme predicts widespread shortages of water in Asia, Africa, and Europe by 2025; the amount of water available per head of population is expected to decline rapidly. And that drastic decline does not take into account the possible impact of global warming on water supplies, nor the impact of dams. So where will the water come from?

It's hard to predict exactly what will happen by 2030, but one sure result of China's water grabbing, megadam building, mining on the grasslands, and other destructive practices in Tibet will be tens of millions of refugees—not only in the People's Republic of China but also downstream in the Indian subcontinent and Southeast Asia. There are already millions of what China terms "ecological migrants." Mining ventures and dam building have displaced more than 2 million Tibetans. Today the world sees large numbers of refugees from political and economic situations, but the future is going to see a dramatic shift to environmental refugees. Their ranks will include those affected by desertification, soil erosion, crop failures, or simply running out water—as in depleted groundwater or loss of glacial meltwater for agriculture and drinking.

Along with a relentless tide of refugees comes the specter of food crisis. How are these people going to survive? Where will the water and food come from? Who will take the refugees? This promises to be a humanitarian crisis on a scale never before seen. It could become the moral dilemma of the twenty-first century.

CHAPTER TEN

Running Wild in Bhutan

Does Bhutan Hold the Key to a Brighter Future?

*L*anding in the kingdom of Bhutan is rather like being dropped into the Scottish Highlands in medieval times. The country is administered by men in robes and argyle socks from a series of *dzongs* (fortresses), a system dating to the seventeenth century. But Bhutan's late development in terms of infrastructure and technology means that its environment has been well preserved.

Bhutan is light years ahead of its Asian neighbors in its environmental vision—a ray of hope for what could be accomplished in terms of preservation. The quixotic nation has become the environmental innovator of Asia: it has banned plastic bags and banished tobacco smoking. In 2009 at the Climate Change Conference in Copenhagen, Bhutan pledged to remain carbon neutral. Bhutan claims to be a net sink for greenhouse gases, saying that it absorbs more carbon in forests than it emits from fossil fuels. In 2013, to reduce oil imports, the Bhutanese government struck a deal with Nissan of Japan to bring in electric vehicles for all officials and taxi drivers in the capital, Thimphu. Bhutan aims to extend the program across the nation in its quest for zero emissions.[1]

Bhutan lies on the edge of the Tibetan Plateau just south of Tibet, bordering India. With an area of 18,147 square miles, the country is roughly the size of Switzerland—and seeks to be just as politically neutral. Bhutan has pledged in its constitution to maintain a 60 percent forest cover, and 25 percent of its land area is set aside for national parks or wildlife sanctuaries. Parks are patrolled by rangers, with strong protection laws in place and stiff penalties for poaching animals or logging in protected areas.

The kingdom of Bhutan has some tremendous advantages over its neighbors. Its population is tiny—under a million. Its people do not need to be convinced about the value of conservation: they follow a sect of Tibetan Buddhism that imbues respect for nature. There is minimal mining and industry, so no real sources of pollution. Here's the lucky part: Bhutan has abundant water resources. Most of its rivers rise on the Bhutanese side of the Himalayan range, although a few transboundary rivers course in from Tibet. Bhutan's real bliss is having full control of its water resources and not having to deal with China: most of Bhutan's economy is linked to India.

There is, however, a potential spanner in the works for Bhutan: hydropower. Bhutan has risen out of poverty without selling off its natural resources like timber, but now seeks to bolster its economy by building dams to produce hydropower for export to India. Here, Bhutan is at a crossroads. Small dams, properly maintained and operated, would have minimal impact. Bhutan uses mini-hydroelectric plants for its own power supply: these are usually run-of-the-river design. Small dams have been constructed in Bhutan with Indian engineering and financing, such as 40 MW Basocho Dam, 60 MW Kurichu Dam, and 126 MW Dagachu Dam. But some larger dams have been built as well, such as 336 MW Chukha Dam and 1,020 MW Tala Dam, both on the same river a few miles apart. Via sales of hydropower to India, these dams are the biggest earners of revenue for Bhutan—a sort of Gross National Hydro. Another megadam, 1,200 MW Punatsangchu, is under construction. The kingdom of Bhutan has signed agreements to provide a minimum 5,000 MW of hydropower to India by 2020. It remains to be seen whether Bhutan can manage hydropower in a way that does not damage its pristine environment.

★ ★ ★

JIGME DORJI NATIONAL PARK, JUNE 2005: MONSOON IN BHUTAN MEANS slippery trails, high rivers, bridges washed away, biting gnats, and leeches. But it also means blue poppies. The only time they flower is during the monsoon rains, from May to July. The blue poppy is the national flower of Bhutan, but that doesn't mean it's easy to find.

And this is what I have set my heart on doing: seeing the rare blue poppy in its remote, high-altitude mountain habitat. Inspiration comes from reading accounts of early twentieth-century Western plant hunters who came to the foothills of the Himalayas in search of gems like the blue poppy as ornamental flowers for European gardens. Five of the 12 blue poppy species growing across the Himalayas are found in Bhutan.

One advantage of trekking in the monsoon season quickly becomes apparent: you have the entire trail to yourself. It's a muggy day in early June, and we are heading into Jigme Dorji National Park, the largest protected area in Bhutan. We plan to complete a 20-day loop of the national park, starting in Paro, a tiny town in the west of the country, and ending east of Thimphu, the capital. "We" means two Canadian trekkers: Eric, an old friend I have talked into joining this expedition, and myself. Eric always dreamed about hiking in the Himalayas, a dream that has been somewhat dampened on this trip by sporadic monsoon downpours. When it rains, it sometimes pours for hours. This is like being thrown into the deep end.

But Eric takes it all in stride and has adapted remarkably well. He is, however, having trouble coming to terms with our unwieldy entourage: a dozen horses and mules, two horse handlers, guide, cook, and assistant. He thinks 1,700 pounds of supplies is a tad over the top. For minimal environmental impact, Bhutanese regulations stipulate that trekking outfits must carry everything they need. It's a pack in, pack out policy: any outfit found dumping garbage stands to lose its operating license.

Jigme Dorji National Park is pristine and remote, with sparse settlements of subsistence farmers in the lowlands and yak and livestock herders in the highlands. Even when villages are encountered, trekkers pass the nights in their own tents at designated campsites. Most of the load is camping gear and food. The rice alone weighs 170 pounds. And there are nine pounds of chilies for our crew. The Bhutanese are very fond of spicy dishes.

We toil upward, through scented pine and oak forests with cypress, spruce, juniper, and birch trees evident. More than 6,000 plant species have been identified in Bhutan, including an astonishing 360 orchid species. In fact, the entire country can be considered to be one great park. Bhutan's poppy species range from smaller varieties in high meadows to taller varieties that grow above the tree line in high-alpine scree. Other rare poppies sighted in Bhutan include the white poppy, the red poppy, and the yellow poppy. This is my second trekking trip to Bhutan. The initial trip merely whetted my appetite for the country's natural beauty, its wildlife and its flora.

Because of a late monsoon arrival, there's a terrific bonus: the rhododendrons are still out in full force. They present a glorious sight as they carpet entire mountainsides with varieties ranging from tiny to tree-sized, including the beautiful, red-flowering *ethometho*. Close to 50 species of rhododendron have been identified in Bhutan. With the rhododendrons in flower, the country turns into a plant lover's paradise. The vastness and silence are broken by birdcalls. In this national park, there are more than 30 mammal species, including takins, snow leopards, musk deer, and Himalayan black bears.

Wildlife is not only protected in Bhutan, it is revered. A striking illustration of this is the protection of the iconic black-necked crane. Every year as winter approaches, some 300 black-necked cranes fly in from Tibet to winter in Bhutan. They descend on wetlands of Phobjikha Valley, to the east side of the country. Phobjikha Conservation Area, covering 63 square miles, has been set aside for the cranes. There are strong protection laws in place: killing a crane in Bhutan could result in a life-term prison sentence. To welcome the cranes, a festival is held at Gangtey Monastery in November. Children wearing crane costumes perform dances, and environmental conservation dramas are enacted.

There are more than 320 bird species in Jigme Dorji National Park (out of 700-plus avian species listed in Bhutan). Tenzin, our guide, has the uncanny ability to spot birds without the aid of binoculars—we zero in on rare species like the ibisbill. This gull-size bird with a gray body and red bill is perfectly camouflaged in the gray rocks of a riverbed, and it's only from its peculiar call that Tenzin is able to locate it. He tells me that he once escorted a birder who spent ten years looking for the ibisbill, and finally arranged to come to Bhutan to see it.

Settling into the rhythm of trekking, you soon develop into a formidable walking machine, and you develop an enormous appetite to keep that machine going. Although the pack animals are carrying the load, and we have only camera gear in daypacks, the elevation proves grueling enough. After several days of arduous trekking on slippery slopes, our small party reaches 11,500 feet, the merciful elevation where the bugs disappear. By the time we get to the Chomolhari region, most plant species have disappeared too. The trees are long gone. But small alpine flowers still flourish, as well as mosses and lichens.

Breakfast in Bhutan: The crew tuck into *ema datsi* (chilies and cheese) while we dine on an array of toast, marmalade, eggs, porridge, fruit juice, and tea laid out on a folding table. This breakfast is a legacy of early British presence in Bhutan. The packhorses are liable to wander over and stick their heads in the porridge if you are not watchful, or if you get distracted by the stupendous views—this morning, it's the snow-capped peak of Chomolhari, a brooding colossus of 23,997 feet.

It has been a long haul this far, but after a week we have finally reached the likely habitat of the blue poppy. Climbing up to a high-altitude lake at 13,450 feet, we sight blue sheep and ruddy shelducks. A mist descends over the lake, reducing visibility to a few yards. The mist turns moody, swirling around. I am about to turn back to camp when, out the corner of my eye, I spot a trace of blue. The mysterious blue poppy has finally surfaced. In such a bleak environment, the flower makes a fantastic sight—a turquoise gem set in a gray landscape. It stands three feet tall and juts out of alpine scree, with snow-capped peaks looming. You wonder how the plant could possibly survive such conditions, let alone produce a gorgeous deep-blue flower. But this hardy alpine poppy can withstand freezing temperatures. It has been observed with its stem hairs encased in ice.

I am gazing at a flower that was once considered to be as mythical as the yeti. Although the blue poppy was identified as early as the 1850s, it was not until 1913 that British explorer Frederic Bailey plucked one in the Tsangpo region of eastern Tibet and pressed it between the pages of a notebook. The specimen was named *Meconopsis baileyi* after him: it aroused considerable interest in Britain. Bailey was a butterfly collector, not a botanist. A decade later in 1924, following precise directions given by Bailey, botanist Frank Kingdon-Ward collected seeds and is credited with introducing the blue poppy to European gardens. In fact, Europeans went crazy over the poppies from the Himalayas. Poppy expert Bill Terry explains why: "Among plants, none display such a palette of primary colors as the Asiatic poppies. There is no red redder than the red of *punicea*, no yellow more buttery than *integrifolia*. The white of *superba* is whiter than white. The imperial purples of *lancifolia* and *delavayi* are unmatched. No blue can compare with the blue of a perfect *grandis* or *betonicifolia*."[2]

Bailey also discovered a huge white poppy (*Meconopsis superba*) while riding into Bhutan through the Ha district in 1922. But the blue poppy remained elusive—its presence in Bhutan was not confirmed until 1933, when British botanist George Sherriff collected specimens in the mountains of Sakteng, at the far eastern border of Bhutan. This variety of blue poppy is known as *Meconopsis grandis*, today the national flower of Bhutan. The seeds that George Sherriff sent back to England flowered in cultivation, and not only that—they cross-fertilized with other species, producing new blue poppy hybrids. In the wilds of Bhutan the different poppy species rarely "meet," so natural hybrids are rare.

Another day of trekking brings us over a high pass to the Lingshi Valley, which is famed for its huge variety of mountain flowers and herbs. Botanists and flower lovers come from as far afield as England or Japan to see these floral wonders. We run into some Bhutanese collectors gathering herbs for the National Institute of Traditional Medicine in Thimphu. They tell me that several rhododendron and blue poppy species are used in traditional medicines.

High on the hillsides above Lingshi, sharp-eyed Tenzin points in excitement to a clump of vegetation. He has found not one blue poppy, but an entire cluster of them. Most blue poppies bear four or five petals, but a larger flower here bears nine petals. It is a thrilling sight, the ultimate reward for undertaking this monsoon quest. The rarity of the blue poppy lies in its fleeting beauty. This variety flowers only once, then seeds and dies. But there is one way to make the bloom last longer—by capturing it on film.

The blue poppy, to my mind, is symbolic of the Tibetan Plateau alpine ecosystem: rare, special, beautiful, fragile, easily damaged. Here in Bhutan, the environment is preserved in a way that no longer happens in Tibet. Plant species thrive, birds thrive, wildlife thrives, forest cover is extensive, national parks are fully protected, environmental laws are strictly enforced. And the rivers run wild and free in Bhutan—for the moment. It's glorious to see, yet it makes me feel sad about the fate of Tibet, lying just across the border from Jigme Dorji National Park.

★ ★ ★

BHUTAN'S ENVIRONMENTAL PATH EVOLVED FROM THE TIBETAN BUDDHIST CONCEPT of sacred landscape: mountains, rivers, lakes, and forests to be left untouched. The world's highest unclimbed peak, Gangkar Punsum, lies within Bhutan, with no plans to allow it to be trammeled by the boots of mountaineers. The same elements present in Bhutan today—very low population; wild rivers and plentiful water resources; abundant wildlife and avian life—were all present in pre-1950 independent Tibet. And I can't help thinking that if the Dalai Lama were still in power, Tibet would be preserved as a region of spectacular natural beauty. Today, restoring full autonomy to Tibetans within the PRC would go a long way toward resolving Asia's water problems. Tibetans would once again be stewards of the Tibetan plateau's mountains, rivers and grasslands—as they have been for thousands of years.

Tibet not only has the grandest mountain scenery on earth with its Himalayan giants of Everest and Cho Oyu, but also the deepest canyons on the planet. The Yarlung Tsangpo gorges are more than double the depth of Arizona's Grand Canyon, where both the Colorado River and canyon were set aside as a national park in 1919. And yet Tibet's magnificent gorges, like those on the Yarlung Tsangpo and the Salween rivers, have been given no such protection.

In 1968, the US government passed into law the Wild and Scenic Rivers Act, guaranteeing protection for certain rivers—or long sections of rivers—with outstanding natural, cultural, or recreational value. The initial act spared eight rivers. The official National Wild and Scenic Rivers System website explains that as of 2011, it protects 12,598 miles on 203 rivers, but this is less than one-quarter of 1 percent of the nation's rivers. By comparison, dams across the country have modified at least 600,000 miles, or about 17 percent, of American rivers.[3]

Today there has been a remarkable shift in thinking about dams in the United States that constitutes a quiet revolution. When they first appeared in the early twentieth century, megadams were glorified as marvels of engineering and the key to efficient energy. But as time passed and the long-term environmental impact of large dams on riverine ecosystems became more evident, attitudes changed. As large dams age and silt up, reaching the end of their lifespan, a number are not being replaced: they are being demolished. The United States is at the center of a movement for freshwater ecological restoration. More than 800 dams have been decommissioned in the last few decades, and thousands more could follow.[4] Once concrete barriers are removed, rivers return to robust health in short order, and millions of fish return to spawn. In 2007, Marmot Dam on the Sandy River in Oregon was removed, giving scientists a chance for close observation. Though Marmot is a small dam, demolition released vast amounts of rocks, sand, and gravel that had accumulated in its reservoir. The river was allowed to process the deluge of sediment itself; some models predicted that it would take years for the river to do this, but it scoured the sediment away in a matter of months. Coho salmon swam upriver the day the dam crumbled. Removal of the aging dam was highly successful in restoring upstream access for Pacific salmon and steelhead trout, feeding an entire food chain and supplying nutrients for plant life.

For Asia, a shift of thinking on rivers and dams is more than an environmental concern: it's a matter of survival. In 2007, the World Wildlife Fund UK published a report, "The World's Top 10 Rivers at Risk."[5] Five of those rivers are in Asia: the Yangtse, Mekong, Salween, Ganges, and Indus. Major risk factors identified include dams, pollution, overextraction, overfishing, and climate change.

For water and food security in Asia, it is essential that Tibet's rivers are not dammed or diverted—and not tainted by pollution from mining. Preserving rivers sourced in Tibet—or lengthy sections of those rivers—to run free is critical for the well-being of the region's ecosystems. Overshadowed by the effects of glacial meltdown, the health of these rivers is of vital concern to all the nations of Asia. Environmental reporter Fred Pearce states the case for international action: "We badly need international law to protect downstream nations—something the UN agreed was necessary a decade ago but has never acted on. But even more, we need international initiatives to protect the ecological integrity of the world's last great wild rivers."[6]

Water Justice

Negotiating Water-Sharing Agreements for Tibet's Rivers

*T*oday, by building megadams and reservoirs in its borderlands, China is working to reengineer the flows of major rivers that are the lifelines of the nations downstream.

Indian geopolitical analyst Brahma Chellaney sums up the situation: "By having its hand on Asia's water tap, China is therefore acquiring tremendous leverage over its neighbours' behaviour. That the country controlling the headwaters of major Asian rivers is also a rising superpower, with a muscular confidence increasingly on open display, only compounds the need for international pressure on Beijing to halt its appropriation of shared waters and accept some form of institutionalised co-operation."[1]

There are river water-sharing treaties in place between India and Pakistan, and between India and Bangladesh. So why can't China be held accountable for its reckless use of water resources, and be brought to the negotiating table to make river water-sharing agreements with nations downstream?

Unfortunately, not even India—in face-to-face talks in Beijing—has been able to negotiate any water-sharing agreements for transboundary rivers such as the Tsangpo-Brahmaputra. The best India has been able to do is to obtain hydrological data from China for certain rivers. Worse still, China has never consulted lower riparian states before undertaking dam construction upstream. China was one of only three countries that voted against the adoption of the United Nations Convention on the Law of Non-Navigational Uses of International Watercourse. In rejecting this 1997 UN Watercourses Convention (UNWC), which lays down rules on shared resources, Beijing asserted its claim that an upstream power has the right to assert absolute territorial sovereignty over the waters on its side of the international boundary—or the right to divert as much water as it wishes for its needs, irrespective of the effects on nations downstream.

Thirty-five signatures were needed for the UNWC to be ratified. In mid-2014, the convention obtained its thirty-fifth signature, from Vietnam, and came into force on August 17, 2014. The UN moves in slow and mysterious ways: it took 17 years for this global treaty to come into force. Such is the level of mistrust among Asian nations that only two have signed: Vietnam and Uzbekistan. Essentially, this makes the UNWC non-binding for the entire region of Asia.

It is imperative that Asia's transboundary water issues be addressed—before they lead to major problems. Following is an appeal emailed to representatives of the nations downstream from Tibet:

World Water Day, 22 March 2013
c/o International Tibet Network
1310 Fillmore Street, #401
San Francisco, CA 94115, USA

To: Environment Ministers of the Governments of India, Pakistan, Cambodia, Laos, Bhutan, Nepal, Bangladesh, Burma, Thailand and Vietnam.

cc Mrs. Irina Bokuva, Director General, UNESCO

Your Excellencies,

Today is World Water Day 2013 in the United Nations International Year of Water Cooperation. We are writing to share our concerns about the impact of China's policies—especially its dam-building programme—on Asia's regional water security, and to urge your government to join forces with other downstream nations to pressure China to enter into appropriate water-sharing agreements.

Over the last sixty years, China's policies in Tibet, often called the earth's "Third Pole" and the source of Asia's great rivers, have led to wide-scale environmental degradation. This includes poisoned river and groundwater through unregulated mining, grasslands ecosystem degradation, and disrupted watershed and ecosystem services in the headwaters of these rivers, which has worsened already acute and chronic flooding downstream from Tibet, including your countries. In turn, global climate change is warming the Tibetan Plateau at twice the rate of the rest of the world, and the impact of this on Asia's water supplies is exacerbated by China's extensive dam-building programme, to harness hydro-power and divert water to mainland China. This programme threatens the safety, security, and sustainable livelihoods of more than one billion people downstream.

By claiming authority over the Water Tower of Asia, China is wielding considerable power over its neighbouring countries, yet it has not signed a single-water sharing agreement. We urge you to act now to secure your future water supplies, by joining together with your counterparts in other

nations downstream of the Tibetan Plateau, and bring China to the negotiating table to sign appropriate regional and international water-sharing
agreements.

Yours faithfully,
Ms. Dhardon Sharling,
Co Chair, on behalf of the International Tibet
Network Secretariat, Tibetan Women's Association and
Tibet Justice Centre

Links

SPECIAL EVENTS

International Day of Action for Rivers

Held annually on March 14; hosted by NGO International Rivers.You can look at a world map to find local activists and activities anywhere from India to Thailand.
www.internationalrivers.org/international-day-of-action-for-rivers/

Tibet Rivers Day

Calling all water warriors! Spinning off from the International Rivers Day of Action, find a Tibet group or create one yourself to celebrate Tibet Rivers Day, on March 10. Become a "yaktivist" and lobby to keep Tibet's rivers free flowing and free from pollution.

World Water Day

Held annually on March 22, this is a UN initiative to raise awareness about water issues.
www.unwater.org/water-cooperation-2013/events/world-water-day/en/

Earth Day

Celebrated worldwide on April 22 each year, Earth Day raises awareness about the environment. Eco-activists see this day as an opportunity to focus on urgent issues and problems. Tibet presents a raft of urgent environmental issues—but these mostly go unreported or under-reported in Western media.
www.earthday.org

World Environment Day

Staged annually on June 5, this event encourages worldwide awareness and action for the environment.
www.unep.org/wed/

World Rivers Day

Held on the last Sunday of September, a Canadian-based initiative that strives to encourage public awareness and encourages improved stewardship of all the rivers around the world. www.worldriversday.com/

CAMPAIGNS

www.internationalrivers.org
International Rivers is a California-based organization that campaigns to save rivers worldwide and stop megadam building; features a China campaign section. Lots of resources and links to other groups such as burmariversnetwork.org and salweenwatch. org/. Through the International Rivers website, you can find a link to a short documentary called Damocracy, which debunks the myth of dams as clean energy, and raises awareness of the impact of monster dams on culture, nature, and people.

www.waterkeeper.org
The Waterkeeper Alliance pushes for the right to clean water on a worldwide basis. There are chapters in China, India, Bangladesh, and Nepal.

www.studentsforafreetibet.org
SFT is a chapter-based network of young people and activists around the world, particularly strong at university campuses. Through education, grassroots organizing, and nonviolent direct action, SFT campaigns on many fronts concerning Tibet, including environmental issues such as mining.

www.savetibet.org
Washington-based International Campaign for Tibet focuses on human rights in Tibet. The long-running NGO has branches in London, Amsterdam, Berlin, and Brussels. Among its many initiatives, ICT monitors and reports on human rights, the environment, and socio-economic conditions in Tibet.

www.Tibet3rdpole.org
An incentive backed by 170 members of the International Tibet Network (www.tibetnet-work.org), advocating fundamental human rights of Tibetans to environmental self-determination as they seek to adapt to climate change.

www.thethirdpole.net
With the main focus is on understanding Asia's water crisis, this website is a project of chinadialogue.net in partnership with Earth Journalism Network. The website provides accurate information and analysis and fosters constructive debate about vital resources from across the region.

www.tibetnature.net/en/
Dharamsala-based site Tibet Nature Environmental Conservation Network has some unique Tibetan takes on the environment.

INTERACTIVE DAM SITES

www.internationalrivers.org/worldsrivers/
The State of the World's Rivers is a brilliant interactive database, comparing ecological health indicators on 50 major river basins. Created by the NGO International Rivers, the database covers river basins sourced from the Tibetan plateau. Turn on the Dam Hotspots filter for a clearer view of dams.

www.dameffects.org
Basic dam impacts: explore the components of healthy rivers—and what happens when a dam is built—at this interactive website.

nationalgeographic.com/geoguide/dams/index.html
Geoguide Dams is an interactive educational website from National Geographic that looks at rivers before, during, and after dam construction.

GLOBAL WATER CRISIS

environment.nationalgeographic.com/environment/freshwater
Freshwater initiative from National Geographic, with a wealth of material on the global water crisis—articles from experts, photos, video, maps, and other media.

www.circleofblue.org
Reporting on the global water crisis, this superb site is backed by water expert Peter Gleick, who runs the Pacific Institute. There are informative sections devoted to Asia, such as Choke Point: China and Choke Point: India.

www.blueplanetproject.net
The Blue Planet Project is a civil society movement begun by the Council of Canadians to protect the world's freshwater from the growing threats of trade and privatization. The project was founded by leading water activist Maude Barlow.

www.rfa.org/english/news/special/thewaterproject/home.html
The Water Project is a brief investigation of drinking water in Asia by Radio Free Asia with photos, video, and links to news stories. Can you survive as a farmer in Asia, dealing with water shortages? To find out, visit the water survival interactive game on this site.

Notes

WHY TIBET MATTERS

1. Dalai Lama, essay in *Heaven and Earth and I, Ethics of Nature Conservation in Asia*, eds.Vivek Menon and Masayuki Sakamoto (New Delhi: Penguin Enterprise, 2002), 20.

CHOPPING TIBET IN HALF

1. "Forestry in Tibet: Problems and Solutions," Tibet Environment Watch, 1996, http://www.tew.org/background/forestry.html.
2. William Laurance, "China's Appetite for Wood Takes a Heavy Toll on Forests," *Yale Environment 360*, November 17, 2011, http://e360.yale.edu/feature/chinas_appetite_for_wood_takes_a_heavy_toll_on_forests/2465/.
3. Ibid.
4. Dalai Lama, *Ancient Wisdom, Modern World: Ethics for the New Millennium* (London: Little, Brown, 1999), 195.
5. Dalai Lama, essay in *Heaven and Earth and I, Ethics of Nature Conservation in Asia*, eds.Vivek Menon and Masayuki Sakamoto (New Delhi: Penguin Enterprise, 2002), 21.

1   RAFTING THE DRIGUNG

1. "China Hikes Defense Budget, to Spend More on Internal Security," Reuters Beijing, March 5, 2013, http://www.reuters.com/article/2013/03/05/us-china-parliament-defence-idUSBRE92403620130305.
2. "China's Challenge: Social Disorder," *Economic Observer*, February 28, 2011, http://www.eeo.com.cn/ens/feature/2011/05/09/200868.shtml. The article gives figures according to Chinese sources. The statistics are unreliable. I went for conservative estimate at 90,000 mass incidents for 2010. Other sources variously give 120,000 and 180,000 mass incidents for 2010.
3. "Does Bombardier's Code of Ethics Include Cultural Genocide?" Press release, Free Tibet, September 13, 2005, http://freetibet.org/news-media/pr/does-bombardiers-code-ethics-include-cultural-genocide.

2   CRISIS AT THE THIRD POLE

1. Rebecca Kessler, "The Most Extreme Migration on Earth?" *Science News*, June 7, 2011, http://news.sciencemag.org/biology/2011/06/most-extreme-migration-earth.
2. Brook Larmer, "The Big Melt," *National Geographic*, April 2010.
3. Ibid.
4. "Black Carbon Deposits on Himalayan Ice Threaten Earth's Third Pole," NASA report, December 14, 2009, http://www.nasa.gov/topics/earth/features/carbon-pole.html.

5. Larmer, "The Big Melt."
6. Henry Pollack, *A World Without Ice* (New York: Penguin, 2010), preface.
7. "It Takes Passion . . . And Patience: High-Altitude Climber Describes Lessons Learned by 'Listening' to the Mountain," remarks delivered at H. B. Johnson Jr. '26 Distinguished Lecture Series, Virginia Military Institute, October 14, 2013, http://staging.vmi.edu/Content.aspx?id=10737425992.
8. Justin Gillis, "Climate Panel Cites Near Certainty on Warming," *New York Times*, August 19, 2013, http://www.nytimes.com/2013/08/20/science/earth/extremely-likely-that-human-activity-is-driving-climate-change-panel-finds.html?pagewanted=all&_r=0.
9. "Black Carbon Deposits on Himalayan Ice Threaten Earth's Third Pole."
10. Ibid.
11. According to a report released January 27, 2014, in the journal *Proceedings of the National Academy of Sciences*, Beijing. Reported by Laura Poppick, "Black Carbon Soot Greater in China, India Than Thought," LiveScience, January 27, 2014, http://www.livescience.com/42872-black-carbon-exposure.html.
12. Veerabhadran Ramanathan is an atmospheric scientist at the Scripps Institution of Oceanography in La Jolla, California. Cited from an article by Jane Qiu, "The Science of the Third Pole," *Nature* 454 (2008): 393–396, republished at EcoBuddhism.org, http://www.ecobuddhism.org/bcp/all_content/3rd_pole/stp.
13. Statistics from the Global Carbon Project, http://www.globalcarbonproject.org/carbonbudget/13/hl-full.htm.
14. Katie Auth, "Record High for Global Greenhouse Gas Emissions," Vital Signs, November 27, 2013, http://vitalsigns.worldwatch.org/vs-trend/record-high-global-greenhouse-gas-emissions.
15. Bryan Walsh, "Greenhouse Effect: CO_2 Concentrations Set to Hit Record High of 400 PPM," *Time*, May 2, 2013, http://science.time.com/2013/05/02/greenhouse-effect-co2-concentrations-set-to-hit-record-high/.
16. Fen Montaigne for Yale Environment 360, "Record 400ppm CO_2 Milestone 'Feels Like We're Moving Into Another Era,'" *The Guardian*, May 14, 2013, http://www.theguardian.com/environment/2013/may/14/record-400ppm-co2-carbon-emissions.
17. Lester R. Brown, "Rising Temperatures Melting Away Global Food Security," Earth Policy Institute, July 6, 2011, http://www.earthpolicy.org/book_bytes/2011/wotech4_ss3.
18. "China's Power Sector Heads toward Cleaner Future," Bloomberg Newswatch, August 27, 2013, http://about.bnef.com/press-releases/chinas-power-sector-heads-towards-a-cleaner-future/.
19. See 2011 chart from US Energy Information Administration, "China Consumes Nearly as Much Coal as the Rest of the World Combined," US Energy Information Administration, January 29, 2013, http://www.eia.gov/todayinenergy/detail.cfm?id=9751.
20. "Chewang Norphel—the Glacier Builder," *The Alternative* (India), January 2, 2013, http://thealternative.in/environment/chewang-norphel-the-glacier-builder/.
21. John Stanley, "Climate Breakdown at the Third Pole: Tibet," in *A Buddhist Response to the Climate Emergency* (Somerville, MA: Wisdom Publications, 2009).
22. Information is from 2009 Air Quality Index: "A Guide to Air Quality and Your Health," brochure from the Environmental Protection Agency, August 2009, http://www.epa.gov/airnow/aqi_brochure_08-09.pdf.
23. Tania Branigan, "Top Tip if You're Going Out in Beijing: Don't Breathe," *Guardian*, January 13, 2013, http://www.theguardian.com/world/2013/jan/13/beijing-breathe-pollution.
24. Li Jing, "Dust Storms and Smog Revisit Streets of Beijing," *South China Morning Post*, March 10, 2013, http://www.scmp.com/news/china/article/1187348/dust-storms-and-smog-revisit-streets-beijing.
25. Christina Larsen, "Tibet's Climate Is Getting Wetter, British and Chinese Scientists Report," *Bloomberg Businessweek*, February 12, 2014, http://www.businessweek.com/articles/2014-02-12/tibets-climate-getting-wetter-british-and-chinese-scientists-report.

3   VALLEYS OF THE DAMMED

1. Bei Hu, "Li Peng's Daughter in Top Power Post," *South China Morning Post*, December 30, 2002, http://www.scmp.com/article/402006/li-pengs-daughter-top-power-post.

2. "Dam the Consequences," *Guardian*, April 6, 2007, http://www.theguardian.com/world/2007/apr/06/outlook.development.

3. "Dammed Rivers, Damned Lives: The Case Against Large Dams," report, International Rivers, 2008, http://www.internationalrivers.org/files/attached-files/irfactsheet_dammed_rivers_lores.pdf.

4. HydroChina Corporation dam inventory map, circa 2003, http://www.hydrochina.com.cn/zgsd/images/ziyuan_b.gif. The map is in Chinese only. The same map has been duplicated with English key and annotations, and can be viewed at http://www.meltdownintibet.com/f_maps_hydrochina.htm.

5. Jonathan Watts, "Chinese Engineers Propose World's Biggest Hydro-Electric Project in Tibet," *Guardian*, May 24, 2010, http://www.theguardian.com/environment/2010/may/24/chinese-hydroengineers-propose-tibet-dam.

6. Ibid.

7. Ibid.

8. Ngo The Vinh, "Global Ecology and the Made in China Dams," Viet Ecology Foundation, July 20, 2010, www.vietecology.org; article appears in Vietnamese language. Available in English via PDF at http://www.livingriversiam.org/4river-tran/4mk/mek_ae18.pdf.

9. Jonathan Watts, *When a Billion Chinese Jump* (New York: Scribner, 2010), 68.

10. Roni Jacobson, "World's Largest Solar Array Set to Crank out 250 MW of Sunshine Power," *Scientific American*, May 9, 2014, http://www.scientificamerican.com/article/world-s-largest-solar-array-set-to-crank-out-290-megawatts-of-sunshine-power/.

11. Tashi Tsering, author interview, summer 2009.

12. "Dam Protest in Tawu County," *Tibet News Digest*, May 24, 2009, http://www.tibetinfonet.net/content/news/11028.

13. "Tibetan Land Seized For Migrant Workers," Tibet Environment Watch, May 6, 2012, http://www.tew.org/archived/2012/06052012_2.htm.

14. Andrew Jacobs, "Tibetan Environmentalist Receives 15-Year Sentence," *New York Times*, June 24, 2010, http://www.nytimes.com/2010/06/25/world/asia/25tibet.html?_r=0.

15. "Three Parallel Rivers of Yunnan Protected Areas," UNESCO World Heritage List, http://whc.unesco.org/en/list/1083.

16. Ibid.

17. Andrew Jacobs, "Plans to Harness China River's Power Threaten a Region," *New York Times*, May 4, 2013, http://www.nytimes.com/2013/05/05/world/asia/plans-to-harness-chinas-nu-river-threaten-a-region.html?_r=0.

18. John Jackson, "Earthquake Hazards and Large Dams in Western China," Probe International, April 2012, http://probeinternational.org/library/wp-content/uploads/2012/04/JohnJacksonFinalReport.pdf.

19. Wang Shanshan, "Three Gorges Dam in Good Shape Despite Quake," *China Daily*, June 2, 2008, http://www.chinadaily.com.cn/china/2008–06/02/content_6727258.htm.

20. Material drawn from several sources, including Fred Pearce, *When the Rivers Run Dry* (Boston: Beacon Press, 2006), 149.

21. "Chinese Criticize State Firm Behind Three Gorges Dam Over Graft Probe," Reuters, February 28, 2014, http://www.reuters.com/article/2014/02/28/us-china-corruption-dam-idUSBREA1R0AJ20140228.

22. Wang Ru, "Battling Against the Current," *China Daily*, July 7, 2011, http://www.chinadaily.com.cn/cndy/2011–07/07/content_12851040.htm.

23. Michael Wines, "China Proceeds on Plans for Disputed Yangtze Dam," *New York Times*, December 29, 2011, http://www.nytimes.com/2011/12/30/world/asia/china-moves-ahead-with-plan-for-dam.html?_r=2&.

24. Katy Yan, "China's Domestic Dam Plans Draw Ire At Home and Abroad," *World Rivers Review*, March 2013, http://www.internationalrivers.org/resources/china%E2%80%99s-domestic-dam-plans-draw-ire-at-home-and-abroad-7882.

25. Ibid.

26. "About Us: Message from Chairman," PowerChina, updated June 27, 2013, http://en.powerchina.cn/2013–06/27/content_16671474.htm.

27. Figures for Bakun Dam are taken from the International Rivers website, http://www.internationalrivers.org/campaigns/bakun-dam.

4 STEALING WATER

1. Gong Jing, "China's Thirst for Water Transfer," *China Dialogue*, January 10, 2012, https://www.chinadialogue.net/article/show/single/en/4722-China-s-thirst-for-water-transfer.

2. Xuyang Jingjing, "Making Rivers Run North," *Global Times*, June 28, 2011, http://www.globaltimes.cn/content/663664.shtml.

3. Elizabeth Economy, "China's Growing Water Crisis, *World Politics Review*, August 9, 2011, http://www.worldpoliticsreview.com/articles/9684/chinas-growing-water-crisis.

4. Keith Schneider, "Choke Point: China—Confronting Water Scarcity and Energy Demand in the World's Largest Country," Circle of Blue, February 16, 2011, http://www.circleofblue.org/waternews/2011/world/choke-point-chinaconfronting-water-scarcity-and-energy-demand-in-the-worlds-largest-country/.

5. "Thirsty China," China Water Risk, 2006, http://chinawaterrisk.org/wp-content/uploads/2011/04/Thirsty-China.pdf.

6. Brook Larmer, "Bitter Waters," *National Geographic*, May 2008.

7. Emily Ford, "28,000 Rivers Vanish From Chinese Map," *Times* (UK), March 29, 2013, http://www.thetimes.co.uk/tto/environment/article3725724.ece.

8. Margaret Wente, "The Real Cost of China Rising," *Globe and Mail*, November 2, 2010, http://www.theglobeandmail.com/globe-debate/the-real-cost-of-china-rising/article1391284/.

9. Diversion figures come from the official South-to-North Water Diversion website. http://www.nsbd.gov.cn/zx/english/wrp.htm.

10. "Water: All Dried Up," *Economist*, October 12, 2013.

11. Quoted from the official government website for the South-to-North Water Diversion project, http://www.nsbd.gov.cn/zx/english/wrp.htm.

12. Yellow River Conservancy Commission website, appearing in Chinese language only, but you can request translation to English via Google Chrome or other browser; http://www.yellowriver.gov.cn/hdpt/wypl/201302/t20130217_128113.html.

13. Details about Ringang are drawn from several sources, including Alex McKay, *Tibet and British Raj* (London: Routledge, 1997).

14. For more information, see Hannah Pearce, "Sacrilege for Power," *Down to Earth*, November 15, 1996, http://www.downtoearth.org.in/node/27011. In *Death of a Sacred Lake* , a recent briefing on Yamdrok and its significance, the UK-based Free Tibet Campaign (FTC) alleges that both these companies have a long track record constructing controversial dam projects such as the Pak Mun dam in Thailand (where 20,000 people were forcibly moved from their land), the Cirata dam in Indonesia (where an estimated 60,000 people were dispossessed) and the Mosul dam in the Kurdish region of northern Iraq (built in an area more or less forcibly cleared of local inhabitants by the military). Despite these claims and the controversy over Yamdrok Tso, neither company has ever tried to justify their involvement in the scheme either to Tibetan or environmental advocacy groups in Europe and elsewhere.

15. Maude Barlow, *The Global Water Crisis* (Toronto: McLelland and Stewart, 2007), 99.

5   VANISHING NOMADS, VANISHING GRASSLANDS

1. Tenzin Norbu, author interview, Dharamsala, November 2010. All subsequent quotes are from this interview.
2. "Three Tibetan Monks Detained for Freeing Yaks Headed to Slaughter," *Radio Free Asia*, February 19, 2014, http://www.rfa.org/english/news/tibet/yaks-02192014162424.html.
3. "Tibet Ecology Declines," *Shanghai Daily*, December 27, 2005, http://www .shanghaidaily.com/news2007/20051227/231566.
4. Jonathan Watts, "Tibetan Nomads Struggle as Grasslands Disappear from the Roof of the World," *Guardian*, September 2, 2010, http://www.theguardian.com/environment/2010/sep/02/tibetan -plateau-climate-change.
5. Julia A. Klein, John Harte, and Xin-Quan Zhao, "Experimental Warming, Not Grazing, Decreases Rangeland Quality on the Tibetan Plateau," *Ecological Applications* 17, no. 2 (2007): 541–557, http://www.case.edu/affil/tibet/documents/JuliaKleinpaper.pdf.
6. Hao Xin, "A Green Fervor Sweeps the Qinghai-Tibet Plateau," *Science* 321 (August 1, 2008): 633–635, http://www-vhosts.tis.cwru.edu/affil/tibet/documents/xin.pdf.
7. Dan Miller, *Drokpa: Nomads of the Tibetan Plateau and Himalaya* (Kathmandu: Vajra Publications, 2008), 129.
8. Ibid.
9. Olivier De Schutter, "Report of the Special Rapporteur on the Right to Food: Mission to China," UN Human Rights Council, 2012, http://www.srfood.org/images/stories/pdf/ officialreports/20120306_china_en.pdf.
10. Tsering Woeser, "The 'Mani Stones' in an Environmental Migrants Village," Tibet service of Radio Free Asia, September 27, 2012. English translation appears at http://highpeakspureearth .com/2013/the-mani-stones-in-an-environmental-migrants-village-by-woeser/.
11. Ibid.
12. Dan Winkler, "Yartsa Gunbu Harvest 2013," *Mushroaming*, March 6, 2014, http://mushroaming. com/content/yartsa-gunbu-harvest-2013.

6   PAPER PARKS, THEME PARKS

1. "Mount Everest Litter Targeted by Nepalese Authorities," Climate Himalaya, March 3, 2014, http://chimalaya.org/2014/03/03/mount-everest-litter-targeted-by-nepalese-authorities/.
2. "Tibet Has China's Largest Proportion of Nature Reserves," *People's Online Daily*, May 17, 2013, http://chinatibet.people.com.cn/8249012.html.
3. Emily Yeh, "Do China's Nature Reserves Only Exist on Paper?" China Dialogue, February 3, 2014, https://www.chinadialogue.net/article/show/single/en/6696-Do-China-s-nature-reserves -only-exist-on-paper-.
4. "Many Chinese National Parks, Reserves Fail To Protect Environment," Radio Free Asia, February 7, 2014, http://www.rfa.org/english/news/china/environment-02072014103456.html.
5. Chris Buckley, "Tibet Prepares Plan to Fight Environmental Hazards," Reuters, June 20, 2008, http://uk.reuters.com/article/2008/06/22/us-china-tibet-idUKPEK21099620080622.
6. George Schaller, *Tibet Wild* (Washington, DC: Island Press, 2012).
7. Ibid.
8. Ibid.
9. *Making Green Development a Choice: China Human Development Report 2002*, United Nations Development Programme, China, http://www.cn.undp.org/content/dam/china/docs/Publications /UNDP-CH-HD-Publication-HDR-2002.pdf.
10. Jane Macartney, "Green Grass of Steppes Falls Victim to West's Stampede for Cashmere," *Times*, August 8, 2009.
11. "Mongolia's Cashmere Industry," Mongolia Briefing, February 24, 2012, http://mongolia -briefing.com/news/2012/02/mongolias-cashmere-industry.html.

12. Keith Bradsher, "After China's Rare Earth Embargo, a New Calculus," *New York Times*, October 29, 2010, http://www.nytimes.com/2010/10/30/business/global/30rare.html?pagewanted =all&_r=0.

13. Harrison Jacobs, "This Chinese City Has Been Devastated by Pollution," *Business Insider*, September 27, 2013, http://www.businessinsider.com/chinese-pollution-photos-2013–9 #ixzz2gEvANmAI.

14. Jonathan Watts, "Gobi Mega-mine Puts Mongolia on Brink of World's Greatest Resource Boom," *Guardian*, November 7, 2011, http://www.theguardian.com/environment/2011/nov/07/gobi-mega -mine-mongolia.

7   PLUNDERING THE TREASURE HOUSE

1. Wang Jun, "A Mining Miracle," China.org, August 30, 2012, http://www.china.org.cn/environment /2012–08/30/content_26381624.htm.

2. Ibid.

3. Ibid.

4. Ibid.

5. "Tibet's Water Pollution and China's 'Global Warming, '"original article appeared on Radio Free Asia, November 19, 2009, and on Woeser's blog in Chinese, December 16, 2009. The English translation is taken from http://highpeakspureearth.com/2009/tibets-water-pollution-and-chinas -global-warming-by-woeser/.

6. Ibid.

7. "Songtsen Gampo's Hometown Is About To Be Completely Excavated," original version appeared on Radio Free Asia on April 14, 2010, and on Woeser's blog in Chinese. The English translation is taken from http://highpeakspureearth.com/2010/songtsen-gampos-hometown-is -about-to-be-completely-excavated-by-woeser/.

8. "Lhasa's Mining Disaster Clearly Shows the Contamination of the Water Supply Will Continue," first appearing on Radio Free Asia in Tibetan in April 2013, and on Woeser's blog in Chinese. The English translation is taken from http://highpeakspureearth.com/2013/lhasas-mining-disaster -clearly-shows-the-contamination-of-the-water-supply-will-continue-by-woeser/.

9. Gabriel Lafitte, *Spoiling Tibet* (London: Zed Books, 2013).

10. "Bill Gates and Warren Buffet Unveil the New BYD Car Model," YouTube video, 2:14, uploaded on June 20, 2011 by How Tech TV, http://www.youtube.com/watch?v=rwVo9cdwbB4.

11. Mark Mackinnon, "Living the Worry-Free Life in China's 'Atomic City,'" *Globe and Mail*, August 13, 2010, http://www.theglobeandmail.com/news/world/living-the-worry-free-life-in-chinas -atomic-city/article1377097/.

12. The original version appeared on Radio Free Asia, August 17, 2011. The English translation is from http://highpeakspureearth.com/2011/impoverished-mato-county-by-woeser/.

13. Tsering Tsomo, author interview, Dharamsala, November 2013. All subsequent quotes are from this interview.

14. The English translation is from http://highpeakspureearth.com/2012/poetry-series-straying -far-from-myself-part-5/.

15. Jonathan Kaiman, "Tibet Self-immolations," *Guardian*, October 17, 2013, http://www.theguardian .com/world/2013/oct/17/tibet-self-immolation-book-woeser-ai-weiwei.

16. Material is taken from report, "'Absurd and Terrifying' New Regulations Escalate Drive to Criminalize Self-Immolations by Targeting Family, Villagers," International Campaign for Tibet, posted February 24, 2014, http://www.savetibet.org/absurd-and-terrifying-new-regulations -escalate-drive-to-criminalize-self-immolations-by-targeting-family-villagers-monasteries/.

17. Tibet 2013 Human Rights Report, International Campaign for Tibet, posted February 27, 2014, http://www.savetibet.org/state-department-report-on-human-rights-2013/.

18. Annual Report: Human Rights Situation in Tibet (Dharamsala, January 2013), 68.

19. "Free Tibet: Machine Guns Used against Environmental Protesters," YouTube video, 1:27, posted by Free Tibet on October 29, 2013, http://www.youtube.com/watch?v=7–6lQyzAi24.

20. Tsering Woeser, "If They Obstruct Mining, Monasteries Will Be Closed and Villagers Arrested," first appearing on Radio Free Asia, June 22, 2013. English version can be viewed at: http://highpeakspureearth.com/2013/chamdo-if-they-obstruct-mining-monasteries-will-be-closed-and-villagers-arrested-by-woeser/.

21. Peiyue Li, Hui Qian, and Jianhua Wu, "Environment: Accelerate Research on Land Creation," Nature, June 4, 2014. http://www.nature.com/news/environment-accelerate-research-on-land-creation-1.15327#/b8

22. Ibid.

23. Ibid.

8 DOWNSTREAM BLUES

1. Nayantara Narayanan, "Dams Responsible for South Asia's Sinking Deltas," The Third Pole, May 6, 2014, http://www.thethirdpole.net/dams-responsible-for-south-asias-sinking-deltas/.

2. Tania Branigan, "One-third of China's Yellow River 'Unfit for Drinking or Agriculture,'" Guardian, November 25, 2008, http://www.theguardian.com/environment/2008/nov/25/water-china.

3. Ma Jun, cited in "Thirsty China: Its Key Resource Constraint Is Water," Water Risk PDF, 2006, http://chinawaterrisk.org/wp-content/uploads/2011/04/Thirsty-China.pdf.

4. "China Risks Environmental Collapse," Washington Post, March 12, 2006, http://www.washingtonpost.com/wp-dyn/content/article/2006/03/11/AR2006031101258.html.

5. Susan Jakes, "When the Yellow River Runs Red," Time, October 24, 2006, http://content.time.com/time/world/article/0,8599,1550046,00.html#ixzz2vA1uSZjz.

6. "China Says More Than 3m Hectares of Land Too Polluted to Farm," South China Morning Post, December 30, 2013, http://www.scmp.com/news/china/article/1393107/china-says-more-3-million-hectares-land-too-polluted-farm.

7. "China Finds 100,000kg of Poisoned Dead Fish in River," Guardian, September 4, 2013, http://www.theguardian.com/world/2013/sep/04/china-poisoned-fish-river.

8. Steve Hirsch, "China's Shadow Looms Over the Mekong," Radio Free Asia, February 4, 2010, http://www.rfa.org/english/news/china/mekong-04022010162623.html.

9. Fred Pearce, When the Rivers Run Dry (Boston: Beacon Press, 2006), 103.

10. Fred Pearce, "The Damming of the Mekong: Major Blow to an Epic River," International Rivers, June 16, 2009, http://www.internationalrivers.org/resources/the-damming-of-the-mekong-major-blow-to-an-epic-river-2813.

11. "Dams or Drought: An Interview," Radio Free Asia, August 24, 2010, http://www.rfa.org/english/news/china/osborne-08232010150911.html.

12. "Cambodia's Snake Slaughter," Geographical Magazine (UK), January 2007, http://www.geographical.co.uk/Magazine/Cambodian_snake_slaughter_-_Jan_07.html.

13. "The Salween River Basin Fact Sheet," International Rivers, May 2012, http://www.internationalrivers.org/resources/the-salween-river-basin-fact-sheet-7481.

14. Information from the Burma Rivers Network website, http://burmariversnetwork.org/index.php/dam-projects/irrawaddynmaimali.

9 HIMALAYAN WATER WARS

1. John Vidal, "China and India 'Water Grab' Dams Put Ecology of Himalayas in Danger," Observer, August 10, 2013, http://www.theguardian.com/global-development/2013/aug/10/china-india-water-grab-dams-himalayas-danger.

2. Xuyang Jingjing, "Making Rivers Run North," Global Times, June 28, 2011, http://www.globaltimes.cn/content/663664.shtml.

3. Jane Qiu, "Flood of Protest Hits Indian Dams," Nature, December 5, 2012, http://www.nature.com/news/flood-of-protest-hits-indian-dams-1.11932.

4. Arundhati Roy, "The Greater Common Good," *World Rivers Review*, vol. 14, no. 4, August 1999, http://www.internationalrivers.org/files/attached-files/wrr.v14.n4.pdf.

5. Arundhati Roy, "Insist on Hope," editorial commentary, *World Rivers Review*, vol. 14, no. 4, August 1999, http://www.internationalrivers.org/files/attached-files/wrr.v14.n4.pdf.

6. Ibid.

7. Jacob Baynham, "India's Development Paradox," *E-International Relations*, February 2, 2009, http://www.e-ir.info/2009/02/02/indias-development-paradox/.

8. Tannoy Sharma, "Fighting India's Mega-dams," *China Dialogue*, March 9, 2012, https://www.chinadialogue.net/article/4799-Fighting-India-s-mega-dams.

9. Don Belt, "The Coming Storm," *National Geographic*, May 2011.

10. Atiq Rahman, interviewed in *The Independent* (Dhaka), June 20, 2008.

11. Yves Marre, author interview, November 2009.

12. "After the Deluge," *Economist*, September 18, 2010.

13. Nayantara Narayanan, "Dams Responsible for South Asia's Sinking Deltas," The Third Pole, May 6, 2014, http://www.thethirdpole.net/dams-responsible-for-south-asias-sinking-deltas/.

14. Gardiner Harris, "Rains or Not, India Is Falling Short on Drinkable Water," *New York Times*, March 12, 2013, http://www.nytimes.com/2013/03/13/world/asia/rains-or-not-india-is-falling-short-on-drinkable-water.html?_r=1&.

15. "Delhi Groundwater May Run Dry in 3–5 Yrs: Study," *Economic Times*, December 19, 2012, http://articles.economictimes.indiatimes.com/2012-12-19/news/35912438_1_ngri-water-levels-delhi-groundwater.

16. According to a report released January 27, 2014, in the journal *Proceedings of the National Academy of Sciences*, Beijing, http://www.livescience.com/42872-black-carbon-exposure.html.

10   RUNNING WILD IN BHUTAN

1. "Bhutan Partners With Automaker Nissan In Carbon-Neutral Quest," February 25, 2014, http://tcktcktck.org/2014/02/bhutan-partners-automaker-nissan-carbon-neutral-quest/60693.

2. Bill Terry, *Blue Heaven* (British Columbia, Canada: Touchwood Editions, 2009), 29.

3. National Wild and Scenic Rivers System website, http://www.rivers.gov/wsr-act.php.

4. Thomas O'Keefe, "Report On Dam Removal in the Pacific Northwest Published," American Whitewater, January 7, 2011, http://www.americanwhitewater.org/content/Article/view/id/30920/.

5. C. M. Wong, C. E. Williams, J. Pittock, U. Collier, and P. Schelle, "World's Top 10 Rivers at Risk," World Wildlife Fund UK Report, March 2007, http://www.unwater.org/downloads/worldstop10riversatriskfinalmarch13_1.pdf.

6. Fred Pearce, "Damming the Mekong—Major Blow to an Epic River," *Yale Environment 360*, June 16, 2009, http://e360.yale.edu/feature/the_damming_of_the_mekong_major_blow_to_an_epic_river/2162/.

WATER JUSTICE

1. Brahma Chellaney, "Water Is the New Weapon in Beijing's Armoury," *Financial Times*, August 30, 2011.

Acknowledgments

My heartfelt thanks go to all those who have assisted with this project, through direct interviews, commentary, providing insights, or setting me on the right path for research. It is testament to the silencing powers of China that many of these sources prefer to remain anonymous. In Tibet and China, prime sources are not identified for safety reasons. In Tibet, much was decoded by courageous guides and others who knew what they said could land them in jail. And yet, they did not hesitate to talk about China's repressive policies in Tibet—and policies leading to destruction of the environment. In nations like Burma, a similar situation prevails under a repressive regime. And in the West, others wish to remain anonymous due to ongoing connections with Tibet. Thanks to Photographers Anonymous for input, and Marcus Rhinelander for the dam photos.

A big high-five to the kayakers who supplied details about rivers and megadams in Tibet, which set things in motion for research. In Dharamsala, India, special thanks to Tenzin Norbu, Jigme Norbu, Tempa Gyaltsen Zamlha, and Tsering Tsomo for interview material. In Bangladesh, thanks to Yves Marre for hospitality, to Jock for expedition expertise, and to Gini for guiding. On the ground, local knowledge proved invaluable, especially with guides Tenzin in Bhutan and Vanna in Cambodia. For research insights, my gratitude to Tashi Tsering, Gabriel Lafitte, Claude Arpi, and Jean-Claude Buhrer. A constant source of motivation was updating a travel guide to Tibet: many thanks to the editors at Bradt Travel Guides in the UK who made that possible. Specialized research for this book was also motivated by the making of short documentaries, which saw the light of day through the dedication of hard-working producer Petr Sevcik, who is no stranger to repressive regimes.

This book would not have made it into print without the perseverance of my agent, Kelly Falconer of Asia Literary Agency, and the skilled direction of Elisabeth Dyssegaard at Palgrave Macmillan, who saw the potential for this work and encouraged me to forge ahead with the manuscript. And finally, kudos to those who inspired this book in the first place— the Tibetans. They are remarkable people with an extraordinary heritage—a heritage that is sadly in danger of disappearing. We have much to learn from their vision of sacred landscape, and their great respect for wildlife—and wild places.

Index

A-bomb testing, 152
Aba, 19
ABB, 54
Adak, Rungye, 100
Africa, 72, 145, 171, 187, 213
Ahai Dam, 64
Ai Wei Wei, 158
Air China, 86
Air Quality Index (AQI), 37–8
air pollution, 33–8
"airpocalypse," 36–7
AK-47, 176
Aksai Chin, 207
All Assam Students Union (AASU), 197
Alstom, 54
altitude, 5, 13, 16, 22, 23–7, 30–1, 36, 51–3, 57, 61, 86, 95, 98, 111, 116, 124, 177, 194, 217, 220
Amdo (northeast Tibet), 5, 24, 101–2, 104, 158, 162, 171
Angkor, 181–2
animism, 25, 58, 81–4, 141, 149, 157, 161–2
Antarctic, 2, 27–8, 32
aquifers, 210
Aral Sea, 78
Arctic, 2, 27–8, 32, 39–50, 122
Argentina, 171
Arjin Shan Reserve, 123
arsenic poisoning, 162, 201
"artificial glaciers," 36
Arun River, 209
Arunachal Pradesh, 189, 194–7
Assam, 51, 195, 197–8, 201
Aufschnaiter, Peter, 82
Australia, 15, 98–100, 145, 171
Avatar (film), 149

Bailey, Frederic, 220–1
Baker, Ian, 48
Bakun Dam, 72–3
Banduo, 52
Bangladesh, 1, 6, 39, 48, 51, 167–8, 190, 193–4, 198–206, 209–10, 212, 225–6, 229; and aquaculture, 203–5;

and *chars* ("river island"), 201; and climate change, 200–1; and corruption, 201–2; and fence, 198–200; and floating solutions, 203–5; and ground water, 200–1; and hand-to-heart gesture, 203; and overpopulation, 202–3; and "sandquakes," 203
Banqiao Dam disaster (1975), 66–7
bar-headed goose, 8–9, 24
Barkhor Bazaar, 126, 128
Barlow, Maude, 87
Beijing, 21–2, 32, 37–8, 47, 61–2, 68, 78, 86–7, 105, 125–7, 133, 142, 158, 195, 197, 225–6
Beijing International School, 38
Bhakra Dam, 207
Bhattacharya, Samujjal, 197
Bhote Kosi, 87–8, 209
Bhutan, 1, 30, 84, 100, 189, 194–5, 215–24, 226; and blue poppy, 217–22; and dams, 216–17; and electric vehicles, 215–16; and environmental awareness, 215–20; and Jigme Dorji National Park, 217–22; and Phobjikha Conservation Area, 219; and rhododendrons, 218–19; and Tibetan Buddhism, 222; and water resources, 216; and wildlife, 218–19
"big-noses," 14
Bill C-300 (Corporate Accountability Act or Responsible Mining Bill), 146
birds, 176–7
black carbon, 31–40
black-necked cranes, 9, 20, 83–4, 116, 219
blue poppy, 217–22
blue sheep, 9, 157, 220
Bohai Pipeline, 76
Bohai Sea, 76
Bombardier, 22
Bon (animist faith), 25, 141; *see* animism
Borneo, 7, 72–3
Bosshard, Peter, 51
bottled water, 22, 86–7
Bradt Travel Guides, 14
Brahmaputra, 48, 167, 175, 190–9, 201, 203, 205, 210, 225; *see* Yarlung Tsangpo

Brazil, 171

British India, 82

Brown, Lester, 35

Brunei, 90

Bruno Manser Fund, 72–3

Buckley, Michael, ix–x

Buddhism, 6–7, 11, 26, 36, 101, 104, 109, 143, 145–6, 187, 216, 222; *see* Tibetan Buddhism

Buffet, Warren, 150

Burma (Myanmar), 1, 7, 39, 52, 62, 72, 89, 165, 167–9, 172–4, 183–7, 190, 205, 226, 229; exploitation of, 183–7

BYD, 150

Cambodia, 1, 72, 168–9, 172, 176–83, 190

Cambodia's Royal Group, 182

Canada, 22, 57, 88, 146–7; and mining, 146–7

Cao Guangjing, 66

Cao Junji, 32

"Captain Ram," 15–7

carbon dioxide, 3, 31–7, 40, 45, 49–50, 70, 92, 130–1, 150, 200, 203, 215; atmospheric, 34–5; and black carbon, 31–2; and largest carbon emitters, 31–4; *see* black carbon

cashmere, 98–9, 121–2, 131–5

cashmere goat, 98, 131–5

Central Tibet, 6

Changtang National Nature Reserve, 121–3

Changu Dam, 66

Chellaney, Brahma, 165, 225

Cheng Xiaotao, 75

Chime Namgyal, 60

China: and air pollution, 33–8; and ethnic unrest, 20; grasslands of, 104–5; and imported food, 171; and internal security budget, 19–20; as largest carbon emitter, 33–4; and meat consumption, 99, 168; and middle class, 168; and military-industrial complex, 19–20, 56–8, 207; population of, 75–6; and secrecy, 18–19, 58, 71–3, 84–5; and social oppression, 18–20, 60–1, 100–1, 126–7; and surveillance, 100–1, 126–7; *see* damming; mining; water stealing

China Central Television, 59

China Daily, 66

China Gold Group, 144

China Gold International Resources, 146

China's Great Wall Motors plans, 150–1

China Human Development Report (2002), 130

China's Hydrolancang International Energy, 182

China Institute of Water Resources and Hydropower Research, 75

China's National Academy of Science, 55

China National Gold Group, 146

China Power International Development, 44

China Railway Express, 86

China Society for Hydropower Engineering, 49

Chinalco, 162

Chinese Academy's Institute of Tibetan Plateau

Research, 28

Chinese Academy of Sciences in Beijing, 32

Chinese Buddhism, 11

Chinese caterpillar fungus (*Cordyceps siniensis*), 111

Chinese Communist Party (CCP), 19, 35, 67, 86, 146

Cho Oyu, 212

Clad, James, 173

clean energy, access to, 33; *see* black carbon

climate change, 2, 13–5, 27–31, 33–4, 36, 40, 49, 57, 77, 83, 92, 105, 112, 120, 131–2, 169, 175, 179, 199–206, 212–3, 215, 223, 228; *see* black carbon; damming; glacial melting; insects; mining; monsoon; refugees; sea level rise

Climate Change Conference in Copenhagen (2009), 215

cloud-seeding, 36

coal, 13, 31–8, 50, 52–3, 70, 76, 80, 89, 112, 120, 134, 151, 161, 197, 200, 298

Conservation International, 119

Construction Crane, 9

Convention on Biological Biodiversity (1992), 108–9

crop yields, 169, 212–13

cuckoo mushroom, 111

cultural genocide, 72–3, 91–2

Cultural Revolution, 145–6

Cyclone Alia (2009), 199

Daduqia, 48

Dai Qing, 55, 67

Dalai Lama, ix–x, 3, 5, 8, 19, 83, 100, 106, 128, 150, 158, 212; message from, vii–viii

damming (Tibet/China), 2, 13–14, 17–18, 21–2, 41, 43–73, 75, 79–81, 84–5, 88–90, 91–2, 104, 106–7, 118–20, 123–6, 141, 154, 159–63, 165, 167–87, 189–90, 193–9, 202, 206–9, 212–13, 216–17, 222–3, 225–7, 228, 229; and Cambodia, 176–9; cascade of, 65–8, 194; and cultural genocide, 72–3; and earthquakes, 64–5; and environmental wreckage, 49–51; and fish, 68–9; and human rights, 45–6, 60, 72–3; and India, 195–7; and indigenous populations, 45–6, 63, 72–3; and land grabs, 58, 67; and Mao Zedong, 54–5; and mining, 194; and mudslides, 64–5; and protesters, 63–4; and risks, 64–7; and secrecy, 58, 71–3; and technology and foreign nations, 53; and U.S., 222–3; *see* hydropower

deforestation, 2–3, 6–7, 34, 25, 72–3, 120, 134, 187, 196

desertification, 2–3, 76–7, 83, 131–5, 156, 213

Dhaka, 199–201, 204

Dharamsala, 101–2

Dingboche, 30

"dirty" glaciers, 32–3; *see* black carbon

documentary making, 88, 90, 92, 96, 203

Drigung River, 15–8

Drolma La pass, 27

Dunhuang caves (Gansu), 11

Dynamic Shangri-La, 124–5

INDEX

Earth Prize, 60
earthquakes, 50–1, 64–6, 71, 161, 190
ecocide, 13, 41
Ecological Buddhism, 36
"ecological migrants," 91, 109–10, 213
ecosystem collapse, and mining, 139–63; *see* mining
electric vehicles, 150, 215–16
Electricity Generation Authority of Thailand (EGAT), 194
ELIN, 64
environmental impact assessment (EIA), 64, 68, 71–2
Ethnic Tibet, 5–6, 20, 61, 63, 101, 158–61

Facebook, 19, 142, 248
Fan Xiao, 64, 76
Fenghuoshan, 21
fertilizers, 50, 77, 106, 168–9, 179, 221
5100 Tibet Glacier Spring Water, 86–7
fish, 68–9, 168–73, 178
Fisher, Richard, 48
floating solutions, 180–1, 203–5
flora, 6, 61–2, 217–21
flooding, 7, 30, 66, 180, 196, 203–5
fluoride poisoning, 210
food security, 2, 35, 45, 167–87, 190, 209, 223–4
Ford Motor Company, 60
Foreign Correspondents' Club (Bangkok, Thailand), 88–9
fossil fuels, 13, 32–5, 215
Free Tibet Campaign, 22
Friends of the Earth Hong Kong, 60
Friends of Nature, 71
Friendship (NGO), 203–4
Friendship Bridge, 78
Fukushima, 2

Galashan Tunnel, 20–1
Ganges, 2, 88, 166–7, 175, 190, 192, 195, 198–9, 205–6, 209–11, 223
Ganges-Brahmaputra Delta, 167, 175, 192, 195, 199–200, 205,
Gansu, 5–6
Ganzi Prefecture, 85
garbage, 25, 116–17, 129, 211–12, 218
Gates, Bill, 150
gazelle (Tibetan), 8
General Electric in India, 83
General Electric USA, 22, 54
genocide, 13, 22, 72–3, 92, 200
geothermal energy, 35, 57
Gezhouba Group, 207
"Ghangjong," the Land of Snows, 27
Ghonkar ("Rugby Boy"), 81–2
glacial lake outburst floods, 30
glacial lakes, 29–30, 83–7
glacial melting, 2, 27–36, 39–40, 70, 83–7, 105, 119, 200, 213, 224; *see* black carbon
glaciers, 2, 11, 14, 23, 26–36, 39–40, 70, 83–7, 105,
119, 130, 161, 169, 200, 202, 206, 213, 224; and
"artificial glaciers," 36; and "dirty" glaciers, 32–3;
and flooding, 29–30, 70; listening to, 11, 29–30;
and survival, 29–30
Global Carbon Project, 34
Globe and Mail (Toronto), 77, 153
Gobi Desert, 38, 133–5
Goes, Frederic, 177
Golok nomad, 101–2
Golmud-to-Lhasa railway, 21
Gongkar, 20, 112
Google, 100
Google Earth, 30, 47, 149–51
Goswami, Dulal, 195
Grand Canal, 54, 68
Grand Canyon, 48, 222
grasslands of Tibet, 2–3, 7–9, 13–14, 25, 38, 77, 90–113,
116–21, 130–5, 140–1, 152, 156–7, 161, 170, 213,
222, 226–7; and carbon, 130–1; and China, 104–5;
and "ecological migrants," 91; future of, 130–1;
and grazing, 105–6; and Mongolia, 131–5; and
predators, 106–7
Great Bend, 47–51, 194
Great Britain/British, 14, 82, 87, 101, 124, 135, 191,
193, 206, 219–21
Great Famine in China (1959 to 1962), 55, 106
Great Leap Forward, 55
Great Sparrow Campaign, 55
Great Wall, 46, 54
"Great Walls of Concrete," 46–7, 67, 72, 209
Greater Tibet, 5
Green Earth Volunteers, 62, 105
Green Watershed, 63
greenhouse gas, 3, 32–3, 40, 49, 162, 169, 215
greenwashing, 116–21
groundwater, 1, 28, 45, 75, 77, 86, 153, 154, 168, 190,
199–201, 204–5, 210, 212–13, 226–7
Guangzhou, 53, 76, 127
Guardian, 49
Guo Kai, 193–4
Guo Qiaoyu, 68
Guwahati University in Assam, 195
Gwadar, 208
Gyama mine, 139–44, 146

Han Chinese, 61, 132, 142–3
Hansen, James, 32
Harbin, 31
Harrer, Heinrich, 82
Hatgyi Dam, 184
Hawaii, 34
Hengduan Mountains, 23, 61
Hilton, James, 124
Himalaya Natural Mineral Water, 86
Himalayas, 2, 6, 9, 13, 23, 26, 28–33, 39, 48–9, 57, 81,
84, 86, 101, 111, 162, 165, 189–213, 216–22; and
water wars, 189–213
Hong Kong, 38

242

Hoover Dam, 53
horses, 8, 27, 92–100, 112, 132, 134, 192, 218–9
Hu Jintao, 56
Huaneng Group, 44–5, 182
Huatailong Mining Group, 140–4
human rights, 45–6, 60–1, 69, 72, 91–2, 142, 145, 147, 156, 163–4, 183–4, 229
Human Rights Watch, 183–4
Hun Sen, 182
Huo Daishan, 118
HydroChina Corporation, 47–8
hydropower, 18, 35, 45–72, 75, 80–5, 118–19, 146–7, 154, 156, 174, 183, 189, 195, 197, 208, 216–17; see damming; ultra-high voltage

ibex (Tibetan wild goat), 121–3
Iceland, 2
Imhof, Aviva, 190
India, 1–2, 13–14, 24, 28, 31–6, 39, 45, 48, 51, 57–8, 82–3, 89, 96–7, 101–2, 106, 121, 156, 165, 167–8, 177, 186–7, 189–202, 206–13, 216–17, 225–6, 228; and Bangladesh fence, 198–200; and damming, 195–7; and democracy, 196; and drivers, 96–7; and the Ganges, 210–11; and groundwater, 210; and hydropower, 196–8; and mapping data, 191; and megadams, 195–6; and monsoon rains, 28; poverty in, 196; and water, 189–196, 209–12; see Arunachal Pradesh; Assam
indigenous populations, 45–6, 63, 72–3, 91; see "ecological migrants"; nomads (Tibetan)
Indochina, 36
Indus, 166–7, 175, 190, 192–3, 205–6, 223
industrial pollution, 37–8, 75–7, 171; see air pollution; water pollution
Inner Mongolia, 35, 38, 104–6, 131–4
Inter-Citic, 119
International Council on Mining and Minerals (ICMM), 145
International Covenant on Economic, Social and Cultural Rights, 108
International Geosphere Biosphere Programme, 206
international law to protect downstream nations, 223–7
International Rivers, 46, 51, 89, 180, 183
Irrawaddy River, 184–5, 191–2
irrigation, 76, 80, 106, 141, 168, 196, 198, 202, 207, 210
Ivanhoe Mines, 135

Jammu and Kashmir, 207
Jamuna, 48, 198
Japan, 2, 7, 111, 205, 215–16, 221
Jigme Dorji National Park, 217–22
Jin River, 76
Jinganqiao Dam, 64
Jinhe Dam, 52
JM Voith AG, 84
Jokhang Temple, 126–7, 143
Jolmolangma (Goddess of the Snows), 115–16
Junggar Basin, 80, 154

justice, and water, 225–7

Kachin ethnic group, 184–6
Kachin Independence Army, 185
Kalachakra 2012, 88–9
Kammu, Matti, 179
Kang Rinpoche, 26
Karnali River, 192, 209
Kashmir, 9, 30, 121–3, 207
Kathmandu, 100
kayaks, 15, 43, 88, 176–80, 201–4, 240
Kazakh nomads, 92
Keeling, Charles, 34
Keeling, Ralph, 34
Kekixili, 123
Kham (eastern Tibet), 5–6, 92–3
Khampa nomads, 93–4, 124–5
Kingdon-Ward, Frank, 220
Kingho Group, 161
Kintup (agent), 192
Kirghiz nomads, 92
Klein, Julia, 105
Kolkata, 199, 210–12
Kyipup ("Rugby Boy"), 81–2
Kyrgyzstan, 24

Ladakh, India, 36, 57–8
Lafitte, Gabriel, 145
lakes (Tibetan), 2, 14, 25–30, 38–40, 50, 58, 83–5, 105, 129–30, 150, 157
Lamosangu Dam, 88
land grabbing, 20, 46, 58, 67, 69, 71, 84, 91–2, 96, 101–2, 104, 107–10, 115–17, 123–4, 131, 146–7, 156, 159, 187; see "ecological migrants"; indigenous populations; "national parks"; nomads
Land of Snows, 27, 95, 125–8, 143
Landsat-8 satellite, 149
landslide, 6, 30, 47, 64, 71, 162, 190
Laohuzui Dam, 52
Laos, 1, 7, 72, 165, 168, 172–5, 178, 190, 226
Laxiwa, 52
Lha Gyalo! Victory to the Gods!, 23
Lhasa, 6, 8–9, 14–15, 20–2, 30–1, 39–40, 52, 56, 81–6, 95, 97, 100–1, 112, 116, 119, 120, 122, 124–9, 139–46, 158, 162, 182–3, 194, 208; and mosquitoes, 30–1; see railway (Lhasa)
Li Bo, 71
Li Ling, 193
Li Peng, 44, 56
Li Xiaolin, 44
Li Xiaopeng, 44
links, 228–30
Litang, 92–6, 99–10, 111, 124; horse-racing festival (Tibet), 92–6
lithium, 150
Liuku Dam, 71
Lonely Planet, 14
Longyangxia, 52

Lost Horizon (Hilton), 124
Lower Sesan 2 Dam, 182
Ludila Dam, 64
Lungge Tsho, 30

Ma Jun, 79, 170
Madagascar, 7
Makar Sankranti, 210–11
Malaysia, 73, 90
mani stone, 109–10
Manwan Dam, 63
Mao Zedong, 7, 19, 54–6, 78, 106, 127
Marmot Dam (Oregon, U.S.), 223
Marre, Yves, 204
mastiff (Tibetan), 99, 112–13
Mauna Loa Observatory, 34
McLeod Ganj, Dharamsala, India, 101
medicinal herbs, 11–1
megadams, 22, 43–50, 56–9, 61, 64–5, 68, 70–2, 75,
     78–9, 89, 118, 120, 154, 160, 162, 170, 172–3, 175,
     179–80, 182–6, 190, 195–7, 207–9, 213, 217–18,
     223, 225, 229, 240; *see* damming
megacities in China, 75–7
Megoe Tso Lake, 85
Mekong: The Occluding River (Ngo The Vinh), 54
Mekong River, 43–5, 52, 54, 61, 63, 65, 70, 79–80, 89,
     118, 154, 166, 167, 172–82, 190, 223; damming,
     172–6
Mekong River Commission (MRC), 89, 173–4
Meltdown in Tibet (documentary), 88–9
MeltdowninTibet.com, 47
methane, 3, 32, 40, 49–50, 162
Metok (Metog), 48; *see* Motuo
Miao, 61
migrant workers, 21–2, 58–9, 126, 148, 155, 207
Miller, Dan, 105–6
mining, 2, 14, 21–2, 25, 40, 45–7, 56, 58, 73, 76, 79–81,
     90, 92, 102, 104–7, 117, 119–20, 123–4, 126,
     133–5, 139–63, 169, 174, 182–9, 194, 211, 213,
     216, 224, 226–7, 229; and asbestos dust, 151;
     and avalanches, 139–41; and Canada, 146–7; and
     copper, 134–5, 139, 154; and damming, 194 (*see*
     water-diversion projects); dangers of, 139–40; and
     ecological devastation, 139–63; and food chain,
     169; and future of Tibet, 163–4; and gold, 119,
     134–5, 139, 141, 155; and Google Earth, 149–51;
     and lithium, 150–1; map of, 136–7; and migrant
     workers, 148–9; in Mongolia, 133–4; and natural
     reserves, 119; and rare earths, 133; and religion,
     141; and salt, 150–1; and self-immolation, 158–9;
     and Tibet as *Xizang*, 145–6; and toxins, 150–3,
     160–1; and uranium, 152; and water pollution, 143
Ministry of Water Resources, 77
Mondo ("Rugby Boy"), 81
Mongolia, 24, 35, 38, 54, 76, 92, 102, 104, 106, 121–2,
     131–5
monks (Tibetan), 8, 19, 84, 93–4, 97, 100, 104, 109,
     124–7, 141, 158–9, 187

monsoon, 6, 15, 28, 39, 169, 178, 199–200, 205, 209–
     10, 217–18, 221
Mooney, Paul, 19
mosquitoes, 30–1
Motuo Dam, 47–51, 194
Mount Everest, 24, 30–1, 86, 115–16, 209, 222
Mount Kailash, 25–6, 48, 83, 130, 191–2, 203, 206,
     209, 211
Mount Meru, 26
mountains, destruction of, 14, 20–1, 155, 157, 162–4
mudslides, 6, 64–5
mushrooms, 111–12

nagas, 84
Namche Bazaar, Napal, 40
Namtso (lake), 129
Namtso Lake Nature Reserve, 129–30
National Bureau of Statistics, 77
National Defense University (Washington, D.C.), 173
National Geographic, 199
National Institute of Traditional Medicine in Thimphu,
     221
"national parks"/nature reserves, 60, 69, 109, 115–23,
     129, 159, 161; as "greenwashing," 116–20
National Wild and Scenic Rivers System, 212–13
Nature Conservancy in Beijing, 68
Nature Reserve Law of 1994, 117–18
Naxi people, 63
Neelum-Jhelum Dam, 207
Neelum River, 207
Nepal, 1, 15–16, 24, 30, 71–2, 87–8, 100, 116–17,
     128, 150, 189, 192, 208–9, 226, 229; and China's
     influence, 208–9; and flashfloods, 30; and
     hydropower, 208
New Guinea, 7
New Zealand, 100
Ngo The Vinh, 54
Nissan of Japan, 215–16
nomads (Mongolian), 131–5
nomads (Tibetan), 13–14, 20, 58–9, 91–135; and
     alcoholism, 108–10; and cashmere, 98–9; Chinese
     policies toward, 91–135; as "curiosity," 126;
     and grasslands, 96–106; and horses, 92–6; and
     mastiffs, 99, 112–13; and medicinal herbs, 11–1;
     and mushrooms, 111–12; and "national parks,"
     115–35; as pastoral, 98; and *tsampa* (roasted barley
     flour), 107–8; and 2008 Tibetan unrest, 100–1;
     and wetlands, 92; and yaks, 95–108, 113; *see* land
     grabbing
nongovernmental organizations (NGOs), 46, 61, 65,
     71, 85, 88–9, 105, 118–19, 145, 183–5, 197, 203,
     228, 229
nor, 99
Norphel, Chewang, 36
Nortel Networks, 22
Nuozhadu Dam, 44, 172
Nyanchen Tanglha range, 129
Nyima Tsering, 143

oil, 1, 34, 49, 80, 89, 137, 144–5, 151, 153, 171, 182, 186–7, 204, 215
Old Tibet (historic Tibet), 5, 7
Open-Up-the-West campaign, 22
Osborne, Milton, 190
Outer Mongolia, 24, 35, 48, 131, 133–5; as "Minegolia," 134–5
Oyu Tolgoi, 134–5

Pakistan, 1, 39, 71–2, 165, 167–8, 189–190, 193, 205–8, 212, 225–6
Panchen Lama, 84, 100
Pando Hydroplant, 52
Pearce, Fred, 224
Pearl River Delta, 76
Pelliot, Paul, 11
People's Armed Police, 59, 84–5
People's Liberation Army (PLA), 20
People's Online Daily, 117
People's Republic of China (PRC), 5, 212
permafrost, 3, 21, 28, 39–40, 83, 162
Perong, 83
pesticides, 77, 169
the Philippines, 7, 89–90
pika poisoning program, 107
pilgrimage, 26, 84, 102, 124, 129–30, 191, 210
Pliocene epoch, 34
poaching, 121–3, 176
Pollack, Henry, 29
Polo, Marco, 31
poor/poverty, 46, 50, 102, 155, 196, 200, 203, 216
population/overpopulation, 6–7, 25, 29, 53, 57, 75, 80, 84, 103, 120, 123, 125–6, 130, 132, 174, 190, 196–7, 199–202, 208, 212–13, 216, 222
Potala Palace, 127–9
Power Construction Corporation of China (PowerChina), 72
Power Corporation, 22
power transmission technology, 52
prayer flags, 23, 47, 93, 109
Preak Toal (Cambodia), 176–81
Princess Wencheng, 128
Probe International, 65
propaganda, 19, 56, 84–5, 106, 128, 142
protests, 19–20, 44, 58–9, 63–4, 67, 70–1, 100–1, 104, 126, 140–6, 156, 158–61, 164, 170, 173, 182–3, 187, 197, 208–9; see self-immolation
Public Security Bureau, 59
Pubugou Dam, 67

Qinghai, 5–6, 24, 52, 59, 66, 104, 107, 109, 113, 117, 119, 123, 127, 143, 151–5, 159, 161, 172–3
Qomolangma (Mount Everest), 86
Qomolangma National Nature Preserve, 115–16

radiation, 152
Radio Free Asia, 59, 118, 142, 230
Rahman, Atiq, 200

railway (Lhasa), 14, 21–2, 31, 40, 56, 86, 120, 125–6, 144–6, 182–3, 208
Rajasthan, 45
Ramanathan, Veerabhadran, 33
rare earths, 133
refugees, 199–200, 205, 213
Reid, J., 83
Reuters, 119–20
rhododendrons, 6, 61, 218, 221
Ringang ("Rugby Boy"), 81–2
Rio Tinto, 73, 135
rioting, 20, 60, 69
Roy, Arundhati, 196
Rugby School, 81
"Rugby Boys," 81–2
Russia, 171

Sagarmartha National Park, 116–17
salt, harvesting, 150–1
saltwater, 76, 78, 150, 175, 199–200, 205–6
Salween River, 61–3, 65, 70–1, 79–80, 154, 183–4, 222–3, 229
Salween River Gorge, 62
Samdrup, Karma, 59–60, 116
Samdrup, Rinchen, 60–1, 116
sandbars, 201–2
Sanjiangyuan National Nature Reserve, 109, 117–19, 159
Sarawak, 72–3
Sautman, Michael, 121–2
Schaller, George, 121–3
Schneider, Keith, 76
Schutter, Olivier de, 108
sea level rise, 199–200
seismic risk, 64–5, 70–1, 190
self-immolation, 15, 158–9
shahtoosh, 121–3
shale-gas, 153–4
Shan Women's Action Network, 183–4
Shangri-La, 124–5
Sharling, Dhardon, 226
Shell, 154
Sherriff, George, 221
Shigatse, 22
Shigatse Spring Water, 86
Siberia, 7
Sichuan, 5–6, 47, 58, 61, 63–8, 76, 85, 95, 117, 142, 154, 158–60
Sichuan Basin, 39
Sichuan earthquake of May 12, 2008, 65
Sichuan Geology and Mineral Bureau, 64, 76
Siemens Energy, 52–4
Sikkim, 189, 196
silt, 168–9, 199
Sina Weibo, 38
Sinohydro (division of PowerChina), 52, 64, 72–3, 174, 182, 184, 209
snow leopard, 9, 24, 99, 113, 218

Snowlands Great Rivers Environmental Protection Association, 59–60
soil erosion, 7, 60, 130, 133, 163, 213
solar panels/energy, 56–7
Songtsen Gampo, 128
South China Morning Post, 171
South China Sea, 49, 89–90, 171, 175
South Korea, 38
South-to-North Water Diversion project, 78–80
Soviet Union, 54, 56, 78, 131
spring water, bottling of, 22, 86–7
Stanley, John, 36
Stein, Auriel, 11
Storm, Ken, 48
strip mining, 163
Survey of India (British), 191
Sutlej River, 192–3, 206–7
Syvitski, James, 206

Taiwan, 90
Taklamakan Desert, 131
Tang Dynasty, 95
Tanggula Mountain, 62, 171
Taoism, 55
Tara (deity), 27
Tarim Basin, 80, 154
Tashi Tsering, 57–8, 85
Tavan Tolgoi, 134
tax havens, 87
tea, 95
Teesta River, 202
temperature warming, 31
Tenzin Gyatso, 8
Tenzin Norbu, 102–4, 107–8, 130–1
"terrorism," 20
Terry, Bill, 223
Thailand, 1, 44, 62, 88–9, 102, 168, 172, 174–5, 182, 184, 186–7, 190, 226, 228
Thein Sein, 186
theme parks, 123–35
"Third Pole," x, 2, 23–40, 226
Thompson, Lonnie, 28
Three Gorges Dam, 44, 46–8, 53–6, 66–70, 73, 184, 209
Three Parallel Rivers, 61–2, 118, 159
Tibet: as "icebox of Asia," 27–8; culture, *see* Tibetans; defined, 5–6; and insects and climate change, 30–1; and lakes, *see* lakes; mapping, 191–2; national bird of, 9; pre-1950, 19, 25, 81–3, 98–9; rafting in, 13–22; rivers of, 43–73
Tibet's Environmental Protection Bureau, 119–20
Tibet's Waters Will Save China (Guo and Li), 193–4
Tibet Autonomous Region (TAR), 5–6, 52, 117, 136–7, 145
Tibetan antelopes, 9, 121–3, 131
Tibetan Centre for Human Rights and Democracy, 156, 163
Tibetan Cham dancing, 125

Tibetan Buddhism, 6–7, 26, 101, 109, 216
"Tibetan Chronicle," 11
Tibetan Magic Water, 86
Tibetan plateau region, ix–x, 1–3, 5, 7, 22–8, 39–40, 51–3, 57, 81, 85, 97–100, 107, 110, 131, 136–7, 143, 153–4, 161, 165, 169, 222
Tibetans, 20, 24–5, 57–8, 80–1, 91–110, 125; and Cham dancing, 125; culture of, 25–7, 99, 109–10, 125–6; in exile, 57–8; physiology of, 24–5; travel methods of, 25–6; and water-diversion projects, 80–1; *see* altitude; animism; grasslands; land grabs; nomads; monks
Tiger Leaping Gorge, 63
Tonle Sap (lake), 176–82
Tongjia Dam, 79
tourism, 21, 31, 38–9, 54, 85, 92–3, 116–17, 124–30, 152; *see* Land of Snows; Shangri-La
Tsaidam Basin, 80, 151–3
tsampa (roasted barley flour), 107–8
Tsangpo Gorges, 192
Tsering Dhondup, 158
Tsering Tsomo, 156–7, 163–4
tsunami, 2, 30, 65–6
tunnels, 14, 18, 20–2, 43, 49, 51, 78–9, 85, 190
Turpan Basin, 80
Turquoise Hill Resources, 135
Twitter, 19
typhoons, 66

U-Tsang (central Tibet), 5
Uighurs, 20
ultra-high voltage (UHV) power transmission lines, 52
UN Convention on the Law of Non-Navigational Uses of International Watercourses, 225
UN Convention on the Law of the Sea, 89
UN Declaration on the Rights of Indigenous Peoples, 73
UN Development Programme, 130
UN Environment Programme, 179–80, 213
UN Intergovernmental Panel on Climate Change (IPCC), 29, 31, 168
UN International Year of Water Cooperation, 226
UN Special Rapporteur on the Right to Food, 108–9
UN World Food Programme, 205
UNESCO World Heritage List, 61–2
UNESCO World Heritage Site, 116–18
United States, 34, 53, 222–3
US Environmental Protection Agency, 37
Upper Yangtse Rare and Endemic Fish Nature Reserve, 69
uranium, 152
Uttar Pradesh, 210

Viesturs, Ed, 29
Vietnam, 1, 54, 89–90, 167–8, 172, 174–6, 181–2, 190, 226
Voices from Tibet (Tsering Woeser and Wang Lixiong), 41

Wang Lixiong, 41, 142
Wang Shucheng, 77
Wang Yongchen, 62, 105
water: and Bhutan, 215–24; crises, and China, 52–3, 75–90; diversion, *see* water-diversion projects; and food security, 167–87; justice, 225–7; pollution, *see* water pollution; sharing, *see* water-sharing agreements; shortages, 212–13; stealing, 75–90; wars, 189–213; as world's most important resource, 1–2
water-diversion projects, 18, 75–80, 119, 124–5, 140–1, 148, 154, 167, 189, 193–4, 212
water pollution, 76–7, 143–4, 169–71, 223–4
water-sharing agreements, 225–6
water stealing, 75–90
water tankers, 211–12
waterbirds, 176–7
Watts, Jonathan, 55
Wen Jiabao, 62–3, 71
West Seti Dam, 209
Western Development Strategy (Open-Up-the-West campaign), 163
Western Mining Company, 151
wetlands, 9, 28, 40, 78, 83, 87, 92, 177, 219
white poppy, 221
wild asses, 8–9
Wild and Scenic Rivers Act (U.S.), 222
wildlife, 7–9, 24–6, 83–4, 96–8, 116–17, 121, 134, 140, 216–23; *see* bar-headed goose; snow leopard; Tibetan antelope; yak
wind power, 36, 57
Winkler, Dan, 112
Woeser, Tsering, 41, 109, 141–4, 155, 158–9, 160
Woolwich Military Academy, 81
World Health Organization, 38
World War I, 81–2
World War II, 193
World Water Day, 226
World Wildlife Fund UK, 223

Xayaburi Dam, 174–5
Xi Jinping, 160

Xiangjiaba Dam, 68
Xiaowan Dam, 43–4, 172
Xichang satellite launch center, 51
Xiluodu Dam, 68
Xinhua News Agency, 113
Xinjiang, 104
Xizang ("Western Storehouse" or "Western Treasure House"), 145
Xizang Province, 5–6

yaks, 8–9, 13–17, 24, 56, 92, 95–108, 113, 116, 125–6, 129, 218
Yamdrok Tso (lake), 9, 83–5
Yamdrok Tso Power Station, 85
Yangtse River, 7, 55, 60–70, 78–9, 118–19, 166–71, 223
Yao Tandong, 28
Yarlung Tsangpo (Brahmaputra), 47–53, 65, 70, 79–80, 85, 94–5, 154, 191–7, 220, 222, 225; large-scale water diversion of, 193–4; *see* Brahmaputra
Yarlung Tsangpo Grand Canyon, 48
Yarlung Tsangpo valley, 22, 48
yartsa gunbu, 111–12
Yeh, Emily, 117
Yellow River, 52, 65, 76, 78–9, 118–19, 134, 161, 169–71; and pollution, 169–71
Yellow River Conservancy Committee, 170
Yellow River Waterway Corridor, 79–80
Yi, 61
YouTube, 19, 150, 160
Yu Xiaogang, 63
Yu, Wallace, 87
Yulong Copper Mine, 154
Yunnan, 6, 43–4, 47, 53, 61–4, 68, 76, 95, 117–18, 124, 159, 172, 175, 179–87

Zhang Boting, 49
Zhang Yongze, 119–20
Zhangmu Dam, 51, 87, 194
Zhikong Dam, 52
Zijin, 145
Zipingpu Dam, 64–6
ZK Group, 160–1

Author Bio

Michael Buckley is a Canadian adventure travel writer, documentary filmmaker, and environmentalist. He has traveled widely in Tibet and the Himalayas, visiting many Tibetan enclaves. He has mounted expeditions to the wilds of high Asia, including mountain biking from Lhasa to Kathmandu, cycling from Gilgit to Kashgar, a jeep safari in Mongolia, and a month-long monsoon trek in Bhutan. Buckley specializes in the Himalayan and Southeast Asian regions. Currently, he divides his time between Canada and Asia. Buckley is author of a number of books about Tibet, including *Eccentric Explorers* (winner of biography category, National Indie Excellence Awards, USA); *Heartlands: Travels in the Tibetan World* (winner, Lowell Thomas Travel Journalism Award, USA); *Shangri-La: A Travel Guide to the Himalayan Dream*; and *Tibet: The Bradt Travel Guide*. Visit the author's book website at www.Himmies.com/.

Buckley is also a filmmaker of several short documentaries about environmental issues in Tibet: *Meltdown in Tibet*, about megadams; *From Nomad to Nobody*, about vanishing grasslands and disappearing nomad culture; and *Plundering Tibet*, about mining in Tibet. For more details, go to www.WildYakFilms.com/. You can visit the author's Facebook page concerning environmental issues in Tibet at www.facebook.com/MeltdowninTibet/.